Pedagogical Grammar

Pedagogical Grammar

Casey Keck

Boise State University

YouJin Kim

Georgia State University

John Benjamins Publishing Company

Amsterdam / Philadelphia

The paper used in this publication meets the minimum requirements of
the American National Standard for Information Sciences – Permanence
of Paper for Printed Library Materials, ANSI z39.48-1984.

Library of Congress Cataloging-in-Publication Data

Keck, Casey M.
  Pedagogical grammar / Casey M. Keck and YouJin Kim.
      p. cm
Includes bibliographical references and index.
1. Language and languages--Study and teaching. 2. Grammar, Comparative and general--
        Study and teaching. 3. Cognitive grammar. 4. Applied linguistics. I. Kim, YouJin
        (Language teacher) II. Title.
P53.412.K43   2014
418--dc23   2014030019
ISBN 978 90 272 1217 7   (Hb ; alk. paper)
ISBN 978 90 272 1218 4   (Pb ; alk. paper)
ISBN 978 90 272 6931 7   (Eb)

John Benjamins Publishing Co. · P.O. Box 36224 · 1020 ME Amsterdam · The Netherlands
John Benjamins North America · P.O. Box 27519 · Philadelphia PA 19118-0519 · USA

Table of contents

Acknowledgements

Over the last decade, we have worked with many in-service and pre-service language teachers, sharing our passion for how to teach grammar effectively in diverse contexts. The idea of teaching descriptive grammar using both corpus tools and communicative tasks arose in the pedagogical grammar seminars that Casey Keck took with Douglas Biber, Lourdes Ortega and Randi Reppen at Northern Arizona University. We are indebted to both Lourdes Ortega and John Norris for encouraging us to write a practical resource book for those who are interested in the teaching and learning of grammar. We are also grateful for the valuable feedback provided by Luke Plonsky, David Olsher, Randi Reppen, and Ute Römer on early drafts of the manuscript. Special thanks go to Kees Vaes, who has provided amazing support and guidance during the entire process.

Our students have been the greatest resource for this book. Without our wonderful students at San Francisco State University (SFSU), Boise State University (BSU), and Georgia State University (GSU), this work would not have been possible. We are also grateful for the support of our SFSU, BSU, and GSU colleagues. Finally, we thank our families, who have always respected our passion for applied linguistics and have provided us with endless support and love.

Casey Keck, Boise State University, Boise, ID, USA
YouJin Kim, Georgia State University, Atlanta, GA, USA

Chapter 1

Pedagogical grammar

A framework for language teachers

> There is great value, it seems to me, for teachers to be able to articulate
> and examine their personal views of language and of grammar – views that,
> like mine, are doubtless influenced by their experiences both as learners
> and as teachers and by the views of their instructors, researchers, and colleagues.
>
> (Larsen-Freeman, 2003, p. xi–x)

In 2003, Diane Larsen-Freeman invited her readers to join her in an exploration of grammar and an examination of how their ideas about grammar influence their approach to language teaching. The present book is a response to this call, a culmination of our own personal explorations of language, grammar, and second language teaching and learning. Like Larsen-Freeman (2003), we believe that teachers' beliefs about grammar – "what it is and what it is not" (p. ix) – can have a profound impact on the ways in which they approach the teaching of grammar in their own classrooms. We also recognize, however, that knowledge and beliefs about grammar are only one piece of the larger puzzle of second language grammar pedagogy. No theory or description of grammar, by itself, "satisfactorily covers the concerns of practitioners" (Odlin, 1994, p. 10). For the teaching of grammar involves not only the description of grammar systems, but the learning and use of grammar in real-world contexts. Approaches to L2 grammar pedagogy are informed not only by one's view of grammar, but also by beliefs about why grammar is (or is not) important, how it can be learned, and in what ways it can (or should) be taught.

Recognizing the multiple concerns of language teachers, many scholars in the field of applied linguistics (e.g., Celce-Murcia, 1991; Ellis, 1998; 2006; Larsen-Freeman, 1989; 2003; Nassaji & Fotos, 2004; 2011; Norris & Ortega, 2000; Odlin, 1994) have highlighted the importance of *pedagogical grammar*, a research domain that is concerned with how grammar can most effectively be taught and learned in the second language (L2) classroom. Odlin (1994) notes that pedagogical grammar is necessarily "a hybrid discipline," one which draws from several areas of study. Similarly, Lourdes Ortega, in her doctoral seminars on pedagogical grammar, has argued that pedagogical grammar is best explored through a "cross-fertilization" of three broad areas of applied linguistics (Ortega, 2003, p. 1): *linguistic description* (data-based accounts of grammar in use), *second language acquisition* (research which explores how and when particular grammar systems are acquired by L2 learners), and *second language instruction* (research which explores the relative effectiveness of different instructional approaches).

Books which aim to synthesize pedagogical grammar research for language teachers, however, rarely provide equal coverage of all three of these important areas. Some books focus on highlighting recent trends in second language acquisition research, some focus on providing practical tips for grammar teaching, and others focus on providing linguistic descriptions of grammatical systems. Perhaps because of the fragmented nature of pedagogical grammar resources, university courses on L2 grammar teaching also tend to cover only one or two of these areas. In a survey of 39 instructors teaching graduate-level pedagogical grammar courses in the US and Canada, for example, Wang (2003) found that the majority of courses emphasized grammar description (i.e., helping pre- and in-service teachers understand the grammar of the target language) over all other considerations. What is more, when asked whether the course covered not only language structure, but also the study of learner language and approaches to explaining grammar to L2 students, only 24% of the instructors surveyed said they were able to address all of these issues. Nevertheless, through an examination of instructors' suggestions for improving future pedagogical grammar courses, Wang was able to identify three key areas of pedagogical grammar which instructors viewed as essential to the training of L2 teachers (p. 75): "*Linguistic description* (reference grammar, linguistic grammar), *Teaching grammar* (methods/techniques, designing/implementing grammar lessons, explaining grammar, materials evaluation/ development) and *Learner grammar* (analyzing/understanding learner errors)." Not surprisingly, this teacher-trainer view of pedagogical grammar overlaps in many ways with Ortega's (2003) conceptualization of pedagogical grammar research. Both the teaching of L2 grammar and research on its effectiveness require a knowledge of not only the "what" of grammar pedagogy, but also the "how" and "when" of L2 grammar acquisition and instruction.

Drawing on the recommendations of Ortega (2003) and Wang (2003), our book proposes a framework for pedagogical grammar which can be used by language teachers to organize both their existing knowledge (of grammar, of second language acquisition, of L2 instruction) and their future explorations of L2 grammar pedagogy. We believe that a framework, rather than a list of recommendations, allows teachers to bring their own beliefs and experiences to the table, to do more than simply receive information about L2 grammar teaching, but to evaluate it in light of their own instructional context. As Fotos and Nassaji (2011) explain, "Teachers are not agents to learn and apply methods, but [rather are] professional decision makers" (p. 140). What "works" in the classroom cannot be defined in advance, but rather is in a constant state of flux, changing from moment to moment, dependent on the learning goals, the classroom environment, student motivations, and so on. We believe that frameworks for professional decision-making allow teachers to develop an approach to L2 grammar instruction that is not only principled, but also flexible and responsive to student needs.

Figure 1.1 displays a framework for pedagogical grammar research that is divided into three major areas highlighted by Ortega (2003) and Wang (2003): *Grammar Description*, *L2 Grammar Acquisition*, and *L2 Grammar Instruction*. These three areas should not be seen as separate entities, but as areas of research that interact with and inform one another. For example, although the grammar of a language can be documented for non-pedagogical purposes, grammars designed for L2 learners necessarily involve both linguistic description and a consideration of learner needs and goals. In the area of second language acquisition research, grammar description also plays a role, particularly when it comes to investigating the nature of learner language and development over time. At the intersection of all three areas, we find research on instructional effectiveness, as such research necessarily involves the design of pedagogical grammar materials, the testing of hypotheses about the nature of L2 acquisition, and the evaluation of instructional interventions and their impact on the acquisition process.

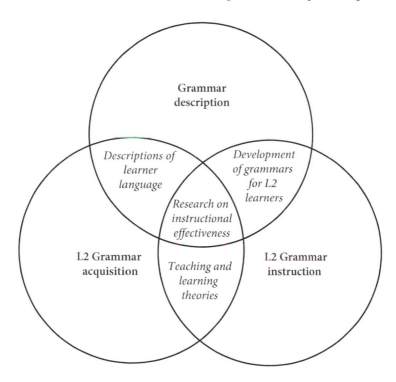

Figure 1.1 A framework for pedagogical grammar research

We would also argue that these three areas of pedagogical grammar can play an important role in the professional decision-making process of L2 teachers. If we take the Venn Diagram in Figure 1.1 and modify it slightly (see Figure 1.2), we can see how these three areas can work together to inform L2 grammar pedagogy. First, as Larsen-Freeman (2003) has so eloquently argued, L2 teachers must examine their beliefs about what grammar is and how it can best be described to their own students. Part of this examination involves a consideration of L2 acquisition. How and when do L2 learners acquire particular grammar forms and systems? In what ways can instruction facilitate this process? Finally, teachers must evaluate what they know about grammar and grammar acquisition in light of their own teaching context. How might a knowledge of pedagogical grammar help to inform the many decisions that teachers make, whether it be choosing a textbook, designing practice activities, or assessing student progress?

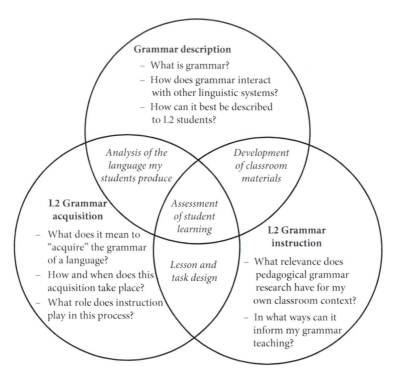

Figure 1.2 A framework for second language grammar pedagogy

Keeping these questions in mind, we have organized our book so that it may serve as a guide through the pedagogical grammar landscape. In Chapter 2, we begin with a historical overview of pedagogical grammar research in the field of applied linguistics and its impact on second language classroom pedagogy. From here, we move to the area of *Grammar Description*, or the "what" of pedagogical grammar. In Chapters 3 and 4, we provide a historical overview of grammar description, with a primary focus on the design of pedagogical grammars for L2 learners. We also highlight recent developments in corpus linguistics and the wealth of information now available regarding the frequency with which particular words or linguistic features occur in a language, the ways in which lexis and grammar work together to create meaning, and the ways in which situational factors (e.g., the mode and purpose of communication) impact the choices we make as writers and speakers of a language. In Chapters 5 and 6, we explore the interface between *Grammar Description* and *L2 Grammar Instruction*, providing guidance in the area of classroom materials development. Chapter 5 discusses the importance of critically evaluating existing grammar resources and adapting these materials to better meet students' needs. Chapter 6 provides an overview of online corpora and related language analysis tools and discusses how teachers might use these resources when developing their own instructional materials.

After a thorough review of *Grammar Description* and its relevance to *L2 Grammar Instruction*, we move to the area of *L2 Grammar Acquisition*. We begin, in Chapter 7, with an exploration of the dynamic nature of learner language. How can we approach the study of learner language? How does learner language change, not just over time, but in real-time, as learners respond to the communication demands of a given situation? In Chapter 8, we shift our attention to research conducted in instructional settings, highlighting six key findings which we feel have particular relevance to L2 grammar pedagogy. Our discussion in this chapter draws on three major theoretical perspectives in second language acquisition research: *interactionist* (e.g., investigations of how communication tasks might promote the acquisition of particular grammatical features), *sociocultural* (e.g., analyses of the ways in which learning occurs through socialization and collaboration with mentors and peers), and *cognitive* (e.g., theoretical models which attempt to explain how attention and memory mediate the language acquisition process). In the final two chapters of the book, just as in Chapters 5 and 6, we provide guidance to L2 teachers, this time in the areas of grammar task design and classroom assessment. Chapter 9 highlights the many recommendations put forth in the literature regarding effective task design, with a focus on the strategies that teachers can use to help students understand, use, and reflect on the grammar they are learning. In Chapter 10, we explore how teachers might assess their students' L2 grammatical ability, not only through traditional grammar tests, but also through alternative approaches, such as task-based performance and dynamic assessment.

Although the primary target audience for this book is second language teachers, we feel that the book can also be a valuable resource for graduate students who hope to conduct research in the area of pedagogical grammar. Just as books for teachers tend to emphasize one area of pedagogical grammar over others, discussions of L2 grammar pedagogy in the applied linguistics literature can also have a somewhat narrow focus. Increasingly, however, scholars are making efforts to explore connections among various theoretical perspectives. For example, as evidenced in a recent colloquium organized by Hulstijn and Schmidt (2013), several L2 researchers are exploring how cognitive and sociocultural orientations might work together to inform our understanding of second language learning and teaching. Corpus linguists are building large collections of learner corpora to aid in the analysis of learner language (see, e.g., Granger, 2002; 2012), and scholars interested in the role of input in L2 acquisition are increasingly turning to corpus-based tools and methodologies (e.g., Wulff, Ellis, Römer, Bardovi-Harlig, & LeBlanc, 2009). In this spirit, we include several theoretical perspectives in this book, as we feel all of these perspectives help to enrich our understanding of L2 grammar pedagogy. We also believe that it is important for pedagogical grammar researchers to consider teacher perspectives at all phases of the research process – design, data collection, analysis, interpretation – so that their studies have relevance to real-world classroom contexts. Thus, we hope that our book can serve as a useful illustration of how these theory-to-practice connections might be made.

Because English is a language that all of our readers share, the majority of the examples we use in this book are in English. Our synthesis of the pedagogical grammar research, however, draws on studies of several languages and thus has relevance for L2 teaching in many target language contexts. And when we say "L2" teaching, this can refer not only to a second language, but any *additional* language – third, fourth, and so on – that is being learned later in life, after one's native language(s) have been mastered. We should also say that the research reviewed here spans many instructional contexts, including K-12 education, university settings, and adult education programs, both where the target language is the official language of the country of residence and where it is not.

In the next chapter of this book, we provide a historical overview of pedagogical grammar in applied linguistics. As we will see in this chapter, the field of applied linguistics emerged shortly after World War II, when there was an increased need in many countries for second language education programs. This demand for effective L2 pedagogy – for immigrants and for military personnel – gave rise to the study of second language acquisition and put in motion a movement towards teaching language for the purpose of communication, rather than simply as a subject to be studied. As these changes unfolded, questions emerged as to whether explicit grammar instruction and practice drills were enough to prepare students for authentic communication, with some scholars calling for an end to grammar instruction altogether. In Chapter 2, we revisit this debate and bring our readers up to the present time, a time in which grammar instruction is again seen as an important component of second language education.

Chapter 2

Pedagogical grammar in applied linguistics

A historical overview

Grammar instruction has always played a central role in the second language class-room. For centuries, to learn a language has meant to learn the vocabulary and grammar of that language. Most of us who have studied a foreign language in school have experienced grammar-focused approaches, through what linguists call a *structural syllabus*. In a structural syllabus, the language class (and typically the corresponding textbook) is organized by grammatical feature. One week of class may focus on simple present tense; the next may move on to the present progressive. Instruction in these classes is typically *explicit* in nature. Rule explanations are given, and students are asked to focus their attention on the grammatical form to be learned. Charts and example sentences are often provided, and students are then given a chance to practice the new rule, through fill-in-the-blank exercises, practice dialogues, or translation activities. After several lessons (and likely several years) students are expected to have built a large repertoire of grammatical rules, and this knowledge, ideally, allows them to both comprehend and produce grammatically well-formed sentences.

The popularity of the structural syllabus today is somewhat surprising, however, if one considers the intense criticism this approach received in the late 20th century. During this time, there were numerous calls to change the current state of affairs in language teaching, to move away from a focus on language-as-object, toward a focus on language for communication. As more people chose to study languages not simply for the purpose of *knowing* them, but for the purpose of *using* them, scholars began to question structure-based approaches to language instruction. Could studying grammar rules in a book and doing fill-in-the-blank exercises really prepare students for real-world tasks like ordering at a restaurant, going to the doctor, or leading a business meeting? Shouldn't a language syllabus be organized according to the everyday tasks that students need to complete in the target language, rather than by a series of discrete grammatical features? Questions like these helped to build momentum for the communicative approach to language teaching. These questions also led many scholars and teachers to reconsider the role that grammar instruction should play in the foreign language classroom.

Grammar teaching's first major challenge: The Audiolingual Method

Prior to the 1950s, grammar teaching in L2 classrooms typically followed some sort of structural syllabus, with many language classes adopting a Grammar Translation approach, which emphasized the use of vocabulary lists, grammar rule explanations, and the translation of foreign language texts into the native language (Brown, 2007). In more recent history, grammar-focused instruction has often been carried out through a three Ps model (Presentation, Practice, and Production), in which the teacher *presents* a grammar rule to the class, asks students to *practice* using the rule in focused grammar exercises, and then gives students a chance to *produce* the grammar structure in activities such as a written essay or a role play (Celce-Murcia & Larsen-Freeman, 1999).

Though Grammar Translation and Presentation, Practice, Production approaches are still practiced in many parts of the world, these methods came under intense scrutiny in the latter half of the 20th century, a time of much innovation, trial-and-error, and debate in the world of second language teaching. Following World War II, many countries began to place a greater emphasis on foreign language education. The United States, in particular, felt that innovations in language pedagogy were needed to increase the oral proficiency of military personnel in a number of languages deemed important to national security. Prior to this time, foreign language education consisted primarily of reading, translation, and grammar instruction; language classes did little to develop functional oral skills. To address this problem, the government sought the help of linguists to develop better teaching methods. Linguists, in turn, drew upon a variety of disciplines, including education and psychology, to explore how theories of language and theories of learning might help to inform second language teaching. The decades that followed saw a marked increase in research focused on how adults learn languages later in life and how carefully designed language classes and materials might speed up the acquisition process. This flurry of research can be said to mark the beginnings of the field of applied linguistics, which would soon take a leading role in the study of second language acquisition and pedagogy (Harris, 2001; Kramsch, 2000).

One of the first and most famous L2 teaching methods to emerge during this time was the Audiolingual Method (ALM), also known as the "Army Method." Its aim was to prepare military personnel for communication with native speakers of other languages (Brown, 2007; Rivers, 1981). It was felt that previously used methods, which emphasized the study of grammar rules and written translation, would not be effective, as these methods did little to develop oral communication skills. A new method was needed which could help students to understand spoken language and communicate fluently with little or no accent.

The demand for this type of language training came at a moment when linguists were re-evaluating their own approaches to the study of language. Prior to the 1940s, the grammar of a language was often described according to existing structures that had already been identified in other languages. Many linguists began to question these methods and advocated instead for a more scientific approach, one that aimed to systematically describe the sound, word, and syntactic patterns of a language as observed in natural language data. This movement gave rise to what is known today as structural linguistics and is largely responsible for the distinction we make today between prescriptive and descriptive approaches to identifying the rules of grammar that a language follows. In a *prescriptive approach*, linguists state what the rules of grammar for the language should be, and these rules are based on what has historically been done in that language, or in classical languages like Greek and Latin. Prescriptive approaches are often used to create grammar references and style guides. In a *descriptive approach*, linguists collect samples of spoken and written language, analyze the grammatical patterns of those samples, and generate rules based on what they observe. In a descriptive approach, what is considered to be "grammatical" may change over time, as speakers and writers use structures in new ways.

As linguists began to place more importance on describing a language based on how it was actually spoken in the real world, they also began to stress the importance of developing teaching materials that prepared students to converse in the language they were learning (Fries, 1955). A push was made to describe a number of languages and to identify useful phrases and structures that native speakers used in conversations with one another. Linguists also turned to current theories of language learning to explore how these useful phrases and structures might be taught to language students. At the time, the most widely accepted views of language acquisition were informed by the behaviorist theories of B. F. Skinner, who characterized language learning as a process of habit formation (Lightbown & Spada, 2013). Children, Skinner argued, received input from their parents and tried to imitate this input. When parents (or others) praised or rewarded children for their own language use, children learned to keep using the words and sentences they had tried. Similarly, if children received negative feedback on an utterance (maybe a confused look or a question), they learned to modify their speech and to try words and phrases that elicited more positive responses. Repeated opportunities to hear language input, imitate language input, and receive positive reinforcement were seen as the primary forces behind child language acquisition.

These new developments in structural linguistics and behaviorist psychology helped to shape the approach to pedagogy taken in the Audiolingual Method. Classroom instruction consisted primarily of oral language drills which were designed to help students unlearn old "habits" (their L1) and develop new habits in the L2. Because fluency and native-like pronunciation were important goals, teaching materials were developed to reflect actual language use. Drawing on linguistic research, such as that of Charles Fries (1940a, 1940b; see also P. Fries, 2010), sample dialogues were constructed to include idioms and other colloquial expressions. The Audiolingual Method also specifically prescribed against the teaching of grammar rules in the classroom. Repeated oral practice was seen as more important and more effective than detailed grammar charts and explanations.

Though the underlying principles of the Audiolingual Method would soon be challenged, its development helped to set in motion a new area of research devoted to the study of the teaching and learning of second languages. The method's emphasis on oral communication and authentic language use also helped to set the stage for the new developments in language teaching that were to follow.

Reflection 2.1

- As an L2 learner, have you ever experienced the Audiolingual Method or a teaching method similar to it? What was this experience like?
- As an L2 teacher, what techniques do you use to provide students with oral practice and repetition? Do you avoid explicit grammar teaching, as was done in the Audiolingual Method? Why or why not?

New theories of language competence: The Chomskyan revolution

Just as the Audiolingual Method was gaining popularity and spreading to foreign language classrooms all over the world, the theories of language and learning upon which the method was based were coming under attack. In the late 1950's, Noam Chomsky took direct aim at both structural linguistics and B. F. Skinner's behaviorist theories of language learning. Chomsky's critique of structural linguistics centered around its focus on identifying the individual component parts of language (e.g., nouns, verbs, adjectives, adverbs) based on language data (e.g., recorded conversations or collections of personal letters). Chomsky believed that such an approach could never fully account for the grammar of a language. In every language, the rules of grammar allow speakers and writers to add sentences together or embed sentences within other sentences, making an infinite number of sentences possible – no sample of language, however large, could possibly allow linguists to adequately describe this infinite variety. What was more important to Chomsky were the rules of grammar that made this infinite variety possible. The aim of linguistics, he argued, was not to describe the surface structure of sentences, but to identify the rules of grammar that make these sentence structures possible. He argued that linguistics should be concerned primarily with language competence, an individual's underlying knowledge of his or her native language system, rather than with performance, or the realization of this knowledge in speech and writing. Chomsky also felt that linguistics should be more than an exercise in cataloguing the grammatical similarities and differences of world languages. Rather, he argued, linguistics should aim to explore the universal properties shared by all languages. These properties, what Chomsky later called Universal Grammar, were the key to understanding language as a distinctly human phenomenon.

Some of Chomsky's evidence for Universal Grammar was derived from observations of child language acquisition, and these observations also helped to build a case against behaviorist views of language learning. In behaviorist models, children were said to learn language through exposure to stimuli, primarily the language spoken by their parents. Chomsky argued, however, that the stimuli (or input) that children received was very poor. Children hear a relatively small set of sentences, compared to what is possible in their language. When children make mistakes, they are often not corrected by their parents, and if they are, they tend to ignore these corrections. Chomsky conceded that children do often repeat sentences they hear; however, he argued that far more often, children generate their own sentences, ones that they have never heard and that have never been uttered before. Even more amazing is the fact that all children (with the exception of extreme cases of neglect or abuse) successfully acquire their native language without formal instruction and without conscious effort. The only way this could be possible, Chomsky argued, is if humans were born with the innate ability to make sense of the language they are exposed to. For Chomsky, this ability is a grammatical one: He argued that all humans possess their own Universal Grammar, which allows them to acquire language despite the "impoverished" nature of the input (Curzan & Adams, 2009; Saxton, 2010).

Chomsky's theories, put forth in a series of publications (e.g., Chomsky, 1959; 1975), led many in the field of language education to question some of the tenets of the Audiolingual Method. As Rivers (1981) notes:

> [In ALM] students may progress like well-trained parrots – able to repeat whole utterances perfectly when given a certain stimulus, but uncertain of the meaning of what they are saying and unable to use memorized materials in contexts other than those in which they have learned them…. If students are trained to make variations on language patterns without being given a very clear idea of what they are supposed to be doing in the process, they may not understand the possibilities and limitations of the operations they are performing. As a result they may have difficulty in using these structural patterns for expressing their own meanings. (p. 47)

In other words, drills that emphasized the memorization and repetition of language chunks were unlikely to help students learn the underlying grammatical system of the language they were studying. If children did not rely on this method to acquire the grammar of their native language, then it was possible that this method would also not be sufficient for classroom learning.

It was not entirely clear, however, how Chomsky's theories of first language acquisition could be used to inform the teaching of foreign languages to adolescents and adults. Certainly, students needed grammatical competence in the language they were studying; without it, they would not be able to generate sentences that could be understood by other speakers of the language. Children seemed to develop this competence effortlessly, simply by virtue of being born into a speech community. However, since children acquired their native language *without* instruction, the question remained as to how (or if) students could, in a classroom setting, develop the grammatical competence needed for effective communication in a second (or third or fourth) language.

Reflection 2.2
- Chomsky's theory of Universal Grammar prompted some scholars to question the tenants of the Audiolingual Method. In what ways does Chomsky's work inform or challenge your own perspectives on second language teaching and learning?

Language competence: More than just grammar?

Chomsky's theories of language competence and Universal Grammar fundamentally changed the nature and direction of linguistics research, and established a new area of linguistics, generative grammar, which was devoted to identifying the underlying, universal properties of human language. At the same time, Chomsky's insistence that linguistic research focus on language competence rather than language performance caused a great deal of upheaval. Structural linguists had devoted entire careers to describing language performance, through the collection and analysis of spoken and written language data. Was it really the case that this body of research would be cast aside as uninteresting and unimportant? Many linguists also called into question Chomsky's insistence that language competence should be seen as a kind of perfect or pure grammatical knowledge unimpeded by external distractions. This seemed to suggest that social factors, such as the purpose of communication and the relationships between speakers, were unrelated to competence; that while social conditions may impact a speaker's performance, they were irrelevant when it came to the study of a speaker's underlying knowledge of the language. As John Searle, a linguist well-known for his work in the area of speech acts argued, Chomsky's theories were limited in that they seemed to suggest that language competence was made up entirely of grammatical competence and did not include knowledge of social conventions and rules of interaction (Searle, 1972).

Another prominent scholar at the time, Dell Hymes, also challenged Chomsky's conception of language competence, arguing that children not only develop the ability to generate grammatically well-formed sentences, but also the ability to make the most *appropriate* linguistic choices in a given situation. To illustrate what competence might look like if it was comprised only of grammatical knowledge, Hymes (1972) asked his readers to imagine a child who could generate an infinite number of sentences, but who generated these sentences in an unsystematic way, speaking when not expected or allowed to do so, saying too much, or saying too little. Such a child would be seen as "at best, a bit odd" (p. 277).

> We have then to account for the fact that a normal child acquires knowledge of sentences, not only as grammatical, but also as appropriate. He or she acquires competence as to when to speak, when not, and as to what to talk about with whom, when, where, in what manner. In short, a child becomes able to accomplish a repertoire of speech acts, to take part in speech events, and to evaluate their accomplishment by others. (p. 278)

In other words, a knowledge of language included not only rules of grammar, but also rules of social interaction. Many of these rules, like the rules of grammar, are not explicitly taught to children, and yet as they mature, children learn to follow these rules without much conscious reflection. If language competence was more than grammatical competence, and Hymes believed it was, then a new framework for studying language competence was needed. Toward this end, Hymes proposed a theory of *communicative competence*, in which a knowledge of social conventions was just as important as knowledge of grammatical rules.

COMMUNICATIVE COMPETENCE (Hymes, 1972)
The ability to discern whether an utterance is:
(1) *Possible*, grammatically speaking;
(2) *Feasible*, considering cognitive constraints like working memory;
(3) *Appropriate*, in terms of what is socially acceptable in a particular situation; and
(4) *Performed*, or typically done by other native speakers in the speech community.
(Hymes, 1972, pp. 284–287)

Uncovering the rules of social interaction required a description of the many social contexts in which we use language, and empirical investigations of how language use varies across these contexts. Several linguists at the time developed new methods for describing language use and language variation, including Hymes, M. A. K Halliday, who helped to establish the field of systemic functional linguistics, and William Labov, who helped to establish the field of sociolinguistics.

Though Chomsky's generative linguistics is still seen as the dominant approach of the late 20th century, Hymes' theories of language competence directly addressed the major concerns of language practitioners at the time, and thus have had a greater overall impact on second language teaching methodology. Despite the movement away from the Audiolingual Method in the late 1970s, many language educators still felt that language classes should emphasize oral skills and authentic communication. Neither grammar charts nor rote memorization and drills were enough to develop this ability. What was missing in the language teaching world was a method that could develop students' abilities to *use* grammar to carry out important communicative functions. In other words, second language learners did not simply need grammatical knowledge or a large repertoire of formulaic expressions, they needed communicative competence. This shift in conceptions of language acquisition and language competence gave birth to a new approach to language teaching. Aptly named the *communicative* approach, it drew directly from Hymes' work and established communicative competence as the most important goal of second language classroom instruction.

Reflection 2.3
- If the goal of second language teaching is to develop students' communicative competence, rather than just their grammatical competence, then what implications does this have for classroom practice?
- As an L2 teacher, how might you help students to develop a sense of what is *possible, feasible, appropriate,* and *performed* in a variety of L2 contexts?

Communicative language teaching

During this tumultuous time in linguistics, the discipline of applied linguistics continued to grow. What started as a small group of (primarily structural) linguists with interests in language education was, by the 1970s, an academic discipline with a well-established journal (*Language Learning*), a research center (the Center for Applied Linguistics), and several new graduate programs. While the larger field of linguistics (without the "applied") focused primarily on first language acquisition and Chomsky's theories of language competence, *applied* linguistics focused primarily on second language acquisition and second language teaching. Many applied linguists were language teachers themselves, and thus their attention was focused on many practical issues: How can teachers improve their students' speaking skills? How can teachers help students to become both fluent and accurate in their production? Although some applied linguists would go on to explore how Chomsky's theory of Universal Grammar might be relevant for second language learning, for many applied linguists, Hymes' theories of communicative competence seemed more immediately relevant to these educational concerns.

The Audiolingual Method's focus on training students to produce perfectly formed sentences in response to particular language stimuli had, by this time, given way to a greater emphasis on developing students' abilities to communicate effectively in a variety of impromptu situations. Sandra Savignon was an early pioneer of communicatively-oriented pedagogy. Just as Hymes was publishing his work on communicative competence, Savignon (1972) was carrying out research to investigate how effective instruction could be when it focused on communication tasks rather than grammar drills. She found that communication tasks could be just as effective as grammar-focused tasks when it came to developing grammatical competence, and *more* effective than grammar-focused tasks when it came to the development of communication skills. Savignon argued that students in foreign language classrooms needed opportunities to interact with one another in authentic and meaningful ways if they were ever going to be able to use the target language for communication purposes.

Following the publication of Savignon (1972) and Hymes (1972), Van Ek (1976) applied Hymes' notion of communicative competence to the development of a foreign language teaching methodology for the European Ministers of Education. Van Ek's proposal was part of a larger effort to promote greater cultural understanding and unity among European nations, and it focused on providing language education to adult learners "who would wish to be able to communicate non-professionally with foreign language speakers in everyday situations on topics of general interest" (p. 2). To meet this communicatively-oriented goal, Van Ek stressed that classes should aim to develop "foreign language ability as a *skill* rather than knowledge" (p. 5). The syllabus for each course, Van Ek argued, should address:

> what the learner will have to be able to *do* in the foreign language and determines only in the second place what *language-forms* (words, structures, etc.) the learners will have to be able to handle in order to *do* all that has been specified. (p. 5, emphasis in original)

Van Ek called what the learner will do "functions," and he called the meanings that could be expressed within each function (e.g., location, time period, quantity) "notions." Core functions to be addressed in a syllabus included:

1. imparting and seeking factual information
2. expressing and finding out intellectual attitudes
3. expressing and finding out emotional attitudes
4. expressing and finding out moral attitudes
5. getting things done (suasion)
6. socializing (pp. 37–38)

Van Ek also outlined topic areas, such as "life at home," "education and career," "free time and entertainment," and "travel" (pp. 28–29). Within each topic were a wide range of more specific functions that could be performed, such as telling a new acquaintance how many children one had, what subjects he or she studied at school, or what hobbies he or she had. Other speech acts like apologizing, expressing pleasure, and accepting/declining an invitation were also included as functions.

For each function, a list of linguistic forms was also provided. For example, in English, when accepting an invitation, the following forms were suggested:

> Thank you [insert person's name]... I shall be very glad [to + V]... that will be very
> nice [insert person's name]... with pleasure!   (p. 45)

In the same year, D. A. Wilkins (1976) put forth a similar proposal, advocating for what he called a *notional syllabus*, in which "the process of deciding what to teach is based on consideration of what the learners should most usefully be able to communicate in the foreign language" (p. 9). Sensing a movement toward communicative approaches to second language teaching, Canale and Swain (1980) synthesized the contributions of Savignon, Hymes, Halliday, Van Ek, and Wilkins (among others) in a paper which served as the opening article for the very first issue of the journal *Applied Linguistics*. In this article, Canale and Swain contrasted two major approaches to second language teaching: a *grammatical approach* (organized according to grammatical forms) a *communicative approach* (organized according to communicative functions). Canale and Swain argued that if second language pedagogy was to embrace communicative approaches over grammatical ones, then it would be crucial to (1) define what was meant by communicative competence and (2) devise methods which could be used to measure students' communicative abilities.

Drawing on Hymes' and other's previous conceptions of communicative competence, Canale and Swain (1980) proposed that communicative competence was made up of three major components: grammatical competence, sociolinguistic competence, and strategic competence. (In 1983, Canale would expand this framework to include a fourth component, discourse competence, or the ability to construct cohesive and coherent texts in a variety of genres.)

COMMUNICATIVE COMPETENCE (Canale & Swain, 1980)
Grammatical competence: Knowledge of lexical items and of rules of morphology, syntax, sentence-grammar semantics, and phonology
Sociolinguistic competence: [Knowledge of] sociocultural rules of use [which are] crucial in interpreting utterances for social meaning, particularly when there is a low level of transparency between the literal meaning of an utterance and the speaker's intention
Strategic competence: Knowledge of verbal and non-verbal communication strategies that may be called into action to compensate for breakdowns in communication due to performance variables or insufficient competence   (Canale & Swain, 1980, pp. 29–30)

Canale and Swain, like Hymes, argued that grammatical competence was not the whole of language competence, but was just one component of communicative competence. They argued that an exclusive focus on grammar in the classroom would not be effective in promoting communication skills. They cautioned, however, against abandoning grammar instruction altogether. The question now facing researchers and teachers was, according to Canale and Swain: How to effectively combine grammar-focused instruction with instruction that aims to develop a larger repertoire of communication skills?

Canale and Swain did not attempt to answer this question, but they did outline several guiding principles for communicative approaches to second language teaching (pp. 27–28):

- Communicative approaches should aim to develop all major areas of communicative competence. No one area should be seen as more important than another, but rather, all areas work together to form a whole.
- Communicative approaches should directly address the needs of learners. These needs will vary from classroom to classroom, and thus it is important for teachers to investigate their own students' language learning needs and goals. Communicative approaches should also draw upon linguistic descriptions of the target language as it is used by native speakers. Curricula should include those speech events that students are most likely to participate in outside of the classroom.
- Communicative approaches must create opportunities for students to participate in authentic communication with speakers of the target language.

These guiding principles had a profound impact on second language teaching methodology. All over the world, syllabi, curricula, and textbooks would be revamped to include more authentic materials and communication tasks. Canale and Swain would also help to shape the focus of applied linguistics research in the decades to follow. If second language instruction was to provide students with information about how native speakers used the language in a variety of situations (at work, at school, at the coffee shop), then rich, linguistic descriptions of language use in these contexts would be needed. Methods for identifying learner needs would need to be developed, and more research on how students acquired communicative competence in a second language would need to be carried out. Researchers would also need to develop new communicative tasks for the classroom, and they would need to investigate whether these tasks did indeed promote language learning. Researchers would also need to take on the challenge described by Canale and Swain regarding the optimal balance of grammar and communication. If syllabi were to be organized by communicative function, and classroom activities focused on authentic interaction, how then, were teachers expected to address grammar in their second language classrooms?

Reflection 2.4

- In your experience as an L2 learner, have your language classes taken a grammatical approach or a communicative approach to L2 teaching? If you have experienced both approaches, which of the two did you prefer, and why?
- As an L2 teacher, how would you characterize your own approach? More grammatical or more communicative?

Reconsidering the role of grammar in the L2 classroom

Though most applied linguists and second language educators agreed that grammatical competence was a necessary component of communicative competence, they disagreed over whether explicit grammar teaching was needed in the classroom to develop this competence. Since children needed only meaningful interaction with native speakers to acquire their grammatical competence, many wondered if second language teaching should also aim to provide as naturalistic an environment as possible to foster L2 grammar acquisition.

One of the most outspoken scholars at this time who argued against the teaching of grammar was Stephen Krashen. In the early 1980s, not long after Canale and Swain proposed their framework for communicative competence, Krashen developed a set of hypotheses about the nature of second language acquisition, which he hoped could be used by teachers to guide their practice. The first of these hypotheses, The Acquisition-Learning Distinction, drew from Chomsky's theories of competence and performance. Krashen argued that only *acquisition*, a process that was unconscious and intuitive and that occurred naturally through interaction with native speakers, could lead to competence in the second language. *Learning*, in contrast, involved conscious reflection and a deliberate attempt to study the grammar and vocabulary of the language. Krashen felt that second language classrooms, particularly those classrooms using Grammar Translation or the Audiolingual Method, engaged students in *learning,* but failed to help students take advantage of their innate ability to *acquire* language through interaction. Krashen argued that while "some second language theorists have assumed that children acquire, while adults can only learn… the ability to "pick-up" languages does not disappear at puberty.… Adults can access the same natural 'language acquisition device' that children use" (Krashen, 1982, p. 10).

ACQUISITION VS. LEARNING IN THE MONITOR MODEL	
Acquisition	*Learning*
– Unconscious	– Conscious
– No Monitor	– Monitor in use
– Supports natural order of development	– Ignores natural order of development
– Achieved through comprehensible input	– Fails to provide comprehensible input
– Anxiety free	– Affective filter is up!
	(Krashen, 1982)

At the time Krashen was writing, there was a growing body of evidence which suggested that adult second language acquisition mirrored child language acquisition in a number of ways, most notably in what linguists call *developmental sequences*. Studies of children acquiring their first language and adults acquiring a second language (e.g., Brown, 1973; Dulay & Burt, 1973; 1974a; 1974b) showed that both children and adults acquired the grammatical forms of the target language in similar orders. For example, for both children and adults learning English, the progressive morpheme –*ing* (I am walking) appears before the past tense morpheme –*ed* (I walked). These studies also showed that explicit error correction, given either by a parent or a teacher, did little to alter the order of acquisition. Correcting a child every time he adds –*ed* to an irregular verb (e.g., I runned) does not have a large impact on the overall order of morpheme acquisition in English. Krashen's second hypothesis, The Natural Order Hypothesis, is based upon this research.

Taking his argument against grammar instruction a step further, in The Monitor Hypothesis, Krashen suggested that conscious reflection on grammar rules actually serves to impede fluent communication. While acquisition in naturalistic contexts allows learners to produce fluent speech in the target language, the learning of grammar rules allows for little more than monitoring, or the analysis of what one wants to say or has said. Krashen argued that all language users have a Monitor, which they use consciously, particularly when they are worried about the grammatical correctness or acceptability of their utterance. While monitoring sometimes serves a useful purpose (e.g., when proofreading an academic essay), Krashen argued that, for the most part, the monitoring process is cumbersome, and mainly serves to interrupt or slow down fluent speech. Second language classrooms that include explicit grammar instruction thus can actually interfere with the acquisition process. An ideal language classroom would foster acquisition and fluent speech; an ineffective one would emphasize the explicit learning of grammar rules, increasing students' dependence on an inefficient and unnatural Monitor.

How then, according to Krashen, could second language classrooms promote acquisition rather than learning? The ideal environment for Krashen was one of rich, engaging, and meaningful interaction. In The Input Hypothesis, Krashen further specifies that classroom interaction should use language that students can understand and engage with. The language input should also be geared approximately one level above their current competence, or what Krashen called *i + 1*. Krashen recognized that *i + 1* was a somewhat fuzzy notion (how to calculate this, exactly?) but he argued that determining every student's exact level (*i*) and the next level above (*i + 1*) was not necessary. Teachers, like parents, should provide what Krashen called "roughly-tuned" input, rather than try to create "finely-tuned" input (p. 22). In child-parent interaction, Krashen explained, it is not the case that parents make careful calculations about which grammatical features their children are ready to acquire next. Rather, they gradually increase the complexity of their language, based on how their children respond and how they interact with parents, siblings, and friends at any given age. Language classroom input should be calibrated in much the same way. If teachers can gage how well students understand the input and how engaged they are with it, they will be likely to hit upon the appropriate *i + 1* for each student at least part of the time. This should be enough to foster second language acquisition, just as it is sufficient for first language acquisition.

The need for comprehensible input became yet another reason to argue against grammar instruction in the L2 classroom. In his discussion of The Input Hypothesis, Krashen outlined four major reasons to abandon grammar-based syllabi and lessons:

1. All students may not be at the same stage. The "structure of the day" may not be *i + 1* for many of the students. With natural communicative input, on the other hand, some *i + 1* or other will be provided for everyone.
2. With a grammatical syllabus, each structure is presented only once. If a student misses it, is absent, is not paying attention, or if there simply has not been enough practice (input), the student may have to wait until next year, when all structures are reviewed! On the other hand, roughly-tuned comprehensible input allows for natural review.
3. A grammatical syllabus assumes we know the order of acquisition. No such assumption is necessary when we rely on comprehensible input, on roughly-tuned natural communication.
4. Finally, a grammatical syllabus, and the resulting grammatical focus, places serious constraints on what can be discussed. Too often, it is difficult, if not impossible, to discuss or read anything of real interest if our underlying motive is to practice a particular structure. In other words, a grammatical focus will usually prevent real communication using the second language (pp. 24–25).

Even Krashen's fifth hypothesis, The Affective Filter Hypothesis, can be said to help build a case against explicit grammar instruction. According to this hypothesis, non-linguistic factors, such as stress or anxiety, can impede the acquisition process. Krashen argued that students with high levels of motivation and self-confidence and low levels of anxiety would be more likely to benefit from exposure to comprehensible input, as they would be more willing to engage with it. Classrooms that provided interesting, comprehensible input were, according to Krashen, much more likely to foster motivation and confidence. In contrast, repetitive drills and boring grammar lessons could likely result in unmotivated students, or, worse, students with anxieties about grammatical correctness.

Krashen's theories resonated with many language educators who felt that grammar charts and drills, still widely used during this time, were failing to help their students to become fluent speakers of the target language. Krashen's emphasis on highly engaging, interactive lessons also fit nicely with the current emphasis on communicative competence. Canale and Swain (1980) had argued that second language classrooms must, at a minimum, provide numerous opportunities for meaningful interaction; classrooms that focused on providing comprehensible input would do just that. For Krashen (1982), and many language teachers around the world, this was not just good theory, but common sense:

The effective language teacher is someone who can provide input and help make it comprehensible in a low anxiety situation. Of course, many teachers have felt this way about their task for years, at least until they were told otherwise by the experts! (p. 32)

Reflection 2.5
- What aspects of Krashen's Monitor Model do you find most persuasive? Least persuasive?
- To what extent do you agree with Krashen's argument that explicit grammar instruction increases anxiety and results in excessive Monitor use?

Making input comprehensible: The role of interaction

Few argued against Krashen's claim that comprehensible input was needed for second language acquisition. What was less clear, however, was how teachers could ensure that students were receiving a sufficient amount of $i + 1$ input in the classroom. What, exactly, did engaging, meaningful, authentic, comprehensible input look like? Intrigued by some of the many conversations he had witnessed between native English-speaking teachers and ESL students, Michael Long began to explore how input could be made comprehensible to L2 learners through a series of negotiations in face-to-face interaction. Long had noticed that native speakers, much like the parents of children, tended to modify their speech when communicating with language learners. As part of his doctoral dissertation, Long (1980) transcribed several of these conversations and described the types of interactional moves that were made by the participants to ensure that meaning was communicated successfully.

LONG'S (1980) INTERACTION HYPOTHESIS

Comprehensible input is a necessary component of successful second language acquisition. *Interactionally modified input* plays a crucial role in making input comprehensible to second language learners. Interactionally modified input often occurs as speakers *negotiate meaning*, using the following strategies to ensure mutual understanding:
- *Requests for clarification*: Asking your conversational partner(s) to clarify or further explain what they mean
- *Confirmation checks*: Making sure you understand what someone has said
- *Comprehension checks*: Making sure someone understands what you have said
- *Repetitions*: Repeating yourself or repeating what your conversational partner has said
- *Repairs*: Correcting an error that you or your conversational partner has made
- *Paraphrase*: Rephrasing what you or conversational partner has said

Long found that several strategies used by native speakers helped to make their language more comprehensible for the L2 users. Native speakers often performed comprehension checks, to make sure the L2 speaker understood. If the native speakers were not understood, they often paraphrased what they had said in a new way. If the L2 speaker said something they did not understand, then native speakers often asked for clarification. In his Interaction Hypothesis, Long (1980) argued that what made input comprehensible was face-to-face interaction. As native and non-native speakers work to understand one another, they go through a series of negotiations, all of which aim to increase comprehension. Thus, interaction was crucial to the second language acquisition process, in that it provided L2 learners with input that was accessible to them.

Reflection 2.6
- As an L2 teacher, what strategies do you use to promote meaningful interaction in the classroom?
- How do you make input comprehensible to your students? In what ways do your students help to make input comprehensible to one another?

Researching the effectiveness of communicative classrooms

Long's (1980) Interaction Hypothesis provided yet another rationale to emphasize meaningful communication in the second language classroom. The question of whether to explicitly teach grammar, however, was far from resolved. While Krashen was advocating for naturalistic classroom environments free from grammar instruction, other applied linguistics researchers were exploring what impact those classroom environments might have on the development of students' grammatical competence over time. Some of the most influential research on communicative language teaching took place in the French immersion programs in Ontario, Canada. These programs were designed for children who spoke English as their native language, and the goal was to develop students' communicative competence in French, so that they would eventually be bilingual in both English and French, the national languages of Canada. Though many classrooms around the world still used grammar-based syllabi to teach second languages, immersion programs in Canada used a combination of communicative language teaching and content-based instruction. All tasks in the classroom were done in French, including content lessons in social studies, science, math, and so on.

To investigate whether students in these immersion programs were developing the communicative competence needed for both academic and professional success, Merrill Swain (of Canale & Swain, 1980) and her colleagues (see, e.g., Swain & Lapkin, 1982; Lapkin, Hart, & Swain, 1991; Swain, 1997) carried out a series of studies that described the type of instruction students received in their immersion classrooms, and then measured the development of students' communicative competence over time. Of interest was not only students' abilities to comprehend French and speak it fluently, but also their ability to speak and write with grammatical accuracy. Could classrooms that focused primarily on meaning, rather than form, still promote the development of students' grammatical competence?

The findings of these studies suggested that while immersion students, after several years of study, were quite fluent in their communication and were confident in their ability to use French in the school setting, analyses of the language produced by these students identified a number of grammatical forms that had not yet been fully acquired.

> The French spoken (and written) by the immersion student is, in many ways, non-native-like. Although the immersion students seem to have little problem understanding or reading French, their spoken and written French clearly identifies them as non-native speakers of the language.   (Swain & Lapkin, 1989)

Swain and Lapkin identified a number of possible reasons for this. First, they found that many of the classrooms they observed were taught by content teachers (e.g., Social Studies experts), not language teachers, and that these teachers taught their subject matter in French much like any content teacher would, through the use of assigned readings, lectures, brief question and answer sessions, and exams. In these classrooms, the range of communicative situations was limited. Students experienced traditional classroom genres, but had little exposure to other speech events in the target language. Though often described, at the time, as "communicative language teaching par excellence," these classrooms provided input that was "functionally restricted"; that is, it did not represent the wide range of communicative situations students would encounter outside of the classroom (Swain & Lapkin, 1989, pp. 153–155).

Not all immersion classrooms were like this, however. Some were more communicative in their approach and based the selection of communication tasks on students' needs and goals. Other classrooms set aside time for grammar-focused lessons. Nevertheless, the general trend was the same. After several years, many students did not display the same grammatical competence of their native French-speaking counterparts.

Swain and Lapkin (1989) concluded that the overarching problem observed in all the immersion settings (whether primarily content-based or communicative; with our without separate grammar lessons) was that they failed to integrate content instruction with language instruction. When grammar was taught, it was done so as a separate lesson, completely unrelated to anything else the students were studying. When classroom activities centered around content, little effort was made on the part of teachers to direct students' attention to form. Error correction was infrequent and inconsistently given. If students made errors in their speech or writing, they were likely unaware of it. As a result, these errors persisted over a period of many years.

While Krashen would likely argue that the French immersion programs were unsuccessful because they did not provide learners with sufficient comprehensible input, many researchers worried that a total focus on meaning, without any attention to form, was not sufficient for the development of grammatical competence. While in many cases, grammatical errors do not impede the flow of communication, educators were well aware that these errors could act as gatekeepers in academic and professional contexts. Using the wrong pronoun or article on the playground may not be a problem, but making these errors in a job interview would be. Many educators felt that a purely communicative classroom left open the possibility that some student errors would go unaddressed, and students would continue to make these errors without realizing it.

Reflection 2.7
- As an L2 learner or a teacher, have you ever experienced a content-based, immersion classroom? If so, in what ways was this context either similar to or different from the contexts studied by Swain and her colleagues?
- How might immersion and content-based programs approach the teaching of L2 grammar?

Beyond input: Pushed output and noticing in L2 development

The French immersion studies prompted many to critically evaluate Krashen's argument that comprehensible input was the primary determinant in language learning success. In many French immersion classrooms, students had plenty of input, yet this was not enough to develop grammatical competence in the target language. Drawing on her extensive research in these settings, Merrill Swain argued that comprehensible input alone was not sufficient for successful second language development. Immersion students in Canada had plenty of input; what they did not have, Swain argued, were opportunities to speak and receive feedback on the accuracy of their production. The fact that these students did not fully develop their grammatical accuracy over a period of several years suggested that both input *and* output played a crucial role in the second language acquisition process. In her Output Hypothesis, Swain (1985) argued that second language classrooms should include activities that "push" learners "toward the delivery of a message that is not only conveyed, but that is conveyed precisely, coherently, and appropriately. Being 'pushed' in output… is a concept parallel to that of the *i +1* of comprehensible input. Indeed, one might call this the 'comprehensible output' hypothesis" (p. 248). For Swain, output was not simply language produced by the learner, but rather was a process in and of itself, a process in which students had opportunities to analyze and reflect on their own language use.

SWAIN'S (1985) OUTPUT HYPOTHESIS
The meaning of 'negotiating meaning' needs to be extended beyond the usual sense of simply 'getting one's message across.' Simply getting one's message across can and does occur with grammatically deviant forms and sociolinguistically inappropriate language. Negotiating meaning needs to incorporate the notion of being pushed toward the delivery of a message that is not only conveyed, but that is conveyed precisely, coherently, and appropriately. Being 'pushed' in output… is a concept parallel to that of the *i +1* of comprehensible input. Indeed, one might call this the 'comprehensible output' hypothesis.   (Swain, 1985, pp. 248–249)

Swain's Output Hypothesis suggested that language classrooms needed to do more than simply provide comprehensible input to students. They needed to also provide opportunities for students to speak and write, to engage more directly with the language they were learning, through the process of using it. It was also crucial for communicatively-oriented classrooms to design lessons and tasks that engaged students in both a focus on content and a focus on language (Swain & Lapkin, 1989). Simply giving students a chance to speak was not enough; teachers also needed to provide students with carefully planned feedback on the comprehensibility and accuracy of their utterances. Without such feedback, students may never notice the ways in which their language production differed from the language of native speakers. Like many immersion students before them, they may complete several years of language study without fully developing their grammatical competence.

Concern over second language student's grammatical competence extended beyond the French immersion classroom. At the same time that Swain and colleagues were investigating the effectiveness of immersion programs in Canada, Richard Schmidt was exploring how adults acquired second languages in both naturalistic and instructed contexts. In 1983, Schmidt published the results of a case study he conducted in Hawaii of a man he called 'Wes,' a professional artist who had recently relocated to Hawaii from Japan. Schmidt describes Wes' exposure to English during the 3-year study period in this way:

> The past three years have been characterized by steadily increasing demands on Wes's ability to communicate in English, and he now lives in an English-speaking world. An extremely friendly and outgoing person, he has a wide circle of friends and acquaintances who are monolingual English speakers, including an American roommate. Contacts with other Japanese speakers have shrunk rather than grown…. I would estimate very roughly that something between 75 and 90 percent of all of Wes's meaningful interactions at the present time are in English.   (Schmidt, 1983, p. 140–141)

Schmidt found, however, that despite the fact that Wes was exposed to a considerable amount of comprehensible input, in a variety of communicative situations, his grammatical competence developed very little during the three-year period of the study. A number of grammatical forms had not been fully acquired by Wes at the start of the study (e.g., progressive *-ing*, auxiliary *be*, plural *-s*, past *-ed*); by the end, his use of these morphemes showed little change. For example, though Wes' use of irregular past tense verbs increased over the course of the study, he had not produced any verbs with the regular *-ed* ending.

In a second study (Schmidt and Frota, 1986), Schmidt investigated his own language learning processes, during a period in which he was studying Portuguese in Brazil. Schmidt took a language class, but also spent a great deal of time engaged in meaningful conversations with native Portuguese speakers. To explore what factors could be said to impact his acquisition process, Schmidt kept a journal of his language learning experiences. Analysis of the journal entries and his own language production revealed an important factor in the learning process that Schmidt and Frota had not anticipated: One of the strongest predictors of Schmidt's use of particular language forms was not whether it was available in the input, but rather whether he had noticed, or paid some kind of attention to, the form. One form of noticing Schmidt and Frota were able to keep track of was Schmidt's mentioning of particular forms in his journal entries. Forms that appeared in the input he received *and* which were mentioned in his written journal entries were most likely to appear later in his language production.

These observations provided support for Swain's argument that input alone was not sufficient for second language development and that output played a crucial role in directing learners' attention toward their own language use. It can be said that Schmidt's journal writing and his conversations with native speakers pushed him to notice aspects of the language he may not have paid attention to otherwise. Schmidt's study also suggested that opportunities to produce output were not, in and of themselves, guarantees that language development would take place. Rather, it was the *noticing* that was key. For example, while Wes had plenty of opportunities to engage in meaningful interaction with native speakers, his grammatical competence changed little over a period of three years. Perhaps, because Wes was not studying the language formally and did not feel pressure to achieve grammatical accuracy, he did not direct a great deal of attention toward specific grammatical forms. His friends and colleagues, for the most part, could understand him, and his English did not stand in the way of his success as an artist. Wes, like the French immersion students, did not receive a great deal of feedback on the accuracy of his utterances. His day-to-day interactions were focused entirely on meaning; little attention was paid to grammatical form.

All of this work helped to lead Schmidt (1990) to propose a theory of the role of consciousness in second language learning. Schmidt argued that "attention is required for all learning" (1995, p. 45), that before a language form can be acquired, it first must be noticed. When learners notice, or detect, a particular word, morpheme, or syntactic pattern, this form becomes available for further processing by the language learner, and thus may eventually be integrated into the learner's own language system. If a form is not noticed, it does not have a chance of being processed or integrated; it cannot be acquired.

NOTICING HYPOTHESIS (Schmidt, 1990; 1995)
What learners notice is constrained by a number of factors, but incidental learning is certainly possible when task demands focus attention on relevant features of the input…. Paying attention to language form is hypothesized to be facilitative in all cases, and may be necessary for adult acquisition of redundant grammatical forms [i.e., forms not crucial to the overall meaning of the message]. In general, the relation between attention and awareness provides a link to the study of individual differences in language learning, as well as to consideration of the role of instruction in making formal features of the target language more salient. (Schmidt, 1990, p. 149)

Such a view of the learning process helped to explain why many second language learners, exposed to authentic language input for many years, still did not fully develop their grammatical competence. A focus on meaning may lead to the noticing of key vocabulary words or formulaic expressions, but may not prompt learners to notice other, less salient features of the input, like grammatical morphemes or word order rules.

Though many questions remained about the role of grammar in the L2 classroom, Schmidt's Noticing Hypothesis emerged at a time in which applied linguists and second language educators had much to agree about. Communicative competence was widely accepted as the primary goal of second language instruction, and grammatical competence was recognized as a crucial component of overall language ability. It was becoming clear that input alone was not enough to develop communicative competence, and that opportunities to both participate in meaningful interaction *and* attend to form were needed. The persistent question of the time, however, was still unanswered. How could teachers promote noticing in a primarily meaning-focused classroom? In an issue celebrating the 25th anniversary of the journal *TESOL Quarterly*, Cecle-Murcia (1991) summed up the state of affairs this way:

> During the past 25 years we have seen grammar move from a position of central importance in language teaching, to pariah status, and back to a position of renewed importance, but with some diminution when compared with the primacy it enjoyed 25 years ago and had enjoyed for so long before then. Grammar is now viewed as but one component in a model of communicative competence (Canale & Swain, 1980; Hymes, 1972), and thus it can no longer be viewed as a central, autonomous system to be taught and learned independent of meaning, social function, and discourse structure. Nor can the grammar of adolescent and adult second and foreign language learners be viewed

as a system that will simply emerge on its own given sufficient input and practice. Grammar, along with lexis – and also phonology for spoken discourse – are resources for creating meaning through text and for negotiating socially motivated communication. These resources need to be learned and sometimes they also need to be taught; however, when taught, they must be taught in a manner that is consonant with grammar's new role. Finding effective ways to do this is the current challenge.

(pp. 476–477)

Reflection 2.8

– What roles do you feel output and noticing have played in your own L2 development?
– Considering the many perspectives reviewed in this chapter (e.g., Krashen, Long, Swain, Schmidt), as well as your own experience, what role do you see for grammar instruction in the L2 classroom?

Focus on form in the second language classroom

Schmidt's and Swain's theories helped to spark a new era of research in the area of second language grammar pedagogy. This research did not focus so much on whether grammar instruction was good or bad for the L2 learner. Rather, the question of whether to teach or not teach grammar was phrased in somewhat different terms: How can teachers prompt students to focus not only on meaning, but also on form, in the L2 classroom? In his (1995) discussion of attention and noticing in second language acquisition, Schmidt outlined a number of options available for teachers, including the use of communication tasks *and* explicit grammar lessons. What was most important, he argued, was to find ways of focusing students' attention on those forms which they had either not yet noticed or were in the process of developing.

Within the field of applied linguistics, however, not all scholars agreed on how teachers could most effectively promote the noticing of grammatical forms in the L2 classroom. Long (1985; 1991; Long & Robinson, 1998), for example, cautioned against a return to explicit instruction, proposing instead a *focus on form* approach to L2 teaching. In a *focus on form* approach, teachers make efforts to draw learners' attention to form in the course of meaningful interaction, not pre-emptively, but reactively. That is, teachers shift learners' attention to word choice or grammar only when difficulties or communication breakdowns occur. Long also made a point to distinguish *focus on form* from what he called a *focus on formS*. In a *focus on formS* approach, the syllabus is organized according to grammatical features, and daily lessons involve the explicit teaching of a target form followed by structured practice (e.g., fill-in-the-blank or error correction exercises). Long argued that a *focus on form* approach is more conducive to L2 learning because it is designed to respond to the learner's communicative needs.

Focus on formS approaches, on the other hand, do not take the learner's needs into account, as target forms are pre-selected and taught regardless of whether the learner needs to or is ready to learn them. A *focus on form* approach, according to Long, also ensures that attention to form occurs within the context of communication, which allows learners to make important links between the linguistic form, its meaning, and its appropriate use.

Other scholars at the time, however, argued that planned, explicit grammar lessons also had a place in the L2 classroom (R. Ellis, 1993; DeKeyser, 1995). If noticing was such a crucial component of the L2 acquisition process, and if learners were found to focus very little on grammatical form when engaged in meaning-focused communication, then perhaps explicit instruction was needed to raise learners' awareness of the grammatical forms they had not yet fully acquired. Fotos (2002) for example, has recommended a three-staged approach to L2 grammar instruction, which involves (1) an explicit grammar lesson, (2) a communication task, and (3) a follow-up discussion of students' use of grammar during the task. This new debate, over how explicit focus on form in the L2 classroom should be, motivated a great deal of SLA research in the years that followed. In Chapters 8 and 9, we review this research, and its corresponding pedagogical recommendations, in more detail. But first, before delving into the "how" of L2 grammar acquisition and teaching, we need to consider the "what." In other words, what is it, exactly, that we teach when we say we are teaching grammar?

Summary

In just 50 short years, a series of major shifts in theory occurred within the fields of linguistics and language teaching. The pioneering work of this era has, in large part, shaped our current understanding grammar use, L2 grammar acquisition, and L2 grammar instruction. Some of the key developments we will revisit in subsequent chapters include:

Descriptions of grammar use
-   From the 1940s onward, linguists have taken a primarily descriptive approach to the study of grammar. Applied linguists are no exception, and as we will see in Chapter 3, the collection and analysis of spoken and written language data still plays a major role in the development of L2 teaching materials and methods.
-   Since the seminal work of Hymes (1972) and Canale and Swain (1980), applied linguists have focused on describing how language is used in a variety of settings: at home, at work, at school, or even at the coffee shop. Of particular interest is how the characteristics of these settings impact the linguistic choices we make. Descriptions of grammar use can include not only rules of morphology and syntax, but also the rules of social interaction.

L2 grammar acquisition
–   Chomsky's theories of child language acquisition prompted many applied linguists to explore how the acquisition of a second language later in life might be similar to, or different from, first language acquisition.
–   One key similarity observed at this time was the phenomenon of developmental sequences. Both children and adults have been found to experience similar stages of acquisition, regardless of whether acquisition occurs in a naturalistic or instructed context. A more extensive review of this research is provided in Chapter 7.
–   The role of input in second language acquisition was also researched extensively during this time. Krashen's hypotheses stressed the importance of comprehensible input, and Long's Interaction Hypothesis highlighted the role that the negotiation of meaning might play in the L2 acquisition process.
–   Studies of French immersion settings suggested, however, that exposure to comprehensible input through meaningful interaction may not be enough to foster the full development of L2 grammatical competence. Swain (1985) argued that comprehensible *output* was also needed; that when pushed to produce the language, students are more likely to analyze their own language use.
–   Schmidt would further argue that in addition to input, interaction, and pushed output, *noticing* was also a necessary condition for successful second language acquisition.

L2 grammar instruction
–   Theoretical shifts in linguistics and second language acquisition led many to question whether grammar instruction should continue to play a central role in the L2 classroom.
–   Many criticized L2 classrooms' use of structural syllabi, which were organized according to grammatical features and which relied primarily on explicit rule explanations. Krashen argued that explicit grammar instruction actually impeded the second language acquisition process.
–   The focus on communicative competence as the ultimate goal of L2 instruction led many to propose alternatives to the structural syllabus, such as the notional syllabi of Van Ek (1976) and Wilkins (1976). Many teachers abandoned grammar instruction altogether, and instead focused on using authentic, meaning-focused, communicative tasks.
–   Continued research in French immersion settings suggested that L2 classrooms which were entirely meaning-focused did not provide students with sufficient opportunities to attend to form.
–   These concerns helped give rise to *focus on form* approaches to second language teaching. Long, who first coined the term, argued that focus on form should always occur in the midst of meaningful interaction, in response to communication difficulties. He warned against a return to *focus on formS*, or teaching approaches which made use of a structural syllabus and explicit grammar lessons. Other researchers, however, argued that *focus on formS* approaches could also be used to draw learners' attention to linguistic forms.

- Though the debate continues over what the ideal balance between form and meaning might be, there is considerable agreement that some focus on form is needed. Precisely how to draw students' attention to grammar while still developing other areas of communicative competence has been a central focus of instructed SLA research over the past two decades.

Suggestions for further reading

Ellis, R. (2006). Current issues in the teaching of grammar: An SLA perspective. *TESOL Quarterly*, *40*(1), 83–107.

Mitchell, R. (2000). Anniversary article. Applied linguistics and evidence-based classroom practice: The case of foreign language grammar pedagogy. *Applied Linguistics*, *21*(3), 281–303.

Chapter 3

What is grammar and how can it be described?

Just as there have been numerous debates over the role that grammar instruction should play in the classroom, several proposals have been put forth regarding what grammar is and how it can be described. The most basic definition offered in many linguistics textbooks is that grammar is a system of rules which governs how words (and smaller morphemes) can be combined to form sentences. Most linguists would agree that, at a minimum, grammar description should involve the analysis of individual sentences, so that the underlying rules that make these sentences possible can be identified. A more complicated issue, however, is whether grammar description should involve *more* than sentence-level analysis. After all, language users rarely utter a single sentence that is disconnected from other sentences. We use grammar to express meaning and to participate in communication. We generate sentences in response to other sentences that have already been uttered, for a particular purpose, in a specific situation. If we consider this larger context, then grammar description may involve more than the study of morphology and syntax.

Debates over whether non-grammatical, contextual factors should be accounted for in the description of grammar are connected to larger debates over the nature of language competence. Chomsky's description of language competence focused on grammatical competence, and his characterization of grammatical competence focused primarily on phrase and clause structure rules. In the generative research that followed, native speakers were typically asked to judge whether individual sentences were either grammatical (possible) or ungrammatical (not possible) in their language.

Grammaticality judgment tasks have also been used in research on second language acquisition. Table 3.1 presents sample items from a grammaticality judgment task developed by Johnson and Newport (1989, p. 73) for a study of age effects on L2 learning. These sentence pairs contrast a grammatical sentence with an ungrammatical one (denoted with an asterisk). In a grammaticality judgment task, sentences like these are distributed randomly (rather than in matched pairs), and test-takers are asked to judge whether a sentence is acceptable or not in the language. While native speakers of a language typically complete grammaticality judgments quickly and with few mistakes, L2 performance is often much more variable, particularly if the L2 user is still in the process of learning the language.

Table 3.1 Sample grammaticality judgment items

Grammatical and ungrammatical sentence pairs
1.   The farmer bought two pigs at the market.   *The farmer bought two pig at the market.
2.   The little boy is speaking to a policeman.   *The little boy is speak to a policemen.
3.   Yesterday the hunter shot a deer.   *Yesterday the hunter shoots a deer.

*Note: An asterisk denotes an ungrammatical sentence.

In grammaticality judgment tasks, ungrammatical sentences violate rules of morphology or syntax. In L2 research, grammaticality judgment tasks are used to assess learners' language competence. The Johnson and Newport study, for example, aimed to investigate whether there was any relationship between the age at which one started learning English and the degree of success achieved in learning the language. L2 users' performance on the grammaticality task was used as a measure of their language ability: participants with lower scores were seen as less ultimately successful than participants with higher scores.

As we saw in Chapter 2, however, not all linguists define language competence in terms of morphology and syntax alone. Hymes' (1972) theory of communicative competence aimed to emphasize the importance of social factors and included the ability to judge not only whether a sentence was grammatical, but also whether it was appropriate in a given context. While word and sentence formation rules help us to understand how native speakers are able to generate an infinite number of sentences in their mother tongue, what was more interesting to many linguists was the fact that they *didn't*. Native speakers had, at their disposal, a vast number of grammatical choices, but with every utterance, they had to choose just one option. How did they make that choice?

This was not a new question in the field of linguistics. It was a question central to much of the structural linguistics research that preceded Chomsky, and it was a question that many linguists, particularly those interested in language education, continued to pursue throughout the latter half of the 20th century. One of the most notable linguists who pursued this question was M. A. K. Halliday, who is credited with founding the field of systemic-functional linguistics. Systemic-functional linguistics (or SFL) aims to describe how speakers and writers use language as a resource for expressing meaning in a social context.

> We use language to interact with one another, to construct and maintain our interpersonal relations and the social order that lies behind them…. Grammar provides us with the basic resource for expressing these speech functions. (Matthiessen & Halliday, p. 1)

In this view of grammar as a resource, grammar description involves more than the description of morphological and syntactic rules. Halliday (1977) did not intend for this functional approach to replace Chomsky's generative approach; rather, he saw the two theories of language as complementary. Whereas Chomsky was primarily interested in the innate human abilities that made language acquisition possible, Halliday was more interested in the external, social factors that helped to shape the course of a person's language development over time.

Halliday's theories, like Chomsky's, were informed by observations of child language acquisition. Halliday (1977) observed children interacting with their parents, from birth into the school-aged years. He noticed that before children developed the ability to use words and grammar, they learned to use their vocal chords to express intentions and desires, or what Halliday called "functions." General functions important in the world of children included "satisfying material needs," "controlling the behavior of others," "getting along with other people," "identifying and expressing the self," "exploring the world," and "communicating new information" (Halliday, 1977, pp. 19–20). Gradually, Halliday argued, children learn what specialized meanings are possible within each function. For example, within the general function of "satisfying material needs," children can request milk, food, comfort, sleep, and so on. Initially, children may indicate these meanings through gestures or sounds. Over time, through interaction with their caregivers, children learn the specific forms (both vocabulary and grammar) that can be used to express these meanings. They also learn which forms are more or less appropriate for a given function, in a particular communicative setting. Halliday (1977) described this process as a process of "learning how to mean":

> If there is anything which the child can be said to be acquiring, it is a range of potential, which we could refer to as his 'meaning potential'. This consists in the mastery of a small number of elementary functions of language, and of a range of choices in meaning within each one. The choices are very few at first, but they expand rapidly as the functional potential of the system is reinforced by success. (p. 19)

This mapping of form to function occurs, Halliday argued, through interaction, as it would be impossible for the child to learn what is or is not appropriate without the experience of communicating in a real context for a real purpose.

In systemic-functional linguistics, then, the starting point for analysis is not the individual sentence, but rather the communicative situation, or what is referred to as *register*. Register is similar to Hymes' (1972) concept of a speech event, and can be defined according to situational factors, such as the institutional setting (the subject matter, the goals of communication, the roles played by participants); the relationship between participants (e.g., whether intimate or not, whether equal in terms of power or not; and the mode (e.g., whether spoken or written). The job of a systemic-functional linguist, according to Matthiessen and Halliday (1997), is to use a knowledge of these contextual factors to explain the grammatical choices made by speakers and writers: "What is a grammarian doing, in working on the grammar of a language? Doing grammar means establishing, and explaining, the principles that lie behind the wordings of a natural language" (n.p.). Matthiessen and Halliday's concept of "principles" was much different from Chomsky's. In Chomsky's generative tradition, the "principles that lie behind the wordings of a natural language" would be primarily syntactic in nature. In systemic-functional linguistics, principles are derived by examining "*which* kinds of situational factor determine *which* kinds of selection in the linguistic system" (Halliday, 1977, p. 32). Identifying important situational factors involves an analysis of the larger register: the mode of communication, the participants, and the purpose.

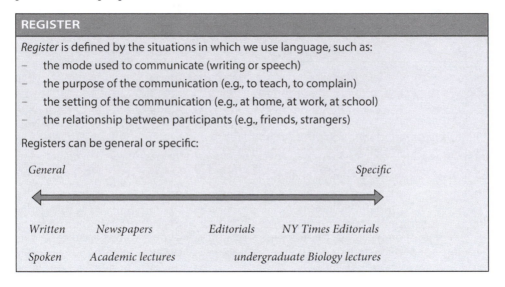

REGISTER

Register is defined by the situations in which we use language, such as:
- the mode used to communicate (writing or speech)
- the purpose of the communication (e.g., to teach, to complain)
- the setting of the communication (e.g., at home, at work, at school)
- the relationship between participants (e.g., friends, strangers)

Registers can be general or specific:

General   Specific

←——→

Written   Newspapers   Editorials   NY Times Editorials

Spoken   Academic lectures   undergraduate Biology lectures

Although individual sentences are analyzed in a systemic-functional approach, they cannot be analyzed in isolation, as the goal of analysis is to explain how the communicative context impacts the wording of the sentence. The unit of analysis is not a sentence, as it would be in a generative tradition, but a text. Each grammatical feature observed within a text (e.g., the use of the past tense or personal pronouns) represents a choice made by the speaker or writer, and each of these choices can be explained by looking at the type of text in which they occurred, as each individual text (e.g., an academic essay or an informal conversation) can be linked to a larger register or social context. Grammar is not so much a collection of sentence-level rules, but rather is a system that can be exploited by speakers and writers for the purpose of communication. Mastering a language means mastering the ability to use language forms for particular purposes in a variety of social contexts, in a way that is not just grammatical, but appropriate and effective.

Reflection 3.1

- What registers are most relevant to your L2 students? Make a list of some specific registers that you feel deserve attention in your classroom.
- Choose one of these registers to reflect on further. What communicative goals or functions are associated with this register? What strategies could you use to raise students' awareness of the grammatical choices that individuals make when communicating in this context?

A pedagogic framework for grammar description

Halliday's systemic-functional approach appealed to many applied linguists working in the area of second language acquisition and pedagogy. Just as Hymes' theory of communicative competence laid the groundwork for communicative language teaching, Halliday's functional approaches provided applied linguists with important tools for describing grammar use. Halliday's and Hymes' theories of language competence and language development also suggested that new approaches were needed not only for linguistic grammars, but for *pedagogical* grammars as well. If the goal of second language teaching was to develop communicative competence, then knowing all of the possible grammatical structures of a language was not enough. Students needed to know which forms were appropriate and typical in a given situation.

To address this need, Diane Larsen-Freeman (1989; 2003; Celce-Murcia & Larsen-Freeman, 1999) proposed a framework for a pedagogical grammar, one that could be used by second language teachers to develop their students' grammatical competence. Larsen-Freeman's framework is made of three major components, which she calls "The Three Dimensions": *Form, Meaning,* and *Use* (see Figure 3.1). Larsen-Freeman (2003, pp. 34–35) defines language *Form* as phonology, graphology (written symbols), semiology (signs), morphology, and syntax. *Meaning,* or semantics, refers to the meaning attached to a particular form when it is presented in isolation, such as a definition of a word, or the concept of "past time" associated with the *–ed* ending in English. *Use,* or pragmatics, refers to a speaker's or writer's intentions in a particular communicative context.

According to Larsen-Freeman, L2 grammar instruction must provide information about all three of these dimensions. Just as Halliday argued that children learn not just isolated forms, but how forms are used to express meaning and fulfill communicative functions, Larsen-Freeman argued that L2 students needed to learn the wide range of meanings a form can express, within a given function and context.

Embedded within this framework is what Larsen-Freeman (2003, p. 1) calls "the grammar of choice." Larsen-Freeman, like Halliday, argues that a good grammar

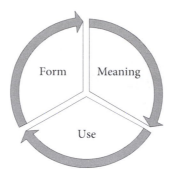

Figure 3.1 Larsen-Freeman's Three Dimensions (2003)

description should include an explanation of why one particular form was chosen over other forms, even when multiple forms may have the same meaning.

> [L2 students] will need to understand that, as speakers or writers, they have choices to make, and that those choices have consequences, so that they can learn to use the language in a way that honors their intentions. Besides, students need to be able to draw inferences about the intentions of others. To the best of our ability, therefore, we should help students understand the linguistic options available. Thus, an understanding of when or why to use a particular grammatical form should be part of teachers' understanding of grammar. (p. 61)

To help language teachers provide more functional descriptions of grammar use, Larsen-Freeman and Marianne Celce-Murcia developed a pedagogical grammar reference titled *The Grammar Book: An ESL/EFL Teacher's Course*. Drawing on individual studies that had been done on each feature, and, in many cases, drawing on their own linguistic analyses, Celce-Murcia and Larsen-Freeman provided descriptions of the form, meaning, and use of a wide range of linguistic features in English. Celce-Murcia and Larsen-Freeman (1983, 1999, forthcoming) also put forth their recommendations regarding grammar descriptions in L2 classrooms, which emphasized the importance of looking at grammar in its discourse context. Grammars for L2 learners, they argued, should include a discussion of how the features of register and the structure of the text itself impact the grammar of individual sentences. A pedagogical grammar should not simply be a collection of rules, but also "reasons," or explanations for *why* writers and speakers might choose one grammar structure over another (Celce-Murcia & Larsen-Freeman, 1999; Larsen-Freeman, 2003, p. 49).

At the time the first edition of *The Grammar Book* was published, however, there were few comprehensive accounts of the grammatical choices made by writers and speakers in a wide range of communicative contexts. The linguistic research at the time typically involved the analysis of a small number of texts of a particular type (e.g., a narrative or a formal essay). Analysis took a great deal of time. (Imagine, for example, trying to look at each instance of the articles *a*, *an*, and *the*, and then attempting to explain why the writer of an essay chose one over the other). In many cases, observations about the use of a grammatical feature could not be generalized – was it the case that a grammatical choice was made because of the nature of the register, or did it have something to do with the author's personal writing style?

To address the uneven nature of functional descriptions of grammar in use, Celce-Murcia (1975; see also 1990, 2000, 2002) developed methods for training teachers to do their own "contextual analysis" of spoken and written texts. Teachers could select the grammatical features that they wanted to learn more about and could analyze their use in texts that were relevant to their students' needs. Contextual analysis empowered teachers to do their own research, but this meant that teachers needed to set aside extra time to carry out their own analyses. As Celce-Murcia explains, once a teacher decided what she wanted to learn, she would need to analyze

> at least 100 tokens of a target form or structure (complete with contextual information and context) to begin making useful generalizations about where the target form occurs (or does not occur), what it means, and why it is used (or not used) by a given speaker/writer in a given piece of discourse.   (Cecle-Murcia, 2002, p. 123)

In addition to time, contextual analysis also requires a great deal of training, the type of training one might find in a TESOL or applied linguistics graduate program. And while this type of analysis allows teachers to investigate specific questions that arise in their classrooms, the findings, like those of the small-scale linguistic studies being carried out at the time, cannot be used to make general claims about how a feature is typically used by most speakers of the language.

Larsen-Freeman's Three Dimensions and Celce-Murcia's contextual analysis provided important frameworks and tools for L2 grammar teaching. In the early 1980s, however, when the first edition of *The Grammar Book* was published, there was still much to be done in the area of functional grammar description. What was needed, in addition to new ways of training teachers to discuss grammar in the classroom, was a comprehensive account of grammar use across a wide range of text types and registers, not only for English, but other languages as well. This was no easy task. It required the analysis of several hundred linguistic features in thousands of texts sampled from all the major domains of daily life: home, work, school, and so on. If done by hand, it would take decades, if not centuries. With the help of computers, however, such large-scale analyses would take place, and, in a few short years, these studies would greatly enrich our understanding of how grammar is used in spoken and written contexts.

> **Reflection 3.2**
> - What aspect of grammar – Form, Meaning, or Use – do you feel is most challenging to learn or to teach? Why?
> - What aspects of grammar have received the most attention in the language classes you have taken? What aspects of grammar do you emphasize most in your own teaching?

Corpus linguistics and the study of language performance

A description of grammar use in a variety of social contexts required the collection and analysis of language performance data, something that had fallen out of favor in the wake of Chomsky's generative revolution. Chomsky had argued that spoken and written language data were limited in that they could not tell us what was, or was not, possible in a language. They only told us what someone had said or written at some time; they did not shine any light on speakers' and writers' underlying competence (Curzan & Adams, 2012; Fillmore, 1992).

The shift in linguistics away from the study of language performance towards a study of language competence did, for a short time, lead to decreased activity in the area of spoken and written text analysis. Two major developments, however, helped to renew interest in collecting language performance data. The first development was a growing call from many linguists for more socially-oriented theories of language. This included Hymes' theory of communicative competence and Halliday's functional approach to grammar description, as well as the study of language variation across social factors pioneered by William Labov. The research methodologies developed by these linguists all required the collection and analysis of language performance data. Second, advances in computer technology had suddenly made it possible not only to store spoken and written texts electronically, but also to perform some analyses (e.g., word counting and retrieval) automatically. This latter development was of particular interest to lexicographers, who previously had to rely on volumes of handwritten notes and text excerpts when selecting words and definitions to include in published dictionaries. But computer technology also showed great promise in the area of functional grammar description, as it was now possible to collect texts from a variety of registers and to use automatic methods of text analysis to compare their linguistic features.

It was during this time period that the field of corpus linguistics emerged. The word "corpus" had been used in linguistics for many years, and simply referred to a collection of texts. In the 1960s, however, corpus linguistics came to be associated with the process of storing and analyzing texts *electronically*, for the purpose of representing specific domains of language use. The first electronic corpus developed during this time was the Brown Corpus, which was compiled by Nelson Francis and Henry Kucera at Brown University. As Kennedy (1998, pp. 23–27) explains in his book, *An Introduction to Corpus Linguistics*, the corpus was organized to represent a variety of written registers, and the texts included in the corpus were sampled from texts published in the United States sometime during the year of 1961. Two major text type categories were created – Informative Prose and Imaginative Prose – and within these categories, further distinctions were made. Text types within Informative prose included newspaper reporting (which was further divided into topic-related categories like politics and sports); newspaper editorials; biographies and memoirs; and "learned" publications (sampled from a variety of academic disciplines: natural sciences, medicine, mathematics, political science, humanities, and so on). In this way, from the very beginning, electronic corpus design was principled in nature, in that texts were sampled from predetermined register categories, and efforts were made to balance different text types. A corpus was designed so that it was representative of a particular domain of use. This domain could be defined in very general terms, such as "Informative Prose," but could also be broken down into smaller categories. Such an approach made it possible to both describe general patterns of grammar use and compare how specific registers (e.g., news writing and academic writing) differed in their grammatical choices.

ELECTRONIC CORPORA

The following websites provide comprehensive lists of corpora, many of which can be accessed for free online.

BYU Corpora

<http://corpus.byu.edu/>

Links to many searchable online corpora, including the Corpus of Contemporary American English, Corpus del Espanõl, and Corpus do Portugues.

Corpora4Learning

<http://www.corpora4learning.net/resources/corpora.html>

Links to corpora of several varieties of English, including Indian English, Philippine English, and Singapore English.

Learner Corpora Around the World

<http://www.uclouvain.be/en-cecl-lcworld.html>

Links to collections of L2 learners' spoken and written texts in several target languages.

Non-English Corpora

<http://www.uow.edu.au/~dlee/corpora2.htm>

Links to corpora in several languages, including parallel corpora (i.e., text collections in one language and their corresponding translations in another language).

Several corpus development projects followed, and by the 1990s there were numerous collections available, which together represented a wide range of dialects and registers in English and other languages (see Hunston, 2002; Kennedy, 1998; and McEnery & Hardie, 2011, for comprehensive reviews). The existence of these electronic collections, together with continued advances in computer technology, made it possible to analyze language use in ways that had never been done before. Three major methodological developments in particular would have a major impact on grammar description, including the development of pedagogic grammars for second language learners:

1. Electronic corpora could be automatically analyzed to generate counts for individual words, phrases, or grammatical structures. This made it possible for linguists to provide more comprehensive descriptions of what was typical or frequent in a particular communicative situation.
2. Electronic corpora could be searched, which allowed linguists to view hundreds of occurrences of a keyword in the context of a sentence, paragraph, or entire text. Lines of text could also be automatically sorted to reveal common phrases and syntactic patterns.
3. The distribution of linguistic features within a register could be compared with that of other registers, which opened the door for large-scale investigations of how situational factors, such as the mode and purpose of communication, impact the choices we make as writers and speakers of a language.

Reflection 3.3

– As an L2 learner or teacher, have you had any opportunities to consult corpora or corpus-based research? If so, what linguistic features did you investigate? What did you learn?
– What types of resources do you regularly use to investigate questions about language use (e.g., online dictionaries, Google)? What resources have been most helpful and why?

Frequency-based descriptions of grammar use

Though it is not possible for computer programs to judge the acceptability or appropriateness of a particular grammatical construction, computers do have the amazing ability to count how many times a particular word or structure occurs in a corpus, even when a corpus is made up of over 500 million words. The computer program will not get tired and it will not make a mistake and it can generate results in a matter of seconds (Biber, Conrad, & Reppen, 1998). This simple technological advancement was in many ways another revolution in language studies. Patterns of use – what is typically done by writers and speakers in particular contexts – could be described on a large scale. In contrast to earlier text analysis studies, which focused on a small number of texts within a single register, corpus-based studies could analyze thousands of texts sampled from a wide range of registers. It was also possible to describe a much wider range of linguistic features, as many large corpora developed after the 1970s were grammatically tagged.

GRAMMATICAL TAGGING

When a text is grammatically tagged by a computer program, each word in the text is annotated to indicate its part of speech and other grammatical properties, as shown in the following example, which uses the CLAWS tagger: < http://ucrel.lancs.ac.uk/claws/trial.html >:

```
This_DT0 sentence_NN1 has_VHZ been_VBN grammatically_AV0 tagged_
VVN._PUN
```

These tags correspond to the following grammatical categories:

```
DT0: general determiner
NN1: singular noun
VHZ: -s form of the verb "have"
VBN: past participle of the verb "be"
AV0: adverb
VVN: past participle of a lexical verb
PUN: punctuation
```

In the generative traditions that dominated linguistics research in the 1960s and 70s, descriptions of the rules of morphology and syntax were based largely on native speaker intuitions, through the use of grammaticality judgment tasks. In the 1980s and 90s, however, corpus-based researchers began to highlight the limitations of native speaker intuition, particularly when it came to judgments about what was typical, or most frequent, in a language. For example, if you were to ask a native speaker of English to name the 10 most frequently used verbs in the English language, and the typical meanings each verb expressed, he or she would likely hesitate – how many of us really stop to think about questions like that? And even if we were to try to name some of these verbs, we would likely suggest some verbs and meanings that are not very frequent at all, and would fail to name other verbs and meanings that are much more frequent than the ones we had thought of.

For many corpus linguists, this inability of humans to describe the nature of their language in quantitative terms underscored the importance of corpus-based research. How could a group of humans, linguists or not, accurately describe the grammar of a language based solely on their intuitions? This realization motivated many corpus linguists to expand corpus research to include not just the description of word frequency, but also the description of grammatical frequency. For example, analysis of grammatically tagged texts could generate lists of the most frequent nouns and verbs in a corpus, which adjectives were typically paired with which nouns, and what types of clauses typically followed different types of verbs.

One of the first comprehensive, corpus-based grammars of a language, the *Collins COBUILD English Grammar*, was developed by John Sinclair and colleagues (see Francis, 1993; Francis & Sinclair, 1994; Hunston & Francis, 1998). This project aimed to develop a grammar of English for language learners, one which was different from traditional grammars in a number of ways. As Francis (1993) explains: (1) the Collins COBUILD grammar uses only real examples from corpora to illustrate grammatical patterns, (2) descriptions of grammar use are based on analysis of corpus data, rather than intuition, and (3) grammar is not described as separate from lexis; *lexico-grammar,* or the tendency of particular words and grammatical structures to occur together in spoken and written texts, is the primary focus.

Building on this work, Biber, Johansson, Leech, Conrad, and Finegan (1999) compiled the *Longman Grammar of Spoken and Written English* (LGSWE). The LGSWE added another important component to corpus-based grammar description: the analysis of variation across registers. The corpus upon which the LGSWE's findings are based was designed to represent four major domains of language use: face-to-face conversation, fiction, news, and academic prose. As with the Brown corpus, further distinctions within these core registers were made (e.g., academic prose included journal articles and textbook samples from a variety of disciplines). The LGSWE corpus also included two dialects of English: British and American. Texts in the corpus were grammatically tagged so that the frequency with which particular grammatical features are used in English could be compared across registers and dialects.

The approach to grammar description taken in the LGSWE is very much a functional one. The LGSWE does not provide frequency counts simply for the sake of counting, but rather aims to provide functional explanations for why some linguistic features are more or less frequently used in particular contexts. As they make clear in the first lines of their introduction, Biber et al. (1999), like Hymes, Halliday, and Larsen-Freeman, are most interested in describing the grammar of choice:

> Every time that we write or speak, we are faced with a myriad of choices: not only choices in what we say but in how we say it. The vocabulary and grammar that we use to communicate are influenced by a number of factors, such as the reason for the communication, the context, the people with whom we are communicating, and whether we are speaking or writing. Taken together, these choices give rise to systematic patterns of use.
> (p. 4)

Biber et al. provided functional accounts of grammar use on a scale that had never been done before. Their corpus-based methodology helped to establish empirical means for describing the "myriad of choices" that language users make every day. These choices could be quantified with the aid of computer programs, allowing linguists to describe "what speakers and writers typically do [versus] what they rarely do" (p. 6). In the LGSWE, frequency counts for over 30 major grammatical features within the four core registers are provided.

The findings of Biber and his colleagues had immediate relevance for pedagogic grammar description. L2 textbook writers are faced with a number of decisions that (ideally) require some knowledge of frequency: What vocabulary words and grammatical forms are students most likely to encounter outside of the classroom? How are these forms typically used in spoken and written contexts? And yet, as Biber and Reppen (2002) note, textbook writers traditionally have not had access to this type of information. "These decisions have usually been based on the author's gut-level impressions and anecdotal evidence of how speakers and writers use language" (p. 200). In other words, the authors of grammar resources for L2 students often rely on their intuitions when describing grammar use. Biber and Reppen admit that "in some cases, our intuitions as authors have turned out to be correct." However, in light of the findings of the LGSWE and other corpus-based studies, Biber and Reppen argue that "in many other cases, we have been wrong" (p. 207).

To illustrate the usefulness of corpus-based findings for pedagogic grammar description, Biber and Reppen (2002) compared the findings of the LGSWE with ESL textbook treatments of grammatical features. They found that high-frequency linguistic features were often not included in the L2 grammar textbooks. Take, for example, the question posed earlier about the 10 most frequently used verbs in English. Ideally, these verbs would appear frequently in ESL textbooks because L2 students are likely to encounter these words when communicating with native speakers of English. Biber and Reppen's analysis of L2 grammar textbooks found, however, that low-frequency verbs were often chosen instead of high-frequency ones. Verbs commonly used in ESL textbooks included "*wear, cry, revolve, arrive, touch, travel, read, rain, shine, write, ring, drive, enjoy, study, build, rise, smoke, close, speak, grow, kiss, stay, own, taste, cause,* and *boil*" (p. 206). These verbs, however, are not among the most frequently used verbs in English. According to the LGSWE, the 12 most common lexical verbs (excluding *be, have,* and *do*) are: *say, get, go, know, think, see, make, come, take, want, give,* and *mean* (Biber & Reppen, 2002, p. 205). Of these 12, only 5 appeared in the textbooks' example sentences. Biber and Reppen suspect that such omissions are quite common, as native speakers are more likely to notice what is infrequent and unusual, rather than what is most commonly done. Several other researchers have noted similar discrepancies between the grammar described in L2 textbooks and the findings of corpus-based research (e.g., Conrad, 2004; Jones, 2000; Meunier & Gouverneur, 2009; Mindt, 1997; Römer, 2005).

For corpus linguists, frequency is important for a number of reasons: (1) the ability to judge what is typically (or most frequently) done in a particular domain of use is a key component of communicative competence, (2) descriptions of grammar should reflect how grammar is actually used in the real world; example sentences and dialogues in L2 textbooks which do not resemble actual language use provide students with inaccurate information and inauthentic input, and (3) high-frequency items make up a large proportion of the language that L2 learners are exposed to; if L2 students are not exposed to these high-frequency items, they will have difficulty comprehending both spoken and written language.

As Biber and his colleagues (Biber et al., 1999; Biber & Reppen, 2002; Biber & Conrad, 2001; Conrad, 1998) have argued, however, the goal of corpus-based research is not simply to provide counts of linguistic features. Rather, corpus linguists aim to provide a comprehensive description of how these features are used in real-world contexts. It is not enough, for example, to know that the verb *get* is the most frequently used verb in LGSWE's collection of face-to-face conversation. What is equally important is how the verb *get* is used in combination with other words to express a variety of meanings, and for what purpose this verb is used (or sometimes avoided) in spoken and written contexts. In corpus linguistics, then, frequency counts are almost always accompanied by contextual analysis and interpretation. This requires that corpus linguists go back to the texts in the corpus to investigate when, why, and how writers and speakers use or avoid particular linguistic features. This analysis takes into account both the immediate discourse context (e.g., Does this feature allow the speaker to politely take a turn in conversation? Does this feature help the writer to smoothly transition from one topic to the next?) and the larger situational context, or register (e.g., What are the goals, values, and expectations of the larger discourse community?). Such functional interpretations allow linguists to build a more comprehensive picture of the many choices that users of a language make each day as they work to achieve their communicative goals.

Reflection 3.4

- What discrepancies have you and your students noticed between your language textbooks and actual language use in the real world? How have you addressed these differences?
- To what extent do you consider frequency when selecting words and grammatical structures to cover in your classes? What resources do you use to learn about frequency and how does this knowledge help to inform your lesson design?

A corpus-informed revolution in L2 grammar teaching?

In the title of a *TESOL Quarterly* article published in the year 2000, Susan Conrad posed a provocative question: "Will corpus linguistics revolutionize grammar teaching in the 21st century?" (Conrad, 2000, p. 548). Citing recent developments in corpus-based approaches to the study of grammar, Conrad predicted that corpus linguistics would have a major impact on how grammar is taught in L2 classrooms:

1. Monolithic descriptions of English grammar will be replaced by register-specific descriptions.
2. The teaching of grammar will become more integrated with the teaching of vocabulary.
3. Emphasis will shift from structural accuracy to the appropriate conditions of use for alternative grammatical constructions.   (Conrad, 2000, p. 549)

Conrad's predictions for L2 grammar teaching emphasize the grammar of choice. Considering what we now know about grammar use, there can be no one-grammar-fits-all approach to language description: "Grammatical study needs to take place within the context of a register or by comparing registers" (p. 552). Conrad illustrates this point with the example of linking adverbials, or transition words such as *however*, *therefore*, and *furthermore*, which are commonly taught in ESL grammar and writing classes. Noting that different registers (e.g., conversation, news, academic prose) exhibit different patterns of use, Conrad argues that general lists of linking adverbials and rules for how to use them do little to prepare students for actual use in real-world contexts. Even discourse-level activities which involve the use of authentic texts can fall short if register variation is not taken into account: "For instance, having students write a newspaper or analyze newspaper articles does not necessarily provide practice in the appropriate use of linking adverbials in academic writing" (p. 552).

Conrad also predicted that future L2 instruction would make a greater effort to integrate grammar teaching with vocabulary teaching, as a large body of corpus-based research has demonstrated that particular grammatical features tend to co-occur with particular lexical items. Take, for example, the high-frequency verb *get*, highlighted previously in this chapter. It is useful to know that *get* is frequently used in conversation but often avoided in academic prose. It is even more useful, however, to know that the verb *get* occurs with particular vocabulary words in particular syntactic patterns. For example, when *get* is used in a copular (linking verb) pattern, it is often followed by negative adjectives (e.g., *get angry, get mad, get upset, get worse*) (Biber et al., 1999). Making appropriate linguistic choices involves not only an awareness of register, but also an awareness of how grammar and vocabulary work together to create meaning. (A point we return to in Chapter 4.)

Finally, Conrad predicted that grammar instruction would emphasize not only accuracy, but also appropriateness. Grammar instruction should aim not only to describe every grammatical feature available to a user of a language, but also how proficient speakers and writers make decisions about which grammatical features to use when. In many ways, Conrad's predictions for L2 grammar teaching in the 20th century echo Larsen-Freeman's recommendations from 15 years earlier: Teaching Form is important, of course, but Form alone is not enough to build language competence. L2 students also need an understanding of Meaning and Use. By the year 2000, corpus linguistics was a well-established field of study, with academic journals and annual conferences devoted to the study of language in use. Surely, this new wealth of information regarding frequency, collocation, and register variation would have a profound impact on grammar description and L2 grammar teaching.

But has it? While Conrad (2000) had argued that corpus linguistics had the *potential* to revolutionize grammar instruction, there was no guarantee it would. The impact of corpus linguistics on L2 pedagogy was dependent on a number of factors. Will L2 teachers have access to corpus-based findings? Will they find corpus-based research to be useful and relevant for their own teaching context? Will publishers incorporate corpus-based findings into their L2 grammar textbooks? Cortes, in a 2013 plenary talk delivered at the American Association for Corpus Linguistics, suggested that she, as well as many other corpus linguists, are still "waiting for the revolution." Similarly, in a comprehensive review of corpus linguistics and language teaching, Römer (2011) writes:

> I would… be hesitant to say that corpora and corpus tools have been fully implemented in pedagogical contexts and would argue that much work still remains to be done in bridging the gap between research and practice. The practice of English language teaching… seems to be only marginally affected by the advances of corpus research, and comparatively few teachers and learners know about the availability of useful resources…. In addition, current language-teaching materials still differ considerably from actual language use as captured in corpora.   (p. 206)

Thus, at the present time, we can, at best, say that yes, *some* L2 teachers and *some* L2 textbooks have made use of corpus-based research. But many have not. There are a number of reasons for this. First, accessing corpus-based research requires some exposure to and training in corpus linguistics, through some amount of coursework, typically at the graduate level (McCarthy, 2008; O'Keefe & Farr, 2003). A number of teacher-training programs now offer courses in corpus linguistics, and several scholars (Aston, 2001; Bennett, 2010; Hunston, 2002; Flowerdew, 2012; O'Keeffe, McCarthy, & Carter, 2007; Reppen, 2010; Sinclair, 2004) have published books that provide an overview of corpus linguistics and its relevance to language teaching, which suggests that over the next few decades, we will likely see a substantial increase in the numbers of L2 teachers who consult corpus-based research as part of their regular teaching practice. In the case of L2 textbooks, the limited impact of corpus linguistics on textbook design is likely due to the textbook industry's strong resistance to change. Several popular L2 grammar textbooks make no use of corpus-based research; nevertheless, they are best-sellers. Significantly altering the content and organization of a top-selling textbook runs the risk of hurting future sales. Change in the grammar textbook industry is likely to be very slow in coming. (See Chapter 5 for some notable exceptions.)

What this means for L2 grammar teachers is that much of the responsibility falls on them. As Conrad (2000) notes:

> The strongest force for change could be a new generation of [L2] teachers who were introduced to corpus-based research in their training programs, who appreciate the scope of the work, and who have practiced conducting their own corpus investigations and designing materials based on corpus research.   (p. 556)

Undoubtedly, as Cortes (2013) points out, corpus linguists must also play a role, as the speed of the "revolution" depends, in large part, on the ability of corpus linguists to make their research both relevant and accessible to L2 teachers and learners. With this in mind, we have included a great deal of discussion of corpus linguistics in this book. In Chapter 4, we focus on the contributions that corpus linguistics has made to our understanding of collocation, phraseology, and formulaic language, and in Chapters 5 and 6, we provide detailed descriptions of how L2 teachers can consult corpus-based resources when designing L2 grammar lessons and materials.

Summary

– In the fields of applied linguistics and second language teaching, the study of grammar includes not only a description of morphology and syntax, but also a description of register, or the situation of use. In Halliday's systemic-functional linguistics, register is defined by a number of contextual factors (e.g., the setting, mode, and purpose for communication), and these factors impact the grammatical choices made by speakers and writers of a language.
– Drawing on the work of Halliday, Larsen-Freeman proposed a framework for pedagogic grammar description which emphasizes Three Dimensions: Form (grammatical morphemes and syntactic patterns), Meaning (the semantic information carried by words, morphemes, and phrases), and Use (information regarding when and why a particular form is used in a given situation). Larsen-Freeman (2003) argues that L2 grammar instruction should aim to address all three Dimensions, so that L2 students have the information they need to use grammar both accurately and appropriately in a variety of real-world contexts.

- L2 teachers can build their own knowledge of Form, Meaning, and Use by consulting linguistic resources and carrying out their own contextual analysis of texts that are relevant to their students' lives. Corpus linguistics research has provided some of the most comprehensive descriptions of Form, Meaning, and Use to date, including information about the frequency of particular grammatical forms, the meanings expressed by particular syntactic patterns, and variation in grammar use across registers.
- As Biber and many others have argued, corpus-based findings often challenge native speaker intuitions and reveal the limitations of existing L2 teaching materials.
- The extent to which corpus linguistics will revolutionize grammar teaching remains to be seen. The continued development of corpus linguistics training programs and resources for L2 teachers will likely play an important role in determining the future course of L2 grammar pedagogy.

Suggestions for further reading

Burns, A. & Knox, J. (2005). Realisation(s): Systemic functional linguistics and the language classroom. In N. Bartels (Ed.), *Applied Linguistics and Language Teacher Education* (pp. 235–260). Dordrecht: Springer.

Conrad, S. (2004). Corpus linguistics, language variation, and language teaching. In Sinclair, J. (Ed.), *How to Use Corpora in Language Teaching* (pp. 67–88). Amsterdam: John Benjamins.

Larsen-Freeman, D. (2003). *From Grammar to Grammaring*. Boston, MA: Heinle & Heinle.

McEnery, T., & Hardie, A. (2011). *Corpus Linguistics: Method, Theory, and Practice*. Cambridge: Cambridge University Press.

Yule, G. (2006). *Explaining English Grammar*. Oxford: Oxford University Press.

Chapter 4

The lexis-grammar interface

Phraseology, collocation, and formulaic sequences

Though corpus-based grammars did not begin to appear until the early 1980s, work on corpus-based dictionaries began almost immediately after the Brown Corpus was compiled. While it might seem that this work is within the realm of vocabulary, rather than grammar, most corpus linguists would argue that lexis and grammar are inseparable; that meaning is not contained within an individual word, but rather is expressed through word combinations. Consider, for example, another high frequency verb in the English language: *make*. If you were to ask a native speaker of English to define this verb, you might get an answer like "to create something." If we look at how *make* is used in sentences, however, it soon becomes clear that the word itself does not carry a great deal of meaning. Instead, its meaning is determined by the phrases and clauses it is a part of. Something can *make sense*, you can *make sure* something gets done, you can *make someone mad*, and you can *make it home* on time. In each of these examples, the word *make* is used to express very different meanings, and it is not possible to attribute these meanings to the individual word itself. Meaning is expressed at the phrase or clause level.

As early as the 1960s, John Sinclair began to study meaning expressed at the level of the phrase, or what is called *phraseology*. Sinclair was a student of M. A. K. Halliday, and, like Halliday, was interested in the grammatical choices available to speakers and writers of a language. For Sinclair, the choices available were not just individual words and grammatical structures, but chunks of language that expressed particular meanings. Sinclair refers to this phenomenon as the *idiom principle*, and he posits that "a language user has available to him or her a large number of semi-preconstructed phrases that constitute single choices" (Sinclair, 1991, p. 110). Though a phrase like *make sure* can be broken down into grammatical components (noun + adj), Sinclair would argue that it is not the case that speakers of English choose the noun and then decide what adjective they'd like to say next. They choose the entire phrase, and in their minds, this phrase represents one lexical item with one particular meaning.

Even when computer technology was in its infancy, Sinclair believed that computer programs could be used to analyze large collections of texts to identify the most frequently occurring phraseological patterns. In the 1980s, when analysis of large electronic corpora became possible, Sinclair began to study phraseology in more

---

EXPLORING THE LEXIS-GRAMMAR INTERFACE

Frequency: the number of times a word (or phrase) appears in a corpus

Phraseology: the tendency of words to occur in particular grammatical patterns

```
make + pronoun + adjective
make   him        angry
```

Collocation: the tendency of words to occur together

```
Make + angry, mad, upset
```

Concordancer: software that allows you to search a corpus for a particular word or phrase

- *Keyword*: the item that is searched for
- *Concordance line*: a single line of text that contains a keyword
- *Key Word in Context (KWIC)*: Concordance lines organized so that the keyword is highlighted (typically centered and in bold).

---

detail, through keyword searches and *concordance line analysis*. In concordance line analysis, a computer program locates each occurrence of a keyword and displays these occurrences as lines of text. The keyword is highlighted in the middle of each line, and lines can be sorted to reveal phraseological patterns. Concordance line analysis can be used to investigate the multiple meanings associated with a word (e.g., all of the meanings expressed by *make*), to distinguish seemingly synonymous words (e.g., phraseologies used with the verb *make* versus phraseologies used with the word *create*), and to describe what Sinclair calls *semantic prosody*, or the positive or negative connotation typically associated with a word or phrase. Figures 4.1 and 4.2 show sample concordance lines, which were generated by doing a KWIC search of the Corpus of Contemporary American English.

Sinclair also developed a method for describing *collocation*, or the tendency for particular words to co-occur with other words. These word associations also help to demonstrate meaning at the phrase, rather than individual word level, as collocations tend to express meanings and connotations that are different from the meanings and connotations of the individual words in isolation.

According to Sinclair, analysis of a word in context, through the use of concordance lines, was crucial to the description of word meaning. Prior to the 1980s, however, learner dictionary development rarely involved the consultation of corpus data.

> The message of a conventional dictionary is that most of the words in daily use have several meanings, and any occurrence of the word could signal any one of the meanings. If this were actually the case communication would be virtually impossible... Every distinct sense of a word is associated with a distinction in form.
>
> (Sinclair, 1987, p. 89)

and the national enquirer tried to	**make**	a big deal out of that and I refused to play
you're actually seeing your audience and	**making**	a connection with the king. and on one level
but they	**made**	a conscious decision to say that he was not conservative on
in tuscany, many farmers struggle to	**make**	a living from olive oil, so they often "pay"
i probably was even thinking that she the coach	**made**	a mistake, o.k., you know, she made
is the u.s. then committed for a number of years to	**make**	certain that there is an infrastructure of democratic
subsequent contributions	**make**	clear that the anthropological figure, unlike the tourist, is
sure the kids, like you guys, huh, will	**make**	fun of him if I tell?
for her birthday but couldn't fool herself into believing they	**made**	her look pretty for these people.
and was back in her apartment around dinnertime. she	**made**	herself a sandwich and later fell asleep on the couch.
If a cowboy	**makes**	it here, he could go all the way to the national
there was regular steamer service to San Francisco,	**making**	it possible to work in the city and live in gentler
Helpful hint to athletes:	**make**	it something easy, and don't hammer your beloved.
I hadn't felt that way ever , the way he	**made**	me feel. being a citizen , you love your country
Sometimes , the scouts of troop 433	**make**	mistakes just like the rest of us. One time ,
I will not enter a pagan temple nor	**make**	sacrifices to your powerless gods . nor will my children . not
calls the manufacturer or simply doesn't use the product .	**make**	sure other parents , teachers , and caregivers know what to do
much protein , not following a kind of atkins diet ,	**make**	sure you're getting adequate calcium intake , not drinking too
are you ? it 's good to have you here .	**making**	them feel comfortable . if they 're going to live in this
're just stingy , " said Tico Tiravante , trying to	**make**	things better and only making them worse . the kids in the
into any of the 200 or so different cell types that	**make**	up the human body . the good news is that evidence is
guys look at all the options , and simply can't	**make**	up their minds . " here are three spots that will help
spring , 1990 my father had begun	**making**	weekly visits : Saturdays to Heather , Richard , and Jeffrey ;

Figure 4.1 Sample concordance lines for the keyword *make*

They 're fighters , they 're not there to	**create**	a bold new society in Haiti , I think you 're saying
there 's a third role here , one of seeking to	**create**	a coherent set of ideas about constitutional law and to
from mass-media campaigns to grassroots organizing , and is	**creating**	a local infrastructure that can be used in off-year local
makes back issues available on-line , its much-repeated goal of	**creating**	a magazine -- currently called HotWired -- that is especially
the freeing of prices in Russia with the aim of rapidly	**creating**	a market economy . He intended to begin priority privatization
Many scholars search eBay out of a desire to	**create**	a mini library devoted to a subject
are taking over the Broadway production this fall . They will	**create**	a new marketing campaign and recast the other principal roles
- Iowa State University has	**created**	a new plan to make diversity a priority , President Martin
tracks : mitigation , adaptation , finance , technology , and	**creating**	a vision for long-term cooperative action .
Show " than to George Carlin . They may not have	**created**	an entirely new form of humor , but collectively they form a
certainly dramatic but only hint at the significance of water in	**creating**	an environment suitable for human habitation
assistance from models . Often , when she has problems	**creating**	an image , she goes to The Metropolitan Museum of Art .
In summer the path is shaded and cool , with foliage	**creating**	an interplay of greens and textures . In autumn brilliant red
The concerns are myriad . Employees who	**create**	blogs set up a direct way to communicate about their company with
Or minestrone or instant almond ? All instant soups are not	**created**	equal . Far too many campers feel they have to settle for
with Indian shops and hunted up individual spices to	**created**	her own special blend . " Instead of the monotony that
such images in a larger context , undercutting some cliches and	**creating**	new frames of reference . The diversity is staggering . Nazar
If you pass them on together , you 've	**created**	something powerful for the individual , the family , and for

Figure 4.2 Sample concordance lines for the keyword *create*

To address the limitations that he saw in dictionaries for English language learn-ers, Sinclair founded the COBUILD language resource series. Word definitions in COBUILD were crafted based on careful analysis of corpus data. Each entry for a word included not only a definition, but also a description of phraseology and collocation. Examples of the word in use were not written by a lexicographer, but came directly from the COBUILD corpus. In a few short years, Sinclair's approach would be adopted by several prominent dictionary makers, and today, the vast majority of L2 learner dictionaries make use of corpus data. As Hunston (2002) explains, "Corpora have so revolutionized the writing of dictionaries… that it is by now virtually unheard of for a large publishing company to produce a learner's dictionary… that does not claim to be based on a corpus" (p. 96).

Attention to phraseological patterns in dictionary development is one example of the inseparability of lexis and grammar; attention to vocabulary in grammar re-source development is another. Both the *Collins COBUILD English Grammar* and the *Longman Grammar of Spoken and Written English* aim to describe not just traditional grammatical structures like verb tenses and clause types, but also the tendency of par-ticular lexical items to co-occur with these structures. In its introduction, the LGSWE devotes several paragraphs to the importance of describing *lexico-grammar.*

> Syntax and lexicon are often treated as independent components of English. Analysis of real texts shows, however, that most syntactic structures tend to have an associated set of words or phrases that are frequently used with them…. These patterns are not merely arbitrary associations; rather, particular grammatical structures often occur with restricted lexical classes because both the structures and the lexical classes serve the same underlying communicative tasks or functions.   (Biber et al., 1999, p. 13)

To illustrate the inseparability of lexis and grammar, Biber et al. compare the types of dependent clauses that most frequently occur with particular verbs in English. While mental verbs like *think, know,* and *believe* are followed by that-complement clauses (e.g., *I think that you should call him*); verbs of desire, such as *want* and *like,* occur with to-clauses (*I want to call him soon*). As Biber et al. argue, these patterns are often related to the underlying communicative functions that each construction fulfills. For example, as Yule (2006) points out in his book *Explaining English Grammar,* we use mental verbs to indicate what we think or believe. The clauses that follow these verbs have a noun-like quality; they are facts and opinions. That-complement clauses allow us to express these statements in sentence form. On the other hand, verbs of desire are used to express what we want or like to do; they indicate action, and the speaker or writer is the agent who carries out that action. To-clauses, by omitting the subject, put the action in central focus: *I want to call, to eat, to run,* and so on. Though it is grammatically possible, we would not typically say, for example, *I want that I will call him soon.* We have preferences regarding which words and grammatical structures go together in a given communicative situation. A descriptive grammar that does not account for these preferences is, in the eyes of most corpus linguists, an incomplete account of grammar in use.

Reflection 4.1

– Examine the concordance lines for the verbs *make* and *create* in Figures 4.1 and 4.2. Do these verbs share any collocates? What collocates occur with the verb *make* but do not occur with *create*? Are there any nouns we use with the verb *create* that we would not typically use with the verb *make*?
– A common phraseology for the verb create is *create + noun phrase*. The verb make, on the other hand, occurs in many different phraseologies. How many phraseologies can you identify in the concordance line sample? How does this difference in phraseology help us to understand the use of these two seemingly synonymous words?
– In what ways might information about phraseology and collocation be integrated into the teaching of L2 grammar?

Formulaic language and grammar description

The strong tendency of individual words to occur frequently in particular grammatical patterns suggests that meaning is expressed not one word at a time, but through word combinations. When communicating with others, language users must not only select the right word, but also the syntactic patterns and collocations that are most closely associated with the meaning they wish to express. On the surface, this seems like a daunting task, a task that involves a great deal of lexical and syntactic analysis. Recent research suggests, however, that in most cases, language users are able to very quickly retrieve the most appropriate phraseologies for a given situation. This is possible because language users have, over time, built up a large repertoire of multiword expressions. These stored language chunks, often referred to as *formulaic sequences*, make efficient, effective, and fluent communication possible. Wray and Perkins (2000) offer the following definition of a formulaic sequence:

> A sequence… of words or other meaning elements, which is, or appears to be, pre-fabricated: that is, stored and retrieved whole from memory at the time of use, rather than being subject to generation or analysis by the language grammar.   (p. 1)

Formulaic sequences include, but are not limited to, idioms like *kick the bucket* or *it's raining cats and dogs*. Many non-idiomatic word strings are also used frequently by speakers and writers to fulfill important communicative functions; for example, we rely heavily on language chunks to express politeness (e.g., *I'm sorry but, I wonder if I could, would you mind if)* and to organize discourse (e.g., *the next point I want to make is, another thing to consider is*). Sinclair (1991) argued that frequent collocations (e.g., *make sure, make sense*) and syntactic frames (e.g., *make + pronoun +action verb + noun*) are also types of formulaic language, as these phraseologies are not typically analyzed piece by piece by language users, but rather are retrieved from memory in the form of language chunks. Wray and Perkins (2000) estimate that, if all of these types of formulaic language are taken into account, "as much as 70% of our adult native language may be formulaic" (p. 2).

The prevalence of formulaic language in speech and writing raises new questions about the role that grammar instruction plays in the L2 classroom. If most of the language used by native speakers is formulaic, then shouldn't second language instruction focus primarily on teaching formulaic sequences? Though few scholars have argued that the teaching of formulaic sequences *replace* the teaching of grammar, many have called for a greater emphasis on formulaic language in the L2 classroom (Biber, Conrad, & Cortes, 2004; Ellis, Simpson-Vlach, & Maynard, 2008; Nattinger & DeCarrico, 1992; Lewis, 1993). Formulaic sequences play an important role in the language acquisition process, as they allow native speakers to both adhere to the norms and expectations of social interaction and to make efficient use of their cognitive resources (N. Ellis, 2002; Martinez & Schmitt, 2012; Wray & Perkins, 2000). Because so many social situations repeat themselves throughout our lives (think, for example, how many times you've approached a counter to order a drink), it is inevitable that certain chunks of language will be used repeatedly over the course of many years. This repetition allows us to retrieve a formulaic sequence automatically when presented with the particular social situation it is associated with.

A great challenge facing L2 learners, however, is that there may be limited opportunity to encounter formulaic language in meaningful contexts (N. Ellis, 2002; Wray & Perkins, 2000). As a result, L2 learners may produce language chunks that are different from the formulaic sequences typically used by native speakers in a given situation. Formulaic sequences also play an important role in the development of L2 fluency. Speakers who use formulaic language are able to communicate at a faster rate than those who do not. Similarly, written prose that contains formulaic language is processed much more quickly by readers than prose without these sequences (Martinez & Schmitt, 2012). When it comes to our personal, professional, and academic needs, Wray and Perkins (2000) argue that formulaic language is something that we "cannot exist without" (p. 12).

It is also true, however, that communication cannot be carried out entirely through the use of formulaic sequences. As Wray (1998) points out, language which relies only on formulae "would be limited in repertoire, clichéd... lacking in imagination and novelty" (p. 64). Wray and Perkins (2000) argue that skilled language users make use of both "creative" and "holistic" processes. Creative processes involve the analysis and generation of novel sentences and rely on the language user's underlying knowledge of grammar rules. Holistic processes, on the other hand, involve the automatic retrieval of language chunks and rely on formulaic sequences that have been stored in memory.

> Our view is that the best deal in communicative language processing is achieved by the establishment of a suitable balance between creative and holistic processes. The advantage of the creative system is the freedom to produce or decode the unexpected. The advantage of the holistic system is economy of effort when dealing with the expected.
>
> (p. 11)

In response to calls for more emphasis on formulaic language in L2 pedagogy, many linguists have aimed to describe the ways in which skilled speakers and writers move in and out of these creative and holistic processes as they work to communicate meaning. Sinclair's early work on phraseology and collocation laid an important foundation for the integration of formulaic language into descriptions of lexis and grammar. Over the past few years, several additional researchers have aimed to describe formulaic language, resulting in the identification of a number of formulaic sequence types. In the following section we focus on four formulaic sequence types that have been studied from an L2 pedagogical perspective: *lexical bundles, idioms, phrasal expressions,* and *multiword verbs.*

Reflection 4.2

- As an L2 learner, did you make a conscious effort to learn idioms and other formulaic expressions? What challenges did you face? What resources and strategies did you find helpful?
- As an L2 teacher, do you integrate lessons on formulaic language into your grammar instruction? If so, how do you do this? What resources do you consult when deciding which formulaic expressions to cover?

Identifying and describing formulaic sequences

Because formulaic language is so prevalent in everyday communication, it is nearly impossible for both teachers and textbook writers to identify all the formulaic sequences that L2 learners need to know in order to communicate fluently and effectively. With the help of computers, however, it is possible to identify those multiword phrases that occur most frequently in a given corpus. One approach to identifying formulaic sequences, then, is to simply generate lists of highly frequent multiword combinations. This approach is taken by Biber and colleagues (Biber et al., 1999; Biber, Conrad, & Cortes, 2004; Cortes, 2004; Csomay, 2004; Csomay & Cortes, 2009), who have compiled several lists of what they call *lexical bundles*. Lexical bundles are multiword strings (e.g., a three-word sequence, a four-word sequence) which meet frequency criteria set by the researcher. For example, Biber et al. (1999) count three- and four-word expressions as lexical bundles only if they occur at least ten times per million words and within at least 5 different texts in one or more registers of the Longman corpus. Because frequency is the only criteria for identifying lexical bundles, these multiword sequences are typically not idiomatic, and they often include incomplete phrases or clauses.

LEXICAL BUNDLES

- Occur with high frequency in a corpus
- Typically do not represent a complete structural unit
  - In conversation, the last two words in the bundle often begin a new clause:
    I want to know   *well that's what I*
  - In academic writing, the last words often begin a new phrase:
    in the case of   *the base of the*
- Fulfill important communicative functions, for example:
  - <u>Stance expressions</u>: *I don't know if, I think that I, I don't want to, I'm not going to, oh I don't know why*
  - <u>Discourse organizers</u>: *if you look at, going to talk about, let's have a look, do you know what*
  - <u>Referential expressions</u>: *that's one of the, and this is a, one of the most, in the United States*   (Biber, Conrad, & Cortes, 2004, p. 377 and pp. 384–388)

While the incomplete nature of lexical bundles make them seem like a somewhat un-natural focus for instruction, Cortes (2004) argues that because these expressions play important roles in both spoken and written discourse, they deserve the attention of L2 teachers and learners. For example, Biber, Conrad, and Cortes (2004), in a study of lexical bundle use in English-speaking, university contexts, were able to classify lexical bundles into three major communicative functions: stance expressions, which allow a speaker or writer to express attitudes and desires; discourse organizers, which allow speakers and writers to indicate the topic or focus of communication; and referential expressions, which allow speakers and writers to direct others' attention toward a specific place, object or idea. Biber, Conrad, and Cortes also found that lexical bundle use varied across academic registers. For example, the majority of the bundles that appear on their frequency list for classroom teaching do not appear on their list for university textbooks. It was also the case that classroom teaching contained the great-est variety of bundle types. While (non-academic) conversation is primarily made up of stance bundles and academic prose is primarily made up of referential bundles, classroom teaching contains roughly equal amounts of both stance and referential bundles. This is not surprising, considering that classroom teaching combines relatively informal conversational elements (*you know what I mean, and stuff like that*) with a heavy load of informational content. Nevertheless, it reveals that students rely on a vast store of multiword chunks when reading, writing, listening, and speaking in their university classes.

The high frequency with which these lexical bundles occur suggests that, over time, speakers and writers commit them to memory and can retrieve them automatically when needed. It is also possible, however, for formulaic sequences to be committed to memory even if they are not highly frequent, as is the case for idioms. Idioms, unlike most lexical bundles, are highly salient. They occur only in very specific communicative situations. We may hear the idiom *it's raining cats and dogs* only a few times in our life; however, the imagery of the idiom, coupled with a violent rain storm, allows us to remember it and retrieve it in the future. Idioms are also different from lexical bundles in that they are difficult to identify in spoken and written corpora. While lexical bundles can be retrieved automatically, based on frequency, human judgment is required to determine exactly what multiword sequences in a language count as idiomatic expressions.

IDIOMS
– Meaning cannot be determined through an analysis of parts
– Widely recognized by a speech community, though not necessarily used with high frequency
– Typically cannot be modified lexically, morphologically, or syntactically; doing so changes the meaning of the expression:

She kicked the bucket	=	She died
The bucket was kicked by her	≠	She died
She kicked the pail	≠	She died
She kicks the bucket	≠	She died (Grant & Bauer, 2004, p. 45)

In a review of several years of research on idioms, Grant and Bauer (2004) highlight three common criteria used to identify idioms in spoken and written discourse: non-compositionality, institutionalization, and frozenness. If a multiword expression is *non-compositional*, then its meaning cannot be derived through an analysis if each individual word in the unit. *Institutionalization* refers to the widespread acceptance of the multiword expression within a particular speech community. The quality of *frozeness*, or fixedness, means that the multiword expression cannot be altered. If a word is replaced by another word, if the syntax is modified, or even if a morphological ending is changed, the meaning of the idiom will be lost. Grant and Bauer argue that non-compositionality, institutionality, and frozenness work together to make a particular multiword expression idiomatic. Unlike many of the phraseological patterns discussed by Sinclair (1991) and the lexical bundles identified by Biber et al. (2004), idioms do not consist of structural frames that allow for word replacements or morpheme changes.

Nevertheless, idioms share an important quality of many multiword expressions: they are not used randomly, simply to make conversation more colorful or interesting, but rather are used to achieve important communicative goals. In an investigation of idiom use in the Michigan Corpus of Academic Spoken Language (MICASE), Simpson and Mendis (2003) found that the idioms used by university professors and students fulfilled important discourse functions. Surprisingly, idioms were used with relatively equal frequency across disciplines and in both monologic speech (e.g., a large class lecture) and interactive speech (e.g., a small class discussion or study group session). In face-threatening situations that required the speaker to give an evaluation, speakers often added an idiom to soften the evaluation. In situations where difficult academic content was being discussed, professors often followed a technical explanation with a paraphrase, using idioms to make the content more friendly and accessible to a student audience. Simpson & Mendis also found that many of the idioms they identified in MICASE were not addressed in ESL textbooks, and, conversely, many idioms featured in ESL textbooks did not occur at all in the spoken academic corpus. Echoing Biber and Reppen (2002), Simpson and Mendis noted: "The selection criteria used by textbook authors for including idioms are somewhat unprincipled and idiosyncratic; thus it is not entirely surprising that there was little overlap between these lists and the idioms found in MICASE" (p. 423).

In Simpson and Mendis' (2003) study, manual reading and analysis of transcripts was used to identify idioms in the corpus. Though this allows the researchers to observe idioms within their discourse context and to evaluate whether a multiword expression meets the criteria of an idiom or not, it is extremely time-consuming. On the one hand, automatic identification of highly frequent formulaic sequences tends to miss less frequent, though still important, idiomatic expressions; on the other hand, manual searches for low-frequency idioms tend to yield only a small list of expressions used in a small sample of specialized language. To address these challenges, Martinez and Schmitt (2012) took an intermediary approach, using, first, automatic means to retrieve multiword expressions, and second, manual coding schemes to separate literal or transparent multiword expressions from more opaque, idiomatic ones. The result of this analysis, carried out using the British National Corpus, was the Phrasal Expressions List. Though not every item in the list would be classified as an idiom (using the criteria outlined above), each item is potentially challenging for L2 learners because its meaning cannot be derived from an analysis of its individual parts. Martinez and Schmitt (2012) point out that transparency versus opacity is not a black and white issue, but rather a continuum ranging from more compositional (more transparent) to less compositional (less transparent). For example, the expression *at all times* is more compositional. One striking feature of the list is that it identifies non-compositional expressions which are not typically thought of as target vocabulary items (e.g., *of course*, *let alone*, *no matter*), but which are also not addressed in L2 grammar materials. Martinez and Schmitt argue that Phrasal Expressions should be included in assessments of vocabulary knowledge and can also be used to gage the difficulty of a particular text. At this point, the items on the Phrasal Expression List have not been classified according to discourse function, as has been done in studies of lexical bundles and idioms. Currently, the list resembles other vocabulary lists, such as the General Service List (West, 1953) or Coxhead's (2000) Academic Word List; analyses of the use of these phrases in spoken and written discourse are sure to follow.

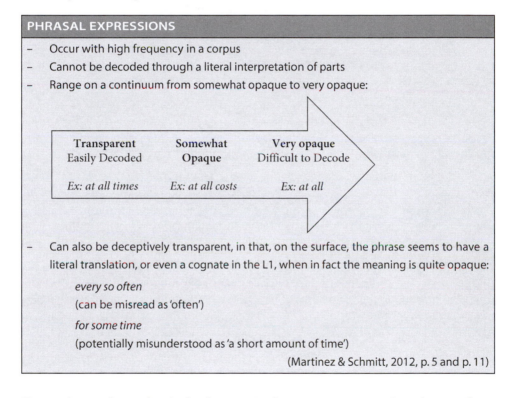

PHRASAL EXPRESSIONS

– Occur with high frequency in a corpus
– Cannot be decoded through a literal interpretation of parts
– Range on a continuum from somewhat opaque to very opaque:

Transparent	Somewhat	Very opaque
Easily Decoded	Opaque	Difficult to Decode
Ex: *at all times*	Ex: *at all costs*	Ex: *at all*

– Can also be deceptively transparent, in that, on the surface, the phrase seems to have a literal translation, or even a cognate in the L1, when in fact the meaning is quite opaque:

 every so often
 (can be misread as 'often')

 for some time
 (potentially misunderstood as 'a short amount of time')

(Martinez & Schmitt, 2012, p. 5 and p. 11)

Yet another multiword unit that has received attention in corpus-based research on English is the multiword verb. This unit, more than any other formulaic expression reviewed thus far, is featured prominently in many grammar textbooks for L2 learners. Multiword verbs, often referred to as phrasal or prepositional verbs in ESL textbooks, tend to be taught as vocabulary items with corresponding one-word definitions; however, multiword verbs can also be inflected to show tense and subject-verb agreement (e.g., I *pick up* my kids from school everyday, I *picked up* my kids yesterday, My mother *picks up* the kids if I am busy) and they come with their own grammatical patterns (some multiword verbs take no direct object, some take a direct object, and some may take more than one object). If textbooks do give grammatical information about multiword verbs, this information tends to focus on whether the verbs are separable or inseparable. For example, it is possible to say either *I pick up my kids from school everyday* or *I pick them up*. However, in the case of the verb *look for*, it is not possible to do this. I *looked for the lost dog* is possible; *I looked it for* is not.

MULTIWORD VERBS
– Consist of a verb + a preposition or adverb particle
– Often have a one-word equivalent in meaning
– Can be inflected to show tense and aspect
– Can be divided into subtypes based on semantic category and syntactic pattern

Coverage of multiword verbs in L2 teaching materials is plagued by many of the same problems observed in textbook treatments of idioms and other multiword expressions. Textbooks seem to choose verbs in a haphazard way, without consideration of frequency of use, grammatical structure, or discourse function. A number of corpus-based investigations have attempted to address these issues. Biber et al. (1999) organize phrasal and prepositional verbs according to syntactic structure and semantic category. Gardner and Davies (2007) have also published a list of phrasal verbs, based on their frequency of occurrence in the British National Corpus, and Liu (2011) published his own phrasal verb list, based on both the Corpus of Contemporary American English and the British National Corpus. Though all of these lists are comprised of frequent multiword verbs in English, no list is the same, and in many cases, the verbs listed at the top of one list do not match the other. These discrepancies do not mean that the lists are invalid; rather, it is important to be aware that what is identified as "most frequent" in English (or any other language) depends on the corpora consulted. Teachers interested in consulting frequency lists (be it a list of phrasal verbs, a list of idioms, a list of lexical bundles, etc.) must keep in mind the registers and dialects represented and the relevance of these registers and dialects for their own L2 students.

Reflection 4.3

– Choose one of the formulaic expressions lists discussed in this chapter (e.g., Biber et al.'s list of lexical bundles, Gardner & Davies' phrasal verbs list). Read over the list with a specific teaching context in mind.
  – In what ways might you use this list when planning lessons and developing materials?
  – Would you share this list (or parts of it) with your students?
  – Would you modify the list in some way before bringing it into the classroom?
  – How does this list compare to other lists you've seen in L2 textbooks?

Frequency, formulae, and phraseology in second language acquisition

As we saw in Chapter 3, advances in computer technology and corpus linguistics methodology have allowed us to investigate how frequently particular grammatical forms occur in spoken and written contexts. This information can help teachers to make decisions about what words, collocations, and phraseologies deserve attention in L2 classrooms. In addition, this information has also helped us to understand the role that language input plays in the language acquisition process. For example, it is often the case that frequently encountered forms are acquired earlier than infrequent ones, and early-learned formulaic expressions can provide a foundation for later grammar development.

It is important to point out, however, that when we talk about the importance of frequency in second language acquisition, we are not simply talking about the number of times a particular word, phrase, or grammatical form occurs in the input. When we encounter a linguistic form, we encounter it in a particular situation. A speaker or writer chooses to use the form for a particular purpose, and the form takes on a particular meaning that is situation-dependent. All of the features of the situation (the setting, the relationship between interlocutors, and so on) co-conspire to create a memorable experience (or not) with this particular form. These situations, or what Tyler (2010, p. 271) calls *usage events*, provide learners with opportunities to make important Form-Meaning-Use connections. Over time, through repeated experiences with similar types of usage events, these connections strengthen, and learners are eventually able to automatically retrieve the linguistic forms needed for particular communicative situations.

Usage-based approaches to the study of language acquisition (Bybee, 2008; N. Ellis, 2008; Eskildsen, 2009; Tomasello, 2009; see also Saxton, 2010; and Tyler, 2010, for reviews) argue that grammar emerges through use in meaningful contexts. Initially, learners are said to remember whole chunks of language (many of which occur as formulaic sequences in the input) and to make one-to-one associations between a particular language chunk and a particular communicative function. For example, learners may acquire the utterance "Hi, how are you?" (a formulaic expression that fulfills the function of greeting) long before they learn to create their own *wh-* questions. Later in development, learners begin to use previously-learned chunks as syntactic frames. Again, frequency plays an important role in this process. Words that frequently co-occur with particular grammatical constructions help to pave the way for future grammar development. In first language acquisition, for example, children learn early on that the verb *give* almost always occurs with two other entities: an object and a person who receives the object. A child's first uses of the ditransitive pattern (S + V + O + O) tend to be with the verb *give*, as this verb frequently occurs in parent-child and child-child interaction. Later, children extend the use of the ditransitive pattern to other verbs. This suggests that frequent collocations and phraseologies in the input help to drive the acquisition process. When children use these language chunks as single utterances with a clear communicative purpose, they make it possible for more interaction and collaboration to occur, which in turn helps to reinforce previously learned patterns and introduce new ones.

Studies of L2 grammar acquisition have observed similar phenomena. N. Ellis and Larsen-Freeman (2009), for example, found that the verbs which emerged first in a corpus of L2 learner language were those verbs which had been used most frequently by the native speakers that the learners interacted with on a regular basis. It was also the case that the L2 learners used these verbs in the constructions they most frequently occurred in. That is, verbs which were almost always used as intransitive verbs in the native speaker input were also used as intransitives by the L2 learners. Table 4.1 displays the verbs and verb-argument constructions which were most frequently used by both the native speakers and, then, subsequently, by the L2 learners.

Table 4.1 Verb constructions which emerged early in L2 learner language

Verb	Verb-Argument construction	Examples
go	Intransitive verb + location (VL)	*I go to school.*
put	Transitive verb + object + location (VOL)	*She put it on the table.*
give	Ditransitive verb + object + object (VOO)	*I gave him the pen.*

The verbs in Table 4.1 can be said to be prototypical of each verb-argument construction. The verb *put*, for example, is almost always used in the VOL pattern (Verb + Object + Location), and, when used in face-to-face conversation, it is easy to see that the meaning involves moving an object to a new location. Ellis and Larsen-Freeman argue that learners first acquire *put* as part of this VOL construction, and this opens the door for learners to eventually extend the use of this construction to other verbs. In this way, the learning that occurs is said to be *item-based*: the item, *put*, a verb that is encountered repeatedly in the input in a particular construction (VOL), drives the acquisition of the VOL pattern.

So what does all of this mean for L2 grammar teaching? First, it suggests, as Krashen (1982) and Long (1980; 1996) argued, that comprehensible input and interaction play a crucial role in the acquisition process. Meaning-focused, goal-oriented interaction provides the necessary conditions for learners to make important Form-Meaning-Use connections. What it adds to this argument is the idea that the frequency of particular words and grammatical constructions greatly influences the emergence of grammar in learner language. L2 learners have the ability to exploit the statistical regularity with which particular words occur in particular constructions – *if* they are exposed to a sufficient number of examples in meaningful contexts. As N. Ellis (2008) and

Wray and Perkins (2000) have noted, however, for many L2 learners, opportunities to interact meaningfully in the target language are often limited by practical constraints, particularly in English as a Foreign Language (EFL) contexts. The amount of input L2 students receive is much, much smaller than what a child receives when learning his or her native language. This challenge is further complicated by the fact that grammatical patterns vary across situational contexts; constructions that are highly frequent in L2 classrooms (e.g., in textbooks and teacher talk) may not be highly frequent in situations outside of the classroom (Lightbown & Spada, 2013). Some effort must be made, then, to identify grammatical patterns that are important to learners' educational and professional goals and to create opportunities for learners to participate in meaningful usage-based events. As we will see in Chapters 5 and 6, corpus-based resources can help teachers to investigate the lexico-grammatical patterns that are most frequent in the registers their students will encounter. And in Chapter 9, we focus more on creating opportunities for students to comprehend and use language forms in meaningful contexts, through the design of grammar-focused tasks.

Summary

-   Corpus-based investigations of vocabulary and grammar have demonstrated that these two linguistic categories are not easily separated. In many cases, meaning is expressed at the phrase or clause level, rather than the level of the individual word.
-   This lexis-grammar interface has been explored through the study of phraseology and collocation. Computer programs, such as concordance line analysis software, allow researchers and teachers to identify the frequency with which particular words co-occur with other words and/or syntactic patterns.
-   Lexico-grammatical patterns are not arbitrary, but rather serve particular communicative functions. Corpus-based approaches to the study of lexico-grammar aim to provide functional descriptions of collocation and phraseology – answering not only the question of how often these patterns occur, but also *why* these patterns occur in particular discourse contexts.
-   In addition to studying collocation and phraseology, linguists have also devoted a great deal of attention to the study of formulaic sequences, or relatively fixed multiword expressions that are stored in memory as single units of meaning.
-   Skilled speakers and writers are able to make efficient use of both holistic (formulaic) and creative (analytical) processes. Fluent, effective communication requires both the ability to create novel grammatical sentences and the ability to comprehend and retrieve appropriate formulaic expressions.

– Corpus-based investigations of formulaic sequences have focused primarily on English. Four major formulaic sequence types that have received attention are lexical bundles, idioms, phrasal expressions, and multiword verbs. One important finding of this research is that formulaic sequences fulfill important discourse functions, allowing speakers and writers to communicate fluently and effectively.

Suggestions for further reading

Huntson, S. (2002). *Corpora in Applied Linguistics*. Cambridge: Cambridge University Press.

Meunier, F., & Granger, S. (2008). *Phraseology in Foreign Language Learning and Teaching*. Amsterdam: John Benjamins.

Römer, U. & Schulze, R. (Eds.). (2009). *Exploring the Lexis-Grammar Interface*. Amsterdam: John Benjamins.

Sinclair, J. (1991). *Corpus, Concordance, Collocation*. Oxford: Oxford University Press.

Chapter 5

Evaluating and adapting existing materials

Thus far in this book, we have reviewed research in the area of grammar description, and we have highlighted some of the implications of this research for L2 grammar pedagogy. In the present chapter, we focus on the evaluation of grammar textbooks and other resources for L2 learners. The goal of this chapter is to help teachers plan, in advance, how they will use existing materials in a particular grammar lesson. We address several of the recommendations put forth in the literature regarding pedagogical grammar description, with a particular emphasis on:

–   Form, Meaning, and Use: As we have seen in previous chapters, learning the grammar of another language involves not only the learning of individual grammar forms, but also the meanings these forms can convey and how these forms are used to accomplish particular communicative goals (Larsen-Freeman, 2003; Celce-Murcia & Larsen-Freeman, 1999).
–   Discourse Context: If students are to understand how grammar is used in particular situations, then pedagogical descriptions of grammar must occur not only at the sentence-level, but also the discourse level (Celce-Murcia, 2000; 2002; Celce-Murcia & Larsen-Freeman, 1999).
–   Frequency, Lexico-grammar, and Register Variation: Over the past few decades, corpus linguistics research has greatly enriched our understanding of how frequently particular grammar structures are used, how grammar and lexis work together to create meaning, and how the use of grammar varies across registers. Grammar descriptions for L2 learners should also strive to include this information (Biber & Reppen, 2002; Hunston & Francis, 2000; Sinclair, 1991; 2004).

Teachers have a number of decisions to make regarding (1) what grammatical features they plan to target in a given instructional lesson, (2) what meanings and uses of these features they plan to cover, and (3) what materials they will use to convey this information (e.g., a textbook chapter, an authentic text sample, a handout they design themselves). In many cases, teachers must use a required textbook; in other cases, they are encouraged to consult multiple textbooks as part of the lesson planning process. This chapter is designed to help teachers make the most effective use of existing L2 grammar materials, through a process of evaluation and adaptation. Because L2 grammar textbooks and websites are designed with a somewhat generic audience in mind, it is likely that the content and style of a given resource will not precisely meet the needs of your own students. Each time you visit a website or open up a grammar textbook to a chapter that covers a topic you hope to teach, you are likely to see aspects of the chapter that you will need to modify – explanations may be too dense or not detailed enough, examples may not represent the registers and dialects your students hope to use, and activities may not reflect the types of tasks your students need to complete outside of the classroom. In this chapter, we encourage you to keep both the needs of your students and the recommendation of L2 grammar scholars in mind as you make decisions about how to use L2 grammar materials in your own classrooms.

Choosing a focus for your lesson

Before a formal evaluation of a website or textbook lesson can begin, it is important for teachers to identify what grammatical form(s) they hope to target and what meanings and uses of those forms they plan to teach. As we will see in Chapter 7, individual grammar forms (e.g., past tense *–ed*, progressive *–ing*) are part of larger grammatical systems (e.g., tense and aspect); acquisition of these forms involves several phases of development. It would be unwise to design a lesson that attempts to teach, for example, the entire tense/aspect system (though some L2 grammar textbooks attempt to do just this!). Instead, teachers (often in consultation with a mandated syllabus or textbook) must select the particular forms within the system they hope to target in a particular lesson, and, ideally, over time, individual lessons build on one another and gradually help students to master entire grammatical systems.

When choosing grammar forms, teachers must also consider the meanings and uses of those forms they plan to target, as one form typically can be used to communicate a variety of meanings, depending on the larger context. One could say, for example, that she is planning to teach her students the simple present tense in English. If our focus were only on form, we might interpret this to mean that the teacher was going to show her students how to conjugate several verbs into simple present tense. However, if we consider meaning in addition to form, then more decisions are in order. Will the focus be on the use of the present tense to express states (e.g., *I am happy, I am a student, I feel nervous*) or habitual actions (e.g., *I eat breakfast every morning, I run three times a week*)? In addition to this, we can also consider use: Is the goal to help students to introduce themselves to new friends? To state opinions in an academic essay? Though it may not be necessary to address all three grammar dimensions in a single class period, identifying target forms, meanings, and uses to be covered within a given time frame can help to facilitate the textbook evaluation and lesson planning process (Larsen-Freeman, 2003).

> **CHOOSING A FOCUS FOR YOUR LESSON**
>
> – What grammatical forms do you plan to focus on for this lesson?
> – What meanings and uses do you plan to target?
> – In what contexts do your learners need to use these forms?
> – What successes and challenges have your learners experienced when trying to use these forms?
> – Based on your knowledge of the forms and your learners' needs (e.g., proficiency level, professional goals), what would you like your learners to know and be able to do with these grammatical forms?

> **Reflection 5.1**
> – As you read through this chapter, we encourage you to try your own textbook evaluation. The first step is choosing a focus for your lesson. Using the guiding questions provided here, identify a target grammatical form, meaning, and/or use you would like to focus on.
> – Next, find an L2 grammar textbook or online resource which includes a lesson on the target form you have chosen. The remaining sections of this chapter will guide you through evaluating and adapting this resource.

Evaluating the quality of textbook and website of explanations

The primary goal of most L2 grammar materials is to *explain* how the grammar of the language works. Grammar materials vary widely, however, in the clarity, completeness, and accuracy of these explanations. Thus, an important first step in evaluating a website or textbook lesson is to examine the quality of explanations provided. Are they written in such a way that my students will understand them? Do they provide all of the essential information I plan to teach? Do they include explanations of not only form but also meaning and use?

Figure 5.1 displays a grammar lesson provided on the British Council's English Grammar website. (We found this resource by googling "present tense English grammar." It was the first hit to appear.) As can be seen in Figure 5.1, the explanations provided are fairly concise, as is common for many online resources. And yet, at the same time, the explanation is complex, covering not just simple present tense, but also present continuous (i.e., progressive), present perfect, and present perfect continuous. In addition, the explanation covers several meanings: "to talk about the present," "to talk about the future," and "to talk about the past." At this point, our students may be wondering why we call it "present" tense!

present tense

There are two tenses in English – past and present.

The present tenses in English are used:

– to talk about the **present**
– to talk about the **future**
– to talk about the **past** when we are telling a story in **spoken** English or when we are summarising a book, film, play etc.

There are **four** present tense forms in English:

Present simple:	I work
Present continuous:	I am working
Present perfect:	I have worked
Present perfect continuous:	I have been working

We use these forms:

– to talk about the **present**:

> He **works** at McDonald's.
> He **has worked** there for three months now.
> He **is working** at McDonald's.
> He **has been working** there for three months now.
> London **is** the capital of Britain.

– to talk about the **future**:

> The next train **leaves** this evening at 1700 hours.
> I'll phone you when I **get** home.
> He's **meeting** Peter in town this afternoon.
> I'll come home as soon as **I have finished** work.
> You will be tired out after you **have been working** all night.

Figure 5.1 Present tense lesson retrieved from: <http://learnenglish.britishcouncil.org/en/english-grammar/verbs/present-tense>

This example helps to highlight not only the issue of clarity, but focus. Lessons which attempt to cover several forms, meanings, and uses at once can quickly become overwhelming and frustrating for L2 learners. Figures 5.2 and 5.3 display textbook excerpts from Books 1 and 2 of the *Grammar Dimensions* textbook series, which is edited by Diane Larsen-Freeman. Not surprisingly, this series organizes grammar explanations according to the Three Dimensions of grammar: Form, Meaning, and Use. The lessons featured in Figures 5.2 and 5.3 also aim to provide a manageable focus for L2 learners, rather than cover all meanings and uses of the simple present tense at once. In Book 1 (Badalamenti & Henner-Stanchina, 2000), for example, the primary focus for the first present tense lesson is using the present tense to tell facts about yourself, for the purpose of introducing yourself to your classmates. In Book 2 (Riggenbach & Samuda, 2000), another meaning of the present tense is introduced, the meaning of habitual action. Here, explanations focus on helping students to see how simple present can be used to describe what you typically do, including study strategies (*I ask questions when I do not understand.*) and daily routines (*Daniela goes to school five days a week.*)

Be: Affirmative statements

SUBJECT	VERB Be		
Monique She Paris The city of Paris	is	single from Paris. in France. beautiful.	singular (one)
Fernando and Isabel They The people in Colombia	are	Colombian. married. friendly.	Plural (more than one)

I	am	single.	
You	are	married.	
He She It	is	Brazilian.	
We You they	are	from Korea.	

Figure 5.2 *Grammar Dimensions 1*: Lesson on Simple Present Tense (pp. 2–4)

Verbs in the Simple Present Tense
Habits and Routines

EXAMPLES	EXPLANATIONS
(a) I ask questions when I do not understand. (b) Elzbieta uses English as much as possible.	Ask, do not understand, and uses are simple present verbs. Use the simple present to talk about habits (things you do again and again)
(c) Our classes start at 9:00 A.M. (d) Daniela goes to school five days a week.	Use the simple present to talk about everyday routines (things you do regularly).

Figure 5.3 *Grammar Dimensions 2*: Lesson on Simple Present Tense (p. 2)

As we will see in Chapter 7, the sequencing of Book 1 and Book 2 also reflects the order of acquisition observed in Bardovi-Harlig's (2000) research on tense and aspect in English: Learners first use simple present with the verb *be* and other verbs expressing states of being, and later learn to use simple present with dynamic verbs (e.g., *work*, *go*). The lesson in Book 2 also includes a focus on adverbs of frequency (e.g., *always*, *sometimes*), which are acquired early by learners and used to express habitual meanings, even before learners start using activity verbs in the simple present tense. Thus, the pairing of these adverbs with activity verbs in the Meaning portion of the grammar explanation helps students to connect a new concept (activity verbs in simple present tense) to a known concept (commonly used adverbs of frequency).

EVALUATING COVERAGE OF FORM, MEANING, AND USE

- To what extent does the textbook address the Form, Meaning, and Use of the target feature?
- Is one Dimension (e.g., Form) emphasized over others?
- Does the textbook provide a manageable focus for the lesson, or are too many forms, meanings, and uses covered at once?
- Are there any explanations that might be confusing to learners? In what ways would you need to modify or supplement the information provided?

In addition to evaluating clarity and focus, teachers can also evaluate L2 grammar materials to determine whether they provide sufficient information about how the target grammatical forms are used in discourse. Many books give examples at the sentence level and save discourse for the practice activities. In her book *Discourse and Context in Language Teaching: A Guide for Language Teachers*, Celce-Murcia (2000) explains how discourse analysis activities might be used to explain grammar use, using a sample text excerpt that contains many instances of the passive voice in English (see Figure 5.4).

Celce-Murcia (2000, p. 65) suggests playing this passage as a radio news report or making copies and distributing to students. Students can first be asked to focus on comprehension (e.g., *How many people were surveyed and where? Which three films were the favorites? What other films were mentioned more than five times? Did men and women like the same films?*). Even though these questions are primarily meaning-focused, they also serve to provide multiple exposures to the target form. After a discussion of content, Celce-Murcia suggests that students move on to an analysis of how and why the passive voice is used in this discourse context:

1. Why is the passive voice so frequent in this text?
2. Who is/are the agent(s) in sentences that have no expressed, explicit agent?
3. Could the passage have been written or spoken using only the active voice? If so,
   a. Would the tone of the reporter be the same?
   b. Would there be the same focus on the films (p. 65)?

> American Film Classics: A survey of 100 People
>
> By Harold Smithers
>
> One hundred Americans (fifty in New York and fifty in Los Angeles) were asked to identify their three faviorite classic films. Casablanca was mentioned most frequently, then Citizen Kane, and the third choice was Gone with the Wind. Only four other movies were named more than five times each. These were Ben Hur, The Birth of a Nation, Sunset Boulevard, and The Ten Commandments. It is interesting to note that while both the male and female respondents mentioned Casablanca as a favorite classic, Gone withthe Wind was suggested mainly by women and Citizen Kane mainly by men.

Figure 5.4 Sample discourse analysis activity from Celce-Murcia (2000, p. 65)

As can be seen in these questions, discourse analysis in the classroom requires a certain level of metalanguage. Teachers using this technique may want to first provide training sessions to students using texts that they can easily understand and providing keywords that can be used to label target forms and their functions. In this way, students learn that a knowledge of grammar can be obtained not only through textbook explanations and charts, but also through their own active engagement with authentic texts. For Celce-Murcia (2000), grammar explanation without discourse context fails to provide students with sufficient information about grammar meaning and use:

> The study of grammar… tends to be restricted to the sentence level…. The problem with this perspective is that there are few grammar choices made by speakers or writers that are strictly sentence level and completely context-free.   (p. 52)

EVALUATING COVERAGE AT THE DISCOURSE LEVEL

- Do explanations include descriptions of the important functions that the grammatical forms fulfill in discourse?
- Are examples provided at the phrase, sentence, and/or discourse level?
- To what extent would you be required to provide additional examples of use in a discourse context?

This view of grammar as context-dependent is also shared by corpus linguists, who feel that information about the frequency of use in particular registers should also be included in L2 grammar materials. An increasing number of resources are making attempts to integrate these findings into L2 grammar textbook design (see the Recommended Resources at the end of this chapter). McCarthy (2008) makes a distinction between corpus-based textbooks and corpus-informed textbooks. A *corpus-based* textbook uses a corpus as the basis for deciding what grammatical forms, meanings, and uses to include in the textbook. More frequently used forms, as well as their collocations and phraseologies, receive more attention than infrequent forms; example sentences are selected from the corpus (not invented by the author); and comparisons of frequency across register are provided. "Corpus-based materials are materials that try to be absolutely faithful to what the computer tells you about language use" (McCarthy, 2008, p. 566). *Corpus-informed* textbooks, on the other hand, may or may not make explicit reference to a corpus, frequency counts, or the distribution of forms across registers, though the textbook designers do consult corpus linguistics research as part of the textbook development process.

> Corpus Informed is a more nuanced approach. It is a way of saying that one is going to do what is useful, what one's students want, what is needed, what is feasible, what is practicable, what is going to be most usable for the students. In this case one takes from the corpus what one believes will fulfill those ambitions, those needs, and the teacher's or material writer's task is essentially to mediate corpus information, filtering it for pedagogical purposes. The 'filters' might include what we know about the learning process, what the constraints of the curriculum are, what the local educational conditions, culture and traditions are, and so on. (McCarthy, 2008, p. 556)

Though we find this distinction useful, we would also say that corpus-based versus corpus-informed is more of a continuum, rather than a dichotomy. Towards the corpus-based end would be books that base the selection and sequencing of grammatical items on the in-depth analysis of a corpus or corpora and which use sample sentences taken directly from these corpora. Towards the corpus-informed end of the continuum would be books which consult corpus-based grammars and research studies, but which do not necessarily base selection and sequencing on these findings and which prefer to create their own example sentences. Somewhere in the middle would be books that make many (but not all) major decisions about selection and sequencing based on corpus research and which often (but not always) use sample sentences from corpora.

Figure 5.5 displays an excerpt from a corpus-based textbook, Conrad and Biber's (2009) *Real Grammar: A Corpus-Based Approach to English*. This grammar lesson focuses on linking verbs (often referred to as copular verbs in linguistic resources), such as *be, become, look,* and *feel.* As can be seen in Figure 5.5, the explanation begins by asking "What have you learned from your grammar book?" In the book's introduction, Biber and Conrad explain that their book is not necessarily designed to replace traditional L2 grammar materials, but rather can be used as a supplement. This allows students to access corpus-based information about a particular grammatical feature that may not be provided in other L2 grammar textbooks.

What have you learned from your grammar textbook?
Linking verbs can be followed by an **adjective**. The adjective describes the subject of the sentence. Linking verbs can describe (1) a **state** of existence, or (2) a **change** to a new state:

      1. He *seems happy*.   2. The weather *became worse*.

What does the corpus show?
The linking verb *be* is common in both conversation and writing. But otherwise, some linking verbs are preferred in conversation; others in writing. Here is a list of the most **common linking verbs** used either in **conversation** or in **writing**:

	Linking Verb	Example
1. conversation	*feel*	I *feel* stupid every time I go over there.
	get	Maybe I should go in a *get* ready.
	go	There was a disease and all the potatoes *went*
	look	bad.
		Lila *looks* good.
2. writing	*become*	It then *became* necessary to discover the cause
	remain	of the change.
	seem	Energy costs have risen since the early 1970s, but fertilizer use *remains* highly cost effective. The second part *seems* more vulnerable than the first.

Most linking verbs describe **specific meanings**, and as a result they occur with a particular **set of adjectives**.

Verb	Describes	Following Adjectives	Example
feel	Physical sensations	*better good tired cold sick uncomfortable*	My hands *feel cold*.
	Mental sensations	*ashamed guilty uneasy bad sure*	I *feel bad* for her.
get	A change to a negative state	*angry mad upset bored sick wet cold tired words lost*	He *got mad* when I told him.
go	A change to a negative state	*bad deaf mad crazy limp wrong*	But something *went wrong*, because they weren't ready.
look	Positive feelings about physical appearance	*good lovely happy nice*	Your hair *looks nice*.
	Negative feelings about physical appearance.	*awful sad terrible pale small tired*	There's some meat in there that *looks* really *awful*.

Figure 5.5 Sample lesson from Conrad & Biber's *Real Grammar* (2009, p. 22)

Figure 5.5 illustrates what a corpus-based grammar explanation for L2 students might look like. First, the explanation highlights frequently used linking verbs, providing two separate lists: one for conversation and one for writing. The explanation then highlights frequent meanings and collocates for each linking verb, noting that it is the combination of the verb with the adjective that gives rise to specific meanings. For example, by itself, the verb *get* does not indicate a change to a negative state, but rather the phraseology *get + negative adjective* does. Corpus-based textbooks also prefer to use sample sentences from the corpus, as opposed to author-created examples. As can be seen in Figure 5.5, the sentences provided in the grammar charts have not been created to sustain a particular theme, but rather have been selected from a corpus to demonstrate a lexico-grammatical pattern. To compensate for a lack of a sustained theme, corpus linguists often select sentences that many people can relate to (e.g., feeling stupid in a particular situation or needing to get ready to go somewhere) and they avoid highly specialized content.

Figures 5.6 and 5.7 display two excerpts from another textbook series, *Grammar and Beyond*, published by Cambridge University Press <http://www.cambridge.org/grammarandbeyond/>. According to the book series website, *Grammar and Beyond* is corpus-based because "The grammar presentations are based on a careful analysis of the billion-word Cambridge English Corpus, so students and teachers can be confident that the information represents real-world use." It is also the case, however, that the textbook series contains features of what McCarthy (2008) would call *corpus-informed*, as it takes into account the learning needs and context of many students studying English for academic purposes, and "filters" corpus findings through its own discourse- and sentence-level examples. Most likely the opening text sample in Figure 5.6 and the sentences in the grammar charts in Figure 5.7 were not taken directly from the corpus, but rather were created with the aim of illustrating important grammatical patterns which were observed by researchers through their corpus analysis. At the same time, *Grammar and Beyond* highlights "data from the real world" through the use of frequency lists.

When evaluating traditional grammar textbooks for their coverage of frequency and lexico-grammar, it is likely that teachers will find that the information provided is based on intuition rather than corpus-based research on collocation and phraseology. Take, for example, the stative verbs lesson provided in Betty Azar's popular grammar textbook, *Understanding and Using English Grammar* (1999, p. 15). In this lesson, sensory linking verbs such as *look, feel, smell, taste,* and *sound* are highlighted, but more frequent linking verbs are not addressed.. As Biber and Reppen (2002) have pointed out, this exclusion of high frequency verbs is common in traditional L2 grammar materials. While less frequent verbs like *smell* and *taste* are important in certain contexts, verbs like *get* and *go* play a vital role in everyday conversation. Thus, while popular

---

1 Grammar in the Real World

Do you know how to give a presentation? What do you do to prepare? Read the article. How many of your ideas are in the web article?

How to Be a Successful Presenter

For many people, giving a presentation can be a **scary** experience. If you feel nervous about giving presentations, here are some helpful tips.

– Prepare your presentation **carefully. Careful** preparation will give you confidence, and this will impress your audience. A **confident** presenter always makes a **good** impression.

– Organize your ideas. Think about what you want to say. Then list your three or four main points on note cards.

– Practice giving your presentation aloud by yourself and with friends, too. Tell your friends to give you **honest** feedback, but make sure they tell you first what you did **well**.

– On the day of the presentation, arrive at the room **early**. Think **positive** thoughts and remember that you can do this.

– Before you start, breathe **deeply** and smile **confidently** at your audience. Speak **slowly** and **clearly**. Make eye contact with people in different parts of the room. Look at your notes **quickly** when you need to. Your audience wants you to do **well**. Then relax and do your best.

– After your presentation, ask people for feedback and advice. Use the ideas in your next presentation. With practice, you will learn to give **good** presentations, and you may even enjoy giving them.

Figure 5.6 *Grammar and Beyond*, Level 1, Adjectives and Adverbs: Opening text sample

textbooks like Azar are often strong in the areas of clarity (many students love Azar's well-organized charts and illustrations), they may be lacking in the area of Use, as these books are typically not informed by linguistic research.

EVALUATING COVERAGE OF FREQUENCY, LEXICO-GRAMMAR, AND REGISTER VARIATION
– Do explanations include information about frequency, collocation, phraseology, and/or use across registers?
– Have the examples been invented by the textbook authors and/or do they come from authentic texts?
– What registers do these examples represent (e.g., informal conversation, academic language)?
– In what ways would you modify or supplement the examples provided, so that they were more representative of the registers that are most relevant to your students?

a. Adjectives give information about nouns. They often come before a noun or after be.	I want your **honest** feedback. The slides were **clear**.
b. Adverbs give information about verbs.	The presenter spoke **clearly**. She prepared her presentation **carefully**.
c. Adverbs of manner usually come after a verb or a verb + object.	Dress **nicely**. She looked at the audience **quickly**.

Data from the Real World

These are the most common adverbs of manner:

well	late	easily	carefully	seriously	automatically
hard	fast	clearly	strongly	differently	properly
early	quickly	slowly	closely	badly	

Figure 5.7 *Grammar and Beyond*, Level 1: Sample Adjectives and Adverbs lesson

Reflection 5.2
- Using the guiding questions provided here, evaluate the explanations provided in your chosen L2 grammar resource (see Reflection 5.1). How well do the explanations address Form, Meaning, and Use? Discourse Context? Frequency, Phraseology, and Register Variation?
- What modifications would you need to make to these explanations before using them in your classroom?

Evaluating the quality of textbook and website practice activities

Included in almost any L2 grammar textbook, in addition to explanations of form, meaning, and use, are follow-up practice activities. These activities can include limited production exercises such as fill-in-the-blank, error correction, and sentence construction; as well as free-production exercises, such as role plays or essays. Larsen-Freeman (2003) argues that these activities, above all, should be *meaningful*, *engaging*, and *focused*. She explains:

> Students will best acquire the structures or patterns when they are put into situations that require them to use structures and patterns for some meaningful purpose other than decontextualized or mechanistic practice. Indeed, a neurological perspective suggests that the kind of language practice in meaningless drills is unavailable for use beyond the classroom.... If [students] are not engaged, then they are probably not attending, and their attention is important. Thus any practice activities have to be independently motivating, seen by learners as worth doing.   (p. 117)

To engage learners, it is necessary to take into account learner needs, interests, and goals, and to evaluate whether the practice activity has relevance to learners' lives. Equally important, according to Larsen-Freemen, is ensuring that grammar practice activities are focused. This relates back to our earlier discussion, in which we encouraged teachers to choose a manageable focus for their lesson prior to evaluating the suitability of L2 materials. Similarly, when evaluating practice activities, it is important to identify what aspect of grammar the activity is focused on. It may be that the activity has a primary focus on form (e.g., practice with forming the present progressive), or meaning (e.g., illustrations of actions in progress), or use (e.g., choosing whether present progressive or simple present is most appropriate). This is not to say that Form, Meaning, and Use are easily separated; however, it is possible to choose or design an activity that emphasizes one dimension more than others.

According to Larsen-Freeman (2003), while Form-focused exercises may strive for repetition and the building of automatic recognition and retrieval skills, Meaning-focused activities (such as a game of charades to demonstrate the present progressive) strive to create memorable scenarios that help students make important form-meaning connections. Activities which emphasize Use should provide students with opportunities to make important grammatical choices in a particular context (e.g., Is simple present or present progressive more appropriate here? Is this phrasal verb more appropriate in conversation or academic writing?)

Figure 5.8 provides an example of a grammar practice activity, taken from Riggenbach and Samuda's (2000) Book 2 lesson on simple present tense. This activity can be said to primarily emphasize form and meaning, as it provides a great deal of repetition (students must use simple present with activity verbs each time they interview a classmate, as well as when they report results) and it helps to make an important form-meaning connection (all but one of the questions deal with habits and routines). To emphasize Use, teachers could create supplemental activities which involve the reading of actual survey data, as this would help students to see that the textbook activity has relevance to the real world and that researchers in social sciences and public health also make this grammatical choice when reporting on the behavior of the people they study.

Activity 1: Speaking/Listening

The purpose of this activity is to prove or disprove the following statements about your classmates. Stand up, walk around the room, and ask your classmates questions to see if the following are true (T) or false (F).

1. Most of the people in this room do not eat breakfast.   T F
2. Women drink more coffee than men.   T F
3. Fifty percent of the people in this room watch TV at night.   T F
4. Somebody in this room wears contact lenses.   T F
5. More than three people read a newspaper in English every day.   T F
6. More than 50% of the people in this room drive a car.   T F
7. Nobody likes opera.   T F
8. More than two people here come to school by bike.   T F
9. Everybody gets more than six hours of sleep a night.   T F
10. Most of the people in this room have a sister.   T F

Figure 5.8 *Grammar Dimensions*, Book 2: Sample practice activity (p. 13)

Figure 5.9 (taken from Benz & Roemer's 1997 Book 2 Workbook, p. 7) is an example of an activity designed to provide practice with making choices among seemingly synonymous grammatical forms. This activity focuses on the choice between present progressive and simple present tense. More specifically, it is intended to highlight the fact that simple present is preferred when a situation is true most of the time (*He's usually very outgoing*) or is a habit or routine (e.g., *He talks and laughs with the other students*), whereas progressive is preferred when an action is temporary in nature (e.g., *[he]'s living in Toronto, he isn't smiling much*). Students are asked to look at the use of these verbs in a discourse context and to explain why simple present is preferred in some cases and present progressive is preferred in others. This type of activity helps students to think through their grammatical choices (and thus can be said to emphasize Use).

Mohammed is an exchange student from Kuwait who's living in Toronto this academic year. His teachers and classmates are worried about him because he looks tired and is acting differently from the way he usually acts. He's usually very outgoing, and he talks and laughs with the other students, inside the classroom and out. But these days he isn't smiling much. Normally Mohammed has lunch in the cafeteria, but today he isn't there eating. He often goes outside to smoke a cigarette, but he's not there smoking today.

Figure 5.9 *Grammar Dimensions*, Book 2, Workbook: Sample practice activity (p. 7)

> **EVALUATING PRACTICE ACTIVITIES: FORM, MEANING, AND USE**
>
> – Do the activities provide students with repeated opportunities to comprehend or use the target feature?
> – Do the activities provide opportunities for learners to make important form-meaning connections?
> – Do the activities push learners to make choices about which grammatical forms would be most appropriate in a given situation?

The activity in Figure 5.9 also illustrates the importance of discourse context. To make the appropriate grammatical choices in this situation, we need to know that Mohammed usually behaves one way but recently has been behaving another. In other words, we need a context that goes beyond the sentence level. All too often, however, as Celce-Murcia (2000) notes, L2 grammar practice is provided at the sentence level only. This not only deprives students of a chance to use the grammar in a meaningful situation, but it also makes it more difficult for students to make appropriate grammatical choices.

One area of grammar that is often practiced at the sentence level is article use in English. When explaining to students how to make choices between the articles *a, an,* and *the,* many textbooks present students with sentence-level fill-in-the-blank exercises, like that displayed in Figure 5.10, an exercises featured on the Purdue Online Writing Lab (OWL) < https://owl.english.purdue.edu/exercises/2/1/12 >.

As can be seen in this exercise, the appropriate choice of article depends largely on the discourse context. In number 1, for example, I want ___ apple from that basket, the correct answer depends on how many apples are in the basket. If there are 2 or more apples, then the a person would likely say "I want an apple from that basket." However, if there is only one apple in the basket, and both the speaker and the listener know what apple is being discussed, a person would likely say "I want the apple from that basket." This ambiguity can be extremely frustrating for students. What is worse, the exercise does not allow students to practice the skill they really need: making article choices based on context.

Another complication of many sentence-level exercises is that they mix up the types of decisions that students have to make when choosing appropriate forms. Article choice in English, for example, involves consideration of numerous issues: Is the noun singular or plural? Countable or non-countable? Generic or specific? Known or unknown to the listener? First mention or subsequent mention in the discourse? Though an eventual goal is for learners to quickly assess a situation and make choices based on all of these considerations, initially, learners will need to practice one type of decision at a time. Thus, as we have seen with other examples in this chapter, explanations and activities which attempt to tackle entire grammatical systems are not ideal, especially for beginning and intermediate students.

Exercise : Articles Exercise 1

Directions: Fill in the blank with the appropriate article, *a*, *an*, or ***the***, or leave the space blank if no article is needed.

1. I want _____ apple from that basket.

2. _____ church on the corner is progressive.

3. Miss Lin speaks _____ Chinese.

4. I borrowed _____ pencil from your pile of pencils and pens.

5. One of the students said, "_____ professor is late today."

6 Eli likes to play _____ volleyball.

7. I bought _____ umbrella to go out in the rain.

8. My daughter is learning to play _____ violin at her school.

9. Please give me _____ cake that is on the counter.

10. I lived on _____ Main Street when I first came to town.

11. Albany is the capital of _____ New York State.

12. My husband's family speaks _____ Polish.

13. _____ apple a day keeps the doctor away.

14. _____ ink in my pen is red.

15. Our neighbors have _____ cat and _____ dog.

Figure 5.10 Purdue On-line Writing Lab (OWL): Articles practice exercise

Examples of more focused practice activities for articles are shown in Figure 5.11. The first activity (from Master, 1997, p. 231) focuses on helping students make a distinction between countable and non-countable nouns (e.g., furniture versus a chair), and the second (also from Master, 1997, p. 231) targets the singular/plural distinction (e.g., a hospital versus people). As students make choices and discuss their choices with the class, they can focus on these distinctions, rather than worrying about other issues (e.g., first versus second mention).

EVALUATING PRACTICE ACTIVITIES: DISCOURSE CONTEXT
– Do the activities require the comprehension and/or use of the target forms at the phrase, sentence, or discourse level?
– To what extent do the activities promote the use of the forms in a meaningful context?
– Is this context authentic? In other words, is it likely that learners will need to use the forms outside the classroom in ways that are similar to the tasks included in the textbook activities?

Exercise 1

Making _a__ Chair

___ carpenter uses a number of tools and products in making ___

furniture. In making ___ chair for example, he uses ___ saw to cut ___

wood and ___ chisel to shape it. He uses ___ hammer to drive in ___ nail

or ___ peg, or ___ screwdriver when ___ screw is required. He also uses

___ glue to give the chair ___ strength and clamps to hold the pieces

together. When the chair has been assembled, it is first sanded with ___

sandpaper and ___ steel wool. Finally, the chair is pained several times

with ___ paint or ___ lacquer, lightly sanding between each coat.

Exercise 2

___ Hospitals

___ hospital is ___ place for the scientific treatment of ___ sick people.

Many modern hospitals are also ___ research centers where ___ doctor

can send __a_ patient for medical treatment or advice. At these centers,

___ new drugs or ___ special surgical procedures and ___ treatments are

developed. In addition, there are ___ training hospitals, which prepare

___ doctors, ___ nurses, and ___ other health personnel for ___ medical

occupations.

Figure 5.11 Sample practice activities for English articles (Master, 1997, p. 231)

Last, but certainly not least, it is important to evaluate the extent to which L2 grammar activities deepen students' understanding of how target forms are used in combination with other lexical words (collocation and phraseology), as well as how the use of the target forms varies across registers. If you have found that the grammar textbook you are using does not include this type of information in its explanations, then it is likely that its practice exercises also do not address these areas of grammar use. In this situation, teachers may need to consult corpus-based resources for relevant frequency lists, phraseologies, and register information. This information can then be incorporated into the design of the practice activity. For example, if a practice activity in a textbook does not include high frequency vocabulary (e.g., most frequent linking verbs), it could be modified to do so. Or, if an activity focuses on word order without mention of collocation (e.g., linking verb + adjective pattern without information about which verbs co-occur with which adjectives), then activities could be designed which allow students to notice or use these lexico-grammatical patterns. Activities that fail to address register variation can be modified to highlight basic register distinctions (e.g., use of the feature in informal conversation versus use of the feature in academic writing).

Ideas for activity modification can also be found by looking at the types of activities provided in corpus-based textbooks. These books often use discourse analysis activities to raise student awareness of important lexical, grammatical and discourse patterns. Books that are closer to the corpus-based end of the design continuum prefer sample texts taken directly from a corpus. The advantage here is that students are given a chance to interact with a text that was produced by a speaker or writer in an authentic context for a specific purpose. Many students enjoy these examples because they provide snapshots of how speakers and writers use grammar to communicate in a variety of settings.

EVALUATING PRACTICE ACTIVITIES: PHRASEOLOGY & REGISTER VARIATION

- To what extent are learners given opportunities to use the target grammatical forms in combination with their frequent collocations and phraseologies?
- Do the scenarios provided for the activities represent the types of registers the forms are typically used in?
- Do the activities help to highlight important differences across registers?

At the same time, however, text samples taken directly from corpora for in-class analysis can present teachers and students with challenges. First, although the sample itself was originally spoken or written in a real context for a real purpose, when taken from a corpus and displayed in a grammar textbook, much of the original context and purpose is lost. Corpus samples that are not accompanied by information about the original discourse context may serve to confuse students, rather than help them learn about the language (Widdowson, 2002). We should note, however, that this is a concern not only for corpus samples, but for any example sentence or paragraph included in a grammar textbook. The less context given (about the speakers/writers and their relationships with listeners/speakers, the setting, the purpose for the communication, and so on), the more difficult it will be for students to understand how and why the target form is being used in the text sample. Thus, teachers may want to consider using text samples that both illustrate important patterns of use and have relevance to students' own lives. For example, a lesson on reported speech may include an analysis of a news article published in a local paper. Features of conversation can be illustrated through the analysis of popular TV shows (see, e.g., Quaglio, 2009), or even through an analysis of conversations that students record themselves.

In addition to developing corpus-based textbooks for language learners, corpus linguists have also devoted a great deal of attention to the use of corpora in the classroom. Many researchers have explored the use of *data-driven learning*, where teachers and students work together to identify important lexico-grammatical patterns in a set of data retrieved from a corpus. In Chapter 6, we highlight the many resources now available to teachers who are interested in using corpora in their own classrooms.

Reflection 5.3

– Using the guiding questions provided here, evaluate the practice activities provided in your chosen L2 grammar resource. How well do these activities address Form, Meaning, and Use? Discourse Context? Frequency, Phraseology, and Register Variation?
– What modifications would you need to make to these activities before using them in your classroom?

Summary

When evaluating and adapting L2 grammar materials, teachers can consider the extent to which the materials:

– Provide a manageable focus for the lesson.
– Address Form, Meaning, and Use in grammar explanations and practice exercises.
– Explain grammatical concepts clearly and accurately.
– Provide examples and activities at both the sentence and discourse level.
– Provide information about frequency of use, lexico-grammar, and register variation.
– Cover situations of use that are relevant to students' needs and goals.

Suggestions for further reading

Lesikin, J. (2000). Complex text in ESL grammar textbooks: Barriers or gateways? *Reading in a Foreign Language, 13*, 431–447.

Kong, K. (2009). A comparison of the linguistic and interactional features of language learning websites and textbooks. *Computer Assisted Language Learning, 22*, 31–55.

Shin, J., Eslami, Z., & Chen, W-C. (2011). Presentation of local and international culture in current international English-language teaching textbooks. *Language, Culture and Curriculum, 24*, 253–268.

Recommended resources

<u>English grammar textbooks</u>

Cambridge University Press – *Grammar and Beyond*
<http://www.cambridge.org/grammarandbeyond/>

Cambridge University Press – *Touchstone*
<http://www.cambridge.org/us/esl/touchstone/sb.htm>

Cengage Learning – *Grammar Connection*
<http://ngl.cengage.com/search/programOverview.do?N=4294918395+&Ntk=P_EPI&Ntt=
    20668193694658426528359480582701 50917>

Cengage Learning – *Grammar Dimensions*
<http://ngl.cengage.com/search/programOverview.do?N=4294918395+&Ntk=P_EPI&N
    tt=107462084366547239116328786131716040203>

Collins – *COBUILD Grammar*
<http://www.collins.co.uk/category/English+Language+Teaching/COBUILD+Reference/
    Collins+COBUILD+Grammar>

Pearson Longman – *Real Grammar*
<http://www.pearsonlongman.com/ae/emac/newsletters/may-2010-grammar.html>

Pearson Longman – *Focus on Grammar*
<http://longmanhomeusa.com/blog/the-role-of-corpus-linguistics-in-focus-on-grammar/>

<u>Materials development resources for other languages</u>

Center for Language Education and Research
<http://store.clear.msu.edu/>

Heritage Languages in America (Center for Applied Linguistics)
<http://www.cal.org/heritage/index.html>

Language Acquisition Resource Center
<http://larc.sdsu.edu/materials/>

Less Commonly Taught Languages Project (The Center for the Advanced Research
on Language Acquisition)
<http://www.carla.umn.edu/lctl/index.html>

National Foreign Language Resource Center Publications
<http://nflrc.hawaii.edu/publications.cfm>

Chapter 6

Investigating grammar use through online corpora

As we saw in Chapter 5, corpus-based resources can play an important role in the L2 grammar lesson planning process, as these resources allow us to evaluate the extent to which existing L2 materials present students with accurate information regarding the use of particular grammatical features in spoken and written registers. In this chapter, we describe the wide array of corpus-based resources available to L2 teachers online, and we provide detailed examples of how teachers might use these tools when designing grammar lessons and activities.

Drawing on recommendations put forth in a number of recent discussions of corpus linguistics in language teaching (Bennett, 2011; Flowerdew, 2009; 2012; Keck, 2013; O'Keefe, McCarthy, & Carter, 2007; Reppen, 2010; Römer, 2011), we present three major options available to language teachers who are interested in the use of corpora in the classroom: (1) the *behind the scenes* approach, in which teachers consult corpus-based resources when planning lessons and creating materials, (2) the *corpora as a classroom resource* approach, in which teachers use online corpus tools to investigate questions as they arise in the midst of instruction, and (3) the *student as researcher approach*, in which teachers regularly engage students in the analysis of corpus data. Of course, it is not necessary for teachers to choose one option over others in a given course; rather, it is likely that teachers will want to explore a variety of approaches as they learn more about corpus linguistics and its relevance to their own classrooms. However, teachers who are new to corpus linguistics may feel most comfortable beginning with option one (consulting corpus-based resources) before they move to using corpus data in the classroom.

The *behind the scenes* approach

A quick tour of many online corpora available to teachers today will show that a considerable amount of training is needed before teachers and students can effectively use these tools to investigate questions about grammar use. In many cases, it is not feasible or appropriate for teachers to engage their students in explorations of online corpora. At the very least, teachers will want some time to explore these corpora on their own, so they can develop effective search strategies that can later be shared with students. In these cases, teachers may wish to take a more *behind the scenes* approach to using corpus resources, developing their own corpus-informed grammar lessons (when needed or when possible) without even mentioning the phrase *corpus linguistics* to their students. As discussed in Chapter 5, teachers can check L2 textbook grammar explanations against corpus-based findings and can modify corpus-based textbook lessons developed by other scholars. In this chapter, we take this approach one step further, and demonstrate how teachers might consult corpora directly when developing L2 grammar lessons and materials.

CONSULTING CORPORA *BEHIND THE SCENES*
–   Teachers consult corpus-based grammars, textbooks, and online resources when planning lessons, designing handouts and tasks, or developing courses and curricula.
–   Teachers integrate information about frequency, collocation, phraseology, and register variation into their L2 grammar lessons.

To illustrate the types of exploration that online corpora make possible, we return here to the linking verb example presented in Chapter 5. In this example, we demonstrated how corpus-based resources could be used to modify and supplement ESL textbook lessons that attempt to explain the use of these verbs. In this section, we'll explore how teachers can also utilize online corpora to further investigate how these verbs are used in spoken and written discourse.

Though it is not possible to directly search the Longman Corpus (the source for Conrad & Biber's 2009 *Real Grammar*), teachers can consult English language corpora through Brigham Young University's website: < http://corpus.byu.edu/ >. Here, one can find a variety of corpora, including the Corpus of Contemporary American English (COCA), the British National Corpus (BNC), the Corpus del Espanol, and the Corpus de Portuguese. These corpora are particularly suitable for L2 grammar teaching because they allow users to search not only keywords, but also grammatical categories. In this chapter, our examples come from COCA; however, a knowledge of COCA can easily be transferred to the other corpora because the search interface for all of the BYU corpora is the same. (At the end of this chapter, we provide a list of additional online corpora with user-friendly interfaces, including corpora of languages other than English.)

To use COCA, it is first necessary to register. (You will be prompted to do this by COCA after 15 search queries.) This process is free and relatively painless, and it allows BYU to keep track of the number of teachers, researchers, and students who consult their corpora on a regular basis. Once you are registered, it is possible to take a number of tutorials which explain and illustrate the many search techniques that can be used to explore the corpus. (See also Reppen, 2010, for a beginner's tutorial.) In this chapter, we will introduce you to a few basic search techniques that relate specifically to the design of L2 grammar lessons and materials.

Because the number and types of searches that can be done with COCA are seemingly limitless, before diving into an exploration, it is important to first consider what questions we have about the keyword or grammatical feature we are interested in. What do we hope to gain from our corpus searches? Do we want to compare the frequency of use across registers? To identify important collocates? The nature of our language-related questions will determine the types of search techniques we use.

If an important part of our lesson on linking verbs is to emphasize that these verbs are often followed by adjectives, then one question we might start with would be: What types of adjectives typically follow the linking verbs I plan to teach? Imagine, for example, that we want to start by investigating the use of the verb *look*, which is one of the most frequently used linking verbs in English. If we were using COCA to learn more about the use of this linking verb in context, we might first begin by simply typing *look* into the Word(s) box, clicking "Search," and seeing what happens. However, there are a few grammatical issues we need to consider before taking this step. If we simply type the word *look* into the Word box and click "Search," we will only retrieve exact matches of this word. Other forms (e.g., *looks, looked, looking*) will not be counted. Also, we will end up counting some instances of "look" that we don't want, mainly, the use of *look* as a noun. So, as a first step, we need to specify that we want all forms of the verb *look*, but not any noun instances. This can be done by using the following syntax: [look].[v*].

To ensure that you are retrieving the right kind of information in your search, it is helpful to use the List option, just above the Word box, as shown in Figure 6.1.

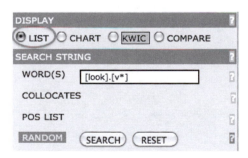

Figure 6.1 Choosing the "List" option in COCA

If we now click Search, we will see a list of all of the forms of *look* that will be retrieved by this syntax (see Figure 6.2).

		CONTEXT	FREQ
1	☐	LOOK	288064
2	☐	LOOKED	135534
3	☐	LOOKING	131150
4	☐	LOOKS	84919
5	☐	LOOKIN	667
		TOTAL	640334

Figure 6.2 "List" search results for the verb *look*

From these results, we can quickly see that *look*, the base form, is the most frequent form that occurs in COCA, followed by the past tense, progressive aspect, and third person singular. We can also click on each verb form to view the concordance line results (see Figure 6.3).

CLICK FOR MORE CONTEXT			
1	2012	ACAD	And I **look** forward this year to further examining new ways for the Association to utilize
2	2012	ACAD	such as help or **look**; or a verb followed by the name of a thing (that is,
3	2012	ACAD	At the same time, other macros can **look** at the id binding and determine that its expansion
4	2012	ACAD	For example, a virtualizationaware NIC could have many personalities that **look** and act as
5	2012	ACAD	When registering new domains, criminals **look** for names similar to the site they want to
6	2012	ACAD	for example, bankofthevvest.com8 uses two vs to **look** like a w. Internationalized domain
7	2012	ACAD	We will also likely see increased spear-phishing and whaling attacks, as phishers **look** for
8	2012	ACAD	While not all technology education laboratories will **look** exactly the same, there are certain
9	2012	ACAD	use a specific aid in your consultation. # ACTIVITY 3 **Look** at the first three consultations in
10	2012	ACAD	a revolution in the clinician/patient relationship where both parties **look** at the evidence and

Figure 6.3 Concordance line results for the verb *look*

Concordance lines can also give us a sense as to whether we are retrieving the uses of *look* that we want. Notice, in Figure 6.3, that many of the instances of *look* that we have retrieved are in fact not what we were looking for! In these cases, *look* is most often not being used as a linking verb, but rather as a multiword verb (*look forward to, look at, look for*). This means that we need to refine our search syntax so that we retrieve linking verb examples, and not these other uses.

To do this, we can specify what kind of word we want to follow the verb *look*. For example, we can say that we want to see only adjectives that come directly after this verb, as shown in Figure 6.4. This would ensure that the uses of look retrieved through our search are indeed linking verb examples.

As shown in Figure 6.4, we can specify adjective forms by using the syntax [j*]. We can then use the Collocate box to indicate where we want the adjective to occur. If we want to see what adjectives come immediately to the right of the verb *look*, then we would set the left context at zero, and the right context at 1. Another feature to note in Figure 6.4 is at the bottom of the screen shot. Here, we have Sorting and Limits. This allows you to choose whether you want to sort search results by frequency (most frequent

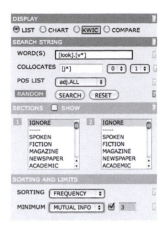

Figure 6.4 Searching for the verb *look* followed by adjectives

to least frequent) or by Mutual Information score. A Mutual Information (MI) score is a statistical measure of how strong a particular collocation is. If the keyword occurs together with another word in the corpus more frequently than would be expected by chance, then the mutual information score for the keyword plus this collocate would be high. Typically, an MI score of 3 or more is considered strong. When you use the Collocates box in COCA, COCA will automatically set an MI requirement of 3. This allows COCA to filter out highly frequent words that co-occur with just about anything (e.g., articles, prepositions, high frequency lexical words). If you are new to COCA, we recommend you not worry about this feature too much (at least initially). As you become more proficient, you may want to experiment with changing the MI settings.

Once we type our keyword in the Word box and our desired collocate (adjectives) in the Collocates box, we can click Search. Figure 6.5 displays some of the results of this query.

		FREQ
1	GOOD	4786
2	GREAT	2115
3	BEAUTIFUL	640
4	TIRED	497
5	FAMILIAR	459
6	SURPRISED	431
7	YOUNGER	385
8	CONFUSED	357
9	PUZZLED	350
10	SAD	245
11	PROMISING	243
12	TERRIBLE	241
13	PALE	237
14	FABULOUS	216
15	TERRIFIC	208
16	RIDICULOUS	195
17	GORGEOUS	192
18	FANTASTIC	184
19	AWFUL	182
20	PLEASED	180

Figure 6.5 *Look* + adjective search results

One pattern we notice immediately when looking at the collocate list is that the adjectives *good* and *great* make up a large proportion of all of the adjective collocates. We can also see that many of the adjectives can roughly be divided into two categories, positive (*good, great, beautiful, fabulous, gorgeous, fantastic*) and negative (*tired, confused, sad, pale, awful*). When providing L2 students with collocational information about a particular keyword or grammatical feature, it is helpful to come up with meaningful collocate categories, rather than simply creating a long list of collocates. At this point in your search process, you might make a quick list of these positive and negative adjectives, or any other meaningful categories you observe. You can also click on any collocate to observe its use in the context of concordance lines.

It is also possible to look at the frequency of these verbs across COCA's five main registers: Spoken, Fiction, Magazine, News, and Academic. This can be done by using the "Chart" option provided just above the keyword search box, as shown in Figure 6.6.

Figure 6.6 Choosing the "Chart" option in COCA

This search query will generate a chart that shows the frequency of *look + adjective* in each register in COCA, as shown in Figure 6.7.

SECTION	ALL	SPOKEN	FICTION	MAGAZINE	NEWSPAPER	ACADEMIC
FREQ	44449	8352	20781	8989	5050	1277
PER MIL	95.73	87.40	229.80	94.07	55.06	14.02
SEE ALL SUB-SECTIONS AT ONCE						

Figure 6.7 "Chart" search results (comparison across registers)

In Figure 6.7, we can see that *look + adjective* occurs in Fiction much more often than it does in the other registers. This use of *look* as a linking verb is also much more frequent in the Spoken register than in the Academic register, which is consistent with the findings of the *Longman Grammar of Spoken and Written English*. There are two separate frequency counts provided in COCA: a raw count (labeled as FREQ) and a normed count (labeled as PER MIL), which indicates the frequency per 1 million words. If we want to see examples of how *look* is used with adjectives in each register, we can click on a bar to see the concordance line results. Figure 6.8 displays some of the concordance line data for the Academic register.

CLICK FOR MORE CONTEXT			
1	2012	ACAD	Treatment of Diseases and Disorders Stem cell research **looks promising** to help fix
2	2012	ACAD	Clarify or you will **look foolish**! 5. Treatment Broadly speaking there are three
3	2012	ACAD	Then what happens? Food will **look different**. There will almost surely be more
4	2012	ACAD	Whether a person is perceived to **look male** or female by others evokes a
5	2012	ACAD	Let them: for once in my life I will **look pretty**. To write in spite of everything, even
6	2012	ACAD	If you **look closed** and distracted when people talk with you, it won't matter that your
7	2012	ACAD	Rowley said. " It **looks promising**. " Rowley adds that, prior to his work with IODP, his
8	2012	ACAD	the MIT professors wrote. At first, those changes **looked temporary**. During the
9	2012	ACAD	Brittney found tattoos satisfying in the sense that " it **looks good**. " Yet, she knew that
10	2012	ACAD	"Hell, however, **looks terrific**: drinking, music, dancing girls. " I'll take Hell,

Figure 6.8 Concordance line results for *look* + adjective in the Academic register

In Figure 6.8, we can see that often, *look* + adjective occurs within a direct quotation, which shows that this combination is even less frequent in academic written prose than the frequency counts indicate.

As these sample searches demonstrate, there are many possible investigations that can be done with just one word – imaging trying to do an in-depth analysis of each linking verb you plan to teach! If we are not careful, behind the scenes investigations can quickly become impractical. At the same time, these investigations have the potential to greatly enrich our L2 grammar teaching.

How then, can teachers make use of online corpora without spending countless hours analyzing frequency counts, concordance lines, and collocate lists? The key, we believe, is focus. Before carrying out an investigation, it is crucial for teachers to articulate their questions and to define a manageable scope for their investigation. These initial parameters can help teachers to refine their search queries and to stay focused throughout the search process. In Table 6.1, we provide an example of a focused, manageable corpus exploration goal.

The next step is to define some parameters for your exploration. Will you be doing general searches of the entire corpus? Will you focus only on one register? Will you be comparing use across 2 or more registers? In terms of collocates, are you interested in only adjective collocates, or do you also want to see what nouns occur after these linking verbs? What about left collocates? The answers to these questions should depend both on your learning goals for the class session and the amount of time you have available for the exploration.

Table 6.1 Steps in the behind the scenes corpus exploration process

---

Step 1: Articulate a manageable focus and goal for the exploration

I am planning a lesson for my Intermediate ESL grammar class on sensory linking verbs. In this lesson, we will focus on the linking verb + adjective pattern and contrast this with the transitive verb pattern (e.g., "you look sad" versus "he is looking for his book"). One key focus of the lesson is that sensory linking verbs are typically used in the simple present tense, while their transitive counterparts (activity verbs) are frequently used in the progressive. I hope to be able to provide my students with many examples of when they'd choose to use a sensory verb in the simple present tense. My primary goal for the corpus exploration is to highlight important collocates and typical uses of five frequently used sensory linking verbs: look, feel, sound, smell, taste.

Step 2: Set parameters for the corpus exploration

Example:
In terms of register, I am mainly interested in use within the Spoken component of COCA because my lesson on linking verbs will focus on comprehending and using them effectively in oral communication. It is also the case that sensory verb + adjective is a pattern that occurs more frequently in speaking than in formal writing. In terms of collocates, I will focus on adjective collocates to the immediate right of the keyword, as adjectives more frequently occur with these linking verbs than do nouns. I will take note of who does the looking and feeling in most of the concordance lines that I view (e.g., Is it typically a pronoun?), but I will not do any formal investigation of frequent left collocates.

Step 3: Determine appropriate search techniques

Example:
My search techniques:
- *Select the Spoken register from the list of possible registers to search*
- *Type [look].[v*] into the Word box*
- *Type [j*] into the Collocate box.*
- *Select 0 for the left context and 1 for the right context.*
- *Repeat these steps for each sensory verb.*

Step 4: Determine appropriate analysis techniques

Example:
My analysis techniques:
- *Scan down the collocate list for each verb. Note any general semantic categories that can be used to characterize the types of collocates associated with each verb (e.g., positive versus negative, adjectives related to appearance, adjectives related to age)*
- *Identify 5 good examples of each major category*
- *Click on these adjectives and scan through the concordance lines. Can I get a sense of important communicative functions that are fulfilled by these verb + adjective combinations?*

Step 5: Identify a possible outcome of the investigation

Example:
Once I finish my analysis, I plan to create a handout that provides a list of key collocates and example sentences for each sensory linking verb.

Once you define your corpus exploration focus, it is important to decide what search techniques you will use to investigate your questions. If you have time to explore a variety of search approaches, that's great; however, if time is limited, it is best to limit the number of search techniques used.

After you generate search results, you will need to decide how to analyze the corpus data. Again, the possibilities here are almost endless. You could, if time were not a factor, click on each adjective in each collocate list, read each concordance line, and write down a brief description of the meaning expressed in these lines. Time, of course, *is* a factor, so we recommend setting, in advance, some limits on how much time you will spend exploring the search results. It is also helpful to have an end product in mind as you work. Your ideas about this may change as you do the investigation, but if you can formulate some tentative plans for how you will share your findings with your students, this will help you to take good notes as you do the exploration.

To summarize, *behind the scenes* corpus explorations allow teachers to investigate their own questions about language use, questions that may not be addressed in existing teaching materials. Online resources like COCA also help to draw our attention to lexico-grammatical patterns we might not otherwise notice, thus allowing language teachers to offer fuller (and more accurate) explanations of how the target language is used in a variety of contexts.

Reflection 6.1

– Try out your own *behind the scenes* investigation. Identify a question you or your students have about the use of a particular word or grammatical structure. Follow the steps provided in Table 6.1.
– What did you learn through your investigation? To what extent were you able to answer your question? How might you present this information to your students?

The *corpora as a classroom resource* approach

As L2 teachers become more comfortable with online corpus resources, they may wish to introduce their students to these resources and make them a more integral part of the L2 classroom. In the *corpora as a classroom resource* approach, students consult not only textbooks and dictionaries when they have language-related questions, but also online corpora and other corpus-based tools.

Integrating corpus consultation into the L2 classroom certainly comes with its challenges. As Chambers (2005) notes, large corpora (like COCA) present learners with many samples of language from a variety of contexts, contexts with which they may or may not be familiar. While traditional resources like grammar textbooks and dictionaries carefully craft explanations and examples that are accessible to language

USING CORPORA AS A CLASSROOM RESOURCE
– Teachers consult corpus-based resources when students ask questions that cannot be answered through traditional resources, and they share these findings with students.
– Teachers recommend and model the use of corpus-based tools to address specific language questions.
– Teachers discuss how corpus-based tools might be used in conjunction with other language resources (e.g., dictionaries).

learners, the language collected in online corpora was not originally intended for an L2 student audience. Rather, it was intended for an audience (a television audience, a reader of fiction, a biologist, a best friend) that is far removed from the classroom context. It is likely that concordance line data will contain language that is unfamiliar to students, which may make it difficult for them to find the "answers" they are looking for.

Nevertheless, studies of corpus consultation in the classroom have found that many L2 students respond positively to the use of corpora in the classroom. Chambers (2005), for example, trained 14 L2 learners studying a variety of languages (English, French, German, Irish, and Spanish) to consult corpora when checking their written work. In a reflective essay at the end of the semester, her students reported that they appreciated the opportunity to work directly with authentic texts:

> As one student wrote, "the French used in these articles is authentic, up to date, and relevant." The word "real" is also used to describe the corpus, in contrast to the invented examples in course books and grammars, which are described by one student as "unreal and sometimes stupid." The up-to-date nature of the contents, relating to news from just a few months previously, was appreciated by many students…. The rich learning environment created by a large number of examples was also appreciated, in contrast to the limited number of examples given in course books, dictionaries, and grammars. As one student wrote, "The sheer amount of entries given by the software was impressive, and it made learning about the choice made [when using demonstrative pronouns in French] much quicker and easier when there were numerous examples to look at.
> (Chambers, 2005, p. 120)

The L2 students in Yoon's (2008) study also expressed positive attitudes towards the use of corpora as a resource. These students, who were pursuing graduate degrees at English-speaking universities, were trained to consult a large general corpus (the Collins COBUILD corpus) as part of their composing process. When students were not sure how to use a particular word, they were encouraged to do a keyword search for this word in the corpus, and they were asked to keep track of their keyword searches in a corpus search log. Yoon found that for many of the L2 students in her study, the corpus consultations helped to raise their awareness of the ways in which lexis and grammar work together to create meaning. As one L2 student explained:

> Learning a language is to learn how the people of that language use the language. Basically, what we learned as grammar is all related to collocation. For example, we just learned "make use of" as a chunk, but the fact that it is not "make use in" or "make usage of" is based on collocation.... Actually, we have to learn words focusing on expressions.... In the past, we taught words and grammar separately. But we can teach them both. (Yoon, 2008, p. 41)

Yoon argues that this increased awareness not only helped her students to improve their writing, but also helped them to develop new approaches to their own language learning: "Developing the awareness that collocations exist or that they are important in language learning/writing is an educational process in itself" (p. 42).

It should be noted that both Chambers (2005) and Yoon (2008) investigated the use of corpora with advanced language learners who were enrolled in credit-bearing university courses, either as undergraduate or graduate students. Indeed, much of the literature to date has focused on the use of corpora with advanced L2 students, and some have questioned whether corpora are an appropriate resource for beginning and intermediate learners. To address this concern, Ishikura (2011) explored the use of corpus-based resources with an L2 student enrolled in an Intensive English Program (IEP). As part of this case study, Ishikura spent a total of 6 hours in one-on-one training sessions with her student, Michelle, introducing her to three corpus-based tools: the *Longman Dictionary of Contemporary English* <http://www.ldoceonline.com>, Just The Word <http://www.just-the-word.com>, and COCA. Ishikura, like Yoon (2008), found that the use of these resources helped to increase her student's awareness of the importance of both lexis and grammar and sparked her student's interest in collocation and phraseology. Ishikura cautions, however, that students in IEP programs may initially feel intimidated by large, general corpora like COCA:

> Michelle had a perception that she did not have enough vocabulary in order to benefit from corpus tools. She seemed to think that she was not ready for the corpus resources, and one of the corpus tools, the COCA corpus, was not quite "ready" for her. (p. 85)

In other words, at this point, COCA is primarily designed for researchers and teachers who already have some amount of corpus training. L2 students who are new to corpora will need a great deal of guidance and support if they are to feel comfortable consulting these resources on a regular basis. To address this challenge, Ishikura recommends gradually introducing learners to corpus-based tools, starting first with tools that use formats they are familiar with (e.g., corpus-based dictionaries) and then gradually moving towards more complicated search interfaces.

To illustrate how L2 teachers might take this approach in the L2 grammar classroom, we will now work through three sample keyword searches in each of the resources Ishikura explored. Figure 6.9 displays an example of a corpus log, which we adapted from the log format used by Ishikura. In this log, students can keep track of each keyword or phrase they decided to look up, why they chose to look it up, and which resources proved to be most useful for the question they posed. The example search included in Figure 6.9, for the word "suggest," is an actual search carried out by Michelle in Ishikura's study.

Date	Keyword	Purpose	My searches
	suggest	to make sure that it is OK to say, "someone suggests + pronoun + to do something" (i.e. Namioka suggested us to make a good decision)	Searches to try: – Longman Learner Dictionary – Just the Word – Keyword search in COCA Which resources were most useful? What did you learn about this word?

Figure 6.9 A sample search log, adapted from Ishikura (2011)

The first resource recommended by Ishikura, the *Longman Dictionary of Contemporary English* (LDCE), allows students to type a keyword and to retrieve a list of definitions, collocations, and example sentences. The definitions and collocations highlighted in each entry are chosen based on the frequency with which they are used in the Longman Corpus. More frequent uses are listed first, followed by less frequent uses. If a student were to type the word *suggest* in the search box, he would be presented with the entry shown in Figure 6.10.

As Figure 6.10 shows, the student's question about the use of *suggest* is directly answered in the GRAMMAR box displayed at the end of the entry. Prior to this, several possible collocational patterns are listed (e.g., *suggest that, suggest –ing, suggest how*). Although students need not work with raw data when consulting the Longman Dictionary, there is still quite a bit of information presented, and students will still need training.

sug·gest [transitive]

1 to tell someone your ideas about what they should do, where they should go etc [↪ propose]:

🔊 *They keep **suggesting ways** to keep my weight down.*

🔊 *She wrote to me and suggested a meeting.*

suggest (that)

🔊 *I suggest you phone before you go round there.*

🔊 ***It has been suggested that** the manager will resign if any more players are sold.*

suggest doing something

🔊 *Joan suggested asking her father for his opinion.*

suggest how/where/what etc

🔊 *The therapist suggested how Tony could cope with his problems.*

can/may I suggest (=used to politely suggest a different idea)

🔊 *May I suggest that you think carefully before rushing into this?*

🔊 *No possible explanation **suggests itself** (=is able to be thought of).*

2 to make someone think that a particular thing is true [= indicate]:

🔊 *Trends in spending and investment suggest a gradual economic recovery.*

suggest (that)

🔊 *Opinion polls suggest that only 10% of the population trusts the government.*

evidence/results/data/studies etc suggest(s) that

🔊 *The evidence suggests that single fathers are more likely to work than single mothers.*

3 to tell someone about someone or something that is suitable for a particular job or activity [= recommend]

suggest somebody/something for something

🔊 *John Roberts has been suggested for the post of manager.*

4 to state something in an indirect way [= imply]:

🔊 *Are you suggesting my husband's been drinking?*

Figure 6.10 Entry in the Longman Dictionary of Contemporary English

5 I'm not suggesting *spoken* used to say that what you have said is not exactly what you intended to say:

🔊 *I'm not suggesting for one moment that these changes will be easy.*

6 to remind someone of something or help them to imagine it:

🔊 *The stage was bare, with only the lighting to suggest a prison.*

GRAMMAR

!! Do not say 'suggest (someone) to do something'. You can use the following structures:

suggest that somebody do something
• *He suggested that we go (NOT suggested us to go) for a drink.*
You can miss out 'that'
• *What do you suggest we do (NOT suggest us to do)?*

suggest doing something
• *I suggest wearing (NOT suggest to wear) something warm.*

suggest something
• *She suggested a walk before dinner.*

Figure 6.10 (*continued*)

Based on recommendations put forth by Flowerdew (2009), Ishikura also trained her students to use Just the Word, a resource which provides feedback to students on multiword combinations, based on the frequency with which these phrases occur in the British National Corpus. As shown in Figure 6.11, if a student is unsure of a word combination they plan to use in writing or speaking, she can type this combination into Just the Word and click on the "Alternatives" button. Selecting "Learner Errors" further tailors feedback to common questions that L2 students have; selecting "Thesaurus" widens the range of suggested alternatives.

PREPARING STUDENTS TO CONSULT CORPUS-BASED DICTIONARIES
Before asking students to conduct their own searches, we recommend:
1. Explaining what a corpus is and how corpora are used to develop dictionaries.
2. Talking through a sample word entry, showing students where to find definitions, information about collocation, and example sentences.
3. Modeling a keyword search, starting with a general question and ending with a tentative answer to the question, based on what was learned from the search.
4. Developing a few guided keyword search activities, so students can practice using the resource in class, with the help of peers.

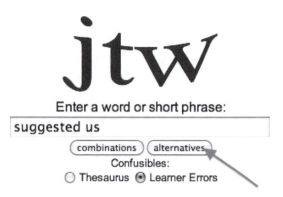

Figure 6.11 Checking a word combination using Just the Word

Once students submit their query, they will then see their phrase and several other suggested phrases, each followed by either a green or a red bar. A green bar indicates a "good" or frequent combination; the longer the bar, the stronger the collocation. A red bar indicates a "bad" or very infrequent combination. Figure 6.12 displays results for the phrase *suggested us*.

suggested us

replacing *suggest* in 'suggest us'

suggest us (0)
advise us (68)
offer us (146)
invite us (112)
introduce us (62)
encourage us (96)

Figure 6.12 Just the Word results for the query *suggested us*

Notice in Figure 6.12 that Just the Word displays verbs in their base form only, and function words are omitted. If students want to see the actual use of these phrases in sentences, they can click on the phrase to view a sample of concordance lines.

Students can also type a single keyword and ask Just the Word to display a list of important collocations. For example, if the student who searched for *suggested us* still wants to know how to use the verb *suggest* (rather than the alternatives provided), she can go back to the home page and do a "Combinations" search, as shown in Figure 6.13. We should warn you, however, that this type of search generates a lot of data, which may be difficult for students to wade through. L2 teachers, however, may find this tool useful, as it quickly highlights frequent syntactic patterns associated with a word.

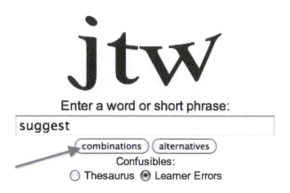

Figure 6.13 The "Combinations" option in Just the Word

suggest ***suggest* obj N**	**suggest**
cluster 1 suggest an approach (22) suggest ways (86) suggest a way (34) cluster 2 suggest the need (27) suggest reason (48) cluster 3 suggest answer (32) suggest solution (32) cluster 4 cluster 5 suggest alternative (24) suggest the possibility (35)	*suggest* obj N , e.g. suggest ways N subj *suggest* , e.g. evidence suggest ADV *suggest* , e.g. also suggest *suggest* ADV , e.g. suggest however *suggest* PREP , e.g. suggest by V and *suggest* , e.g. be and suggest *suggest* and V , e.g. suggest and be *suggest* or V , e.g. suggest or be

Figure 6.14 Results for *suggest* using the "Combination" option

As shown in Figure 6.14, a Combinations search in Just the Word will generate a list of collocates organized by syntactic pattern. Each major syntactic pattern associated with the keyword will be listed in the upper right-hand corner of the page, and users can click on each of these patterns to be taken to the appropriate collocate list. Collocate lists are also organized by semantic domain (e.g., *approach* and *way*; *answer* and *solution*; *alternative* and *possibility*). Again, as with the *Longman Dictionary*, there is a potential for students to be overwhelmed by the amount of information they are being presented with. In-class training prior to at-home use is crucial. If students have already been introduced to the *Longman Dictionary*, then Just the Word could be used to build on their knowledge of corpus-based resources. Teachers can point out, for example, that corpora are designed to represent different dialects and domains of use. The Longman Corpus used by the *Longman Dictionary* is a corpus of American English, while the corpus used by Just the Word is the British National Corpus. Teachers will also need to introduce students to frequency lists. While the Longman Dictionary lists definitions, Just the Word provides only lists of collocates and syntactic patterns. Because this format will be very different from formats used in dictionaries and L2 textbooks, teachers will need to spend time in class talking through sample keyword searches and explaining how to use the red and green bars, the collocate lists, the syntactic jargon, and the concordance line samples.

The third resource used by Ishikura in her case study was COCA. As we have seen in this chapter, COCA allows uses to conduct a wide range of lexical and grammatical searches, and the amount of data displayed can be overwhelming – even to experienced corpus linguists! Nevertheless, there are a few search techniques that can yield relatively quick answers to some types of language use questions.

If we return to the question about *suggest* and whether one can say *Namioka suggested us to make a good decision*, it is possible for students to check this syntactic pattern in COCA. The question of "Is it ok to say this?" can be answered by looking at the frequency with which this pattern occurs. For example, a student could type "suggested us to" into the Word box in COCA, as shown in Figure 6.15.

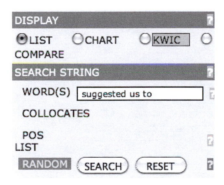

Figure 6.15 Searching for *suggested us to* in COCA

COCA will then display the number of times this word combination occurs in the corpus. Though the corpus is comprised of over 40 million words, *suggested us to* occurs only once.

This is a strong indication that this combination is not typically done in American English. To see what words can follow the verb *suggested*, a student could type *suggested ** into the Word box, as shown in Figure 6.16. This search will generate a list of two-word phrases that all begin with the word *suggested*.

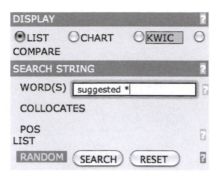

Figure 6.16 Searching for words that follow the word *suggest* in COCA

		FREQ
1	SUGGESTED THAT	11443
2	SUGGESTED ,	2118
3	SUGGESTED BY	1928
4	SUGGESTED .	1770
5	SUGGESTED A	1296
6	SUGGESTED THE	1247
7	SUGGESTED TO	929
8	SUGGESTED IN	623
9	SUGGESTED HE	503
10	SUGGESTED IT	426
11	SUGGESTED THEY	380
12	SUGGESTED WE	332
13	SUGGESTED I	299
14	SUGGESTED SHE	297
15	SUGGESTED RETAIL	293

Figure 6.17 Search results for *suggest* *

As we can see in Figure 6.17, suggested is followed by *that* much more frequently than any other collocate. Figure 6.17 also shows that when a pronoun is used, it is a subject pronoun (he, they, we), not an object pronoun like *us*. To see the fuller phraseology of *suggested that*, a student could click on this collocation to see concordance line examples.

As the sample searches presented here demonstrate, bringing corpora into the classroom requires a considerable time investment. Teachers must first learn what resources are available, how each search interface works, and what search strategies are most effective for investigating students' questions. From there, teachers need to develop classroom lessons which train students in the use of online corpus tools. Nevertheless, it is also clear that when students are given the chance to consult corpora first-hand, they respond quite positively and they develop a deeper understanding of how lexis and grammar work together to create meaning. These tools also allow students and teachers to take a more active role in the language learning process, by providing them with direct access to language data. In the following section, we build on this idea of corpora as a resource and describe how teachers might integrate corpus analysis directly into their L2 grammar lessons. The use of corpora in L2 grammar teaching need not always be reactive, or a last resort when other more traditional resources fail. Corpus analysis can also be planned in advance, for the purpose of enriching, supplementing, or challenging grammar textbook explanations.

Reflection 6.2

– Using Ishikura's search log, identify a keyword or set of keywords you want to investigate. Define a purpose for your investigation, through the creation of a research question. Focus your question on collocation, phraseology, or register variation.
– Carry out an investigation of your research question using the three types of resources highlighted here:
    – An online, corpus-based dictionary
    – Just the Word (or a similar resource)
    – A searchable, online corpus
– Which resources were most helpful in your investigation? What did you learn about the use of your keyword(s)? What challenges did you face as you conducted your research?

The *student as researcher* approach

As we have seen thus far, corpus tools not only allow students to check the accuracy or acceptability of their grammar use, but they also have the potential to change the ways in which L2 students approach their grammar learning. A *student as researcher* approach aims to capitalize on this potential, through the routine use of corpus analysis tasks in the classroom. As a number of corpus linguists have argued, when put in the position of language researcher, rather than language student, L2 learners feel in charge of their own learning, and thus motivation is increased (Aston, 2001); learners feel empowered to challenge textbook explanations and native-speaker intuitions (Lorenz, 2000; Mair, 2000); and learners make "serendipitous" discoveries about language use that, without the use of corpora, would not have been possible (Bernardini, 2000).

In addition to stimulating learners' curiosity about the target language, corpus analysis tasks may also provide learners with important opportunities to 'notice the gap' between their own interlanguage and the target (Aston, 2001; Meunier, 2002; Gavioli,

2001). Drawing on theories of second language acquisition that emphasize the role of input, noticing, and output in the language learning process (e.g., Schmidt, 1990; Swain, 2000), corpus linguists have pointed out that corpus-based tasks allow learners to test their hypotheses about language use against the data that they observe, and this noticing, in turn, may help learners to modify their output so that it more closely approximates target language norms, or the conventions of particular disciplines or genres (Aston, 2001; Gavioli, 2001; Meunier, 2002; Zanettin, 2001).

THE STUDENT AS LANGUAGE RESEARCHER

Teacher-directed research
- Teachers develop L2 grammar lessons that make use of corpus data (e.g., frequency lists, concordance line results)
- Teachers engage students in guided analysis tasks which help them to notice particular patterns of language use

Student-directed research
- Teachers train students in corpus search and analysis techniques
- Teachers allow students to generate research questions, conduct searches, analyze results, and draw conclusions about language use

---

One of the earliest proponents of bringing corpus data into the classroom was Tim Johns (1991), who coined the term *data-driven learning* (DDL). In John's conception of DDL, which we refer to as *teacher-led DDL*, learners engage in the analysis of concordance lines that have been selected, arranged, and possibly edited by the teacher in order to draw learners' attention to patterns of language use. Johns advocates both an inductive and deductive approach to concordance line analysis. In an inductive approach, learners may be asked to notice important collocations, words, grammatical forms, or semantic categories that immediately precede or follow the keyword. In a deductive approach, learners might fill in missing elements of concordance lines based on patterns they have already studied.

As in the *behind the scenes* approach, teachers using Johns' DDL approach conduct their own analyses outside of class, make decisions regarding which findings to share with students, and design classroom materials that present these findings in an understandable way. Unlike teachers using the *behind the scenes* approach, however, teachers using DDL make explicit reference to corpora and they include corpus data (e.g., word frequency lists, concordance lines) in their instructional materials.

Johns (1991) argues that teacher-led DDL can be an effective way of introducing students to corpus analysis. As both Chambers (2005) and Ishikura (2011) note, large, general corpora can be intimidating and overwhelming for learners. If learners are viewing concordance lines for the very first time, then teachers may want to present those concordance lines in such a way as to minimize cognitive overload. For example, teachers can delete lines that contain too many unfamiliar vocabulary words and sort concordance lines so that patterns of use are more apparent.

In a study of teacher-led data-driven learning, Boulton (2010) explored the use of prepared DDL handouts with low-intermediate L2 learners and compared the effectiveness of these materials with more traditional, dictionary-based materials. To identify challenging areas of grammar shared by many French learners of English, Boulton collected argumentative essays from 79 French university students writing in English. Based on errors made in the essays and input from other English teachers at the university, Boutlon selected 15 language items (e.g., use of *good* versus *right*, *say* versus *tell*) to focus on in the DDL and traditional materials. Participants in the study then received instruction on 10 of these items. Five items were taught using traditional materials (see Figure 6.18) and five items were taught using DDL materials (see Figure 6.19). The remaining five items were not taught to participants, so these items could serve as a control.

Prior to the instructional treatment, participants took a pretest which targeted the 15 language items. After the instructional treatment, participants took another test. Boulton found that participants improved their scores on items that were taught using DDL and items taught using traditional methods. Items that were not taught (the control) showed no improvement. Boulton argues that these findings show that even low-intermediate students "are capable of detecting at least some patterns and applying them to new contexts" (p. 557), suggesting that not just advanced, but also beginning and intermediate students may benefit from DDL activities. Boulton further argues that paper-based, teacher-prepared DDL activities play an important role in training L2 students to eventually consult corpora themselves.

Designing DDL materials, like consulting corpora-based tools, can take a considerable amount of time. Studies like Boulton (2010) suggest, however, that this time investment may be worth it. Many of the steps involved in creating DDL materials are similar to those outlined in Table 6.1 for *behind the scenes* investigations. An added step, however, is selecting samples of corpus data to share with students in class. Concordance lines should use language that students are familiar with and should be arranged in such a way as to highlight important collocational and phraseological patterns.

Collections of graded readers provide an excellent resource for gathering concordance line data that is accessible to beginner and intermediate students. One useful resource for English is Tom Cobb's website, The Compleat Lexical Tutor, which provides access to an English Graded Reader Corpus. Graded readers are designed to target a particular reading level (e.g., elementary school grade levels, different levels of English proficiency). Vocabulary is carefully controlled so that readers at each level are not overwhelmed by too many unfamiliar words.

RIGHT (group A: DDL).

Introduction:

The adjective *right* has several meanings in English.

a) How would you translate *la bonne réponse* into English?
b) How would you translate *the right side* into French?

Main materials:

c) Below are some of the most common nouns which follow *right*, e.g. 1) *right hand* or 2) *right time*.
For each one, decide how you would probably translate it.

1. hand _____   7. place _____
2. time _____   8. angles _____
3. side _____   9. wing _____
4. thing _____   10. arm _____
5. way _____   11. hemisphere _____
6. direction _____   12. leg _____

d) How many translations did you have for *the right side*?
        Why do you think we often say *the right hand side*?

e) Look at the words to the left of *right answer* and *good answer* in the concordance lines below.
        What do you think is the difference in meaning and use?
        Would you translate them differently in French?

1. Corporate strategists point out that there is no single **right answer**. The correct strategy will be industry specific. This is what the
2. are made. These answers should not be viewed as the " **right answer**" and we would suggest that wherever possible the students are
3. , and avoid making them feel that they have to search for the **right answer**, hidden somewhere in the teacher's head. Open questions
4. in a number of respects although he may have reached the **right answer** by the wrong route. I do not agree. His conclusion that there
5. a set of facts and techniques --; in which questions have one **right answer** and prescribed methods of solution. Hand-in-hand with this
6. much children have taken in. In drama there is rarely a single **right answer**, and it's often more appropriate to phrase questions so that it is
7. the right question is usually more difficult than to find the **right answer**. The questions which are tackled at Advanced level reflect the
8. argument and "yes" more quickly when "yes" is the **right answer**," he said. Of the 40,000 asylum applications made last year,
9. "Closer study shows that there is no simple solution, no one **right answer**, no single "management style" that delivers better results." He
10. answer. However, I think we are more likely to find the **right answer** if we ask the right question. We should not ask "Why are

11. don't have any meetings. Well yeah, that's a very **good answer** to that, yeah, but when, how would you do research? Yeah
12. there was next. To see what animals came next. Yes. **Good answer**. And what about you. You'd live in? You'd live in
13. that answer your question? I mean, it's not a very **good answer**, because frankly we don't know, th the full reasons for this,
14. it that a causal circumstance makes an effect happen? A **good answer** is that we regard the causal circumstance as leaving no room
15. I've got a right." Nutty could not think of a **good answer** and nor could Mr Sylvester, so Nails was allowed to come.
16. : the Godfather's name is that. Will-power supreme" "A **good answer** to a question that has no simple answer. A reverend answer. A
17. "Hanging about waiting to die is not my idea of a **good answer**!" "Visual sighting of parasite at grid mark four by five,"
18. more grass," said the aunt. It was not a very **good answer**, and the boy knew it. "But there is lots of grass in
19. Susan smiled. "Well ..." But she couldn't find a **good answer** to Karen's question. A week later, when the workers had to
20. so angry with him?" Lydia was evasive, not having a **good answer** ready. "Mmm," she said shiftily, "I just thought it

Look at questions (a) and (b) again. How would you answer them now?

(Corpus: *BYU-BNC: British National Corpus*. Davies, 2004, online)

Figure 6.18 Sample DDL lesson used by Boulton (2010, p. 567)

RIGHT (group B: Traditional).

Introduction:
The adjective *right* has several meanings in English.

a) How would you translate *la bonne réponse* into English?

b) How would you translate *the right side* into French?

Main materials:

c) What common nouns can you think of which frequently follow *right*? For each one, decide which translation is the best.

right	hand		*main droite*
right	time		
right			
right			
right			
right			
right			
right			

d) How would you translate *the right side*? Why do you think we often say *the right hand side*?

e) Look at the dictionary entries below. What do you think is the difference in meaning and use between *right answer* and *good answer*? Would you translate them differently in French?

right
adj
  (not left) **droit**(e)
  (=correct) [answer, road, direction, address,
  number] **bon(bonne)**
  (=accurate) [time] **juste**
  (=most suitable) [moment, choice] **bon(bonne)**
  (=morally good) **bien** inv
  (in normal or satisfactory condition) I don't feel right today.
  Je ne me sens pas bien aujourd'hui.
  (=socially acceptable) the right people les gens bien placés
  (British) * *(=total)* **sacré**(e) *

right adj
1 equitable, ethical, fair, good, honest, honourable, just, lawful, moral, proper, righteous, true, upright, virtuous
2 accurate, admissible, authentic, correct, exact, factual, genuine, on the money (U.S.) precise, satisfactory, sound, spot-on (Brit. informal) true, unerring, valid, veracious
3 advantageous, appropriate, becoming, comme il faut, convenient, deserved, desirable, done, due, favourable, fit, fitting, ideal, opportune, proper, propitious, rightful, seemly, suitable
4 all there (informal) balanced, compos mentis, fine, fit, healthy, in good health, in the pink, lucid, normal, rational, reasonable, sane, sound, unimpaired, up to par, well
5 conservative, reactionary, Tory
6 absolute, complete, out-and-out, outright, pure, real, thorough, thoroughgoing, utter **adv**
7 accurately, aright, correctly, exactly, factually, genuinely, precisely, truly
8 appropriately, aptly, befittingly, fittingly, properly, satisfactorily, suitably
9 directly, immediately, instantly, promptly, quickly, straight, straightaway, without delay
10 bang, exactly, precisely, slap-bang (informal) squarely
11 absolutely, all the way, altogether, completely, entirely, perfectly, quite, thoroughly, totally, utterly, wholly
12 ethically, fairly, honestly, honourably, justly, morally, properly, righteously, virtuously
13 advantageously, beneficially, favourably, for the better, fortunately, to advantage, well **n**

14 authority, business, claim, due, freedom, interest, liberty, licence, permission, power, prerogative, privilege, title
15 equity, good, goodness, honour, integrity, justice, lawfulness, legality, morality, propriety, reason, rectitude, righteousness, truth, uprightness, virtue
16 by rights equitably
17 to rights arranged **vb**
18 compensate for, correct, fix, put right, rectify, redress, repair, settle, set upright, sort out, straighten, vindicate **adj**

1 bad, dishonest, immoral, improper, indecent, unethical, unfair, unjust, wrong
2 counterfeit, erroneous, fake, false, fraudulent, illegal, illicit, inaccurate, incorrect, inexact, invalid, mistaken, questionable, uncertain, unlawful, untruthful, wrong
3 disadvantageous, inappropriate, inconvenient, undesirable, unfitting, unseemly, unsuitable, wrong
4 abnormal, unsound
5 left, leftist, left-wing, liberal, radical, right-on (informal) socialist **adv**
7 inaccurately, incorrectly
8 improperly
9 incompletely, indirectly, slowly
13 badly, poorly, unfavourably **n**
15 badness, dishonour, evil, immorality, impropriety **vb**
18 make crooked, topple

Look at questions (a) and (b) again. How would you answer them now?

(Dictionaries: *Collins English French Electronic Dictionary*, 2005, online;
Collins COBUILD English Dictionary for Advanced Learners, 2003, on-line)

Figure 6.19 Sample traditional lesson used by Boulton (2010, p. 568)

To access graded reader material through Tom Cobb's website, teachers can first go to the websites main page: <http://www.lextutor.ca/>. From the website's main page, users can click on Concordance, as shown in Figure 6.20. From here, users can choose to generate concordances in English, French, German, and Spanish, as shown in Figure 6.21.

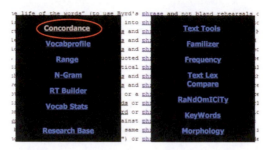

Figure 6.20 Choosing the "Concordance" option in the Compleat Lexical Tutor

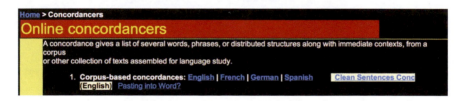

Figure 6.21 Choosing a language to work with

Once users choose a language, they will be presented with a number of search options for generating concordance lines. Tom Cobb's search interface differs from COCA's in a number of ways. First, the corpora available through the Compleat Lexical Tutor are not grammatically tagged, so you will not be able to search for specific grammatical categories. However, you can sort concordance lines so that collocates are listed in alphabetical order. This means that concordance lines will be organized so that instances of *make a* will all come first, and later, you will be able to clearly see all instances of *make the*. We recommend experimenting with different settings and clicking Submit, to learn how each parameter impacts the concordance line display.

Here, we will demonstrate a sample search using the keywords *make* and *do*, two seemingly synonymous words that ESL students often have questions about. To begin our search, we can type *make* into the Keyword box and Sort By 1 word to the right. We can also choose a corpus of simplified language. For example, the 1k Graded Corpus shown in Figure 6.22 is a corpus of graded readers which use only the first 1,000 words of English.

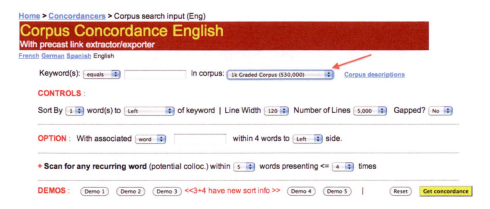

Figure 6.22 Choosing to search a corpus of graded readers

The search query displayed in Figure 6.22 generates over 1,000 hits. When you scroll down these concordance lines, you will notice that many important collocates of make (e.g., *difference, mistake, money*). To generate a smaller sample of concordance lines which highlight the patterns you want to present to your students, you can search for specific collocates that occur near the keyword. Figure 6.23 shows how to generate concordance lines which contain the verb *make* and the collocate *decisions*, and Figure 6.24 displays the results.

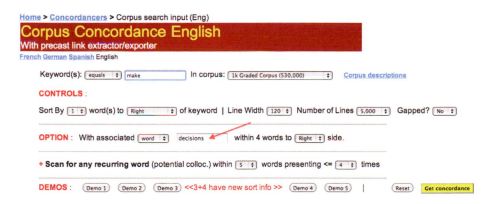

Figure 6.23 Searching for *make + decisions*

He can wait. I won't	**MAKE**	**any** quick <u>decisions</u>.
'Every day Max, we	**MAKE**	**decisions**. Lots of <u>decisions.</u>
'Oh, I have a difficult decision to	**MAKE**	I hate making <u>decisions</u> like this.
But I think I must	**MAKE**	**the** <u>decisions</u>, and you must obey my orders.
It was written down, but judges could	**MAKE**	**their** own <u>decisions</u> in special cases.

Figure 6.24 Concordance lines for *make + decisions*

Once you identify the concordance lines you want to share with your students, you will also need to decide how to display them. First, you will want to clean up the lines to eliminate examples that are not appropriate and to take out any distracting symbols. You may also consider arranging concordance lines so that they do not contain any incomplete sentences. Finally, you want to think about how to structure the language analysis activity. It is important to provide students with clear instructions about what you want them to do with the data you have presented them. Figures 6.25 and 6.26 present a staged language analysis task that could be used to raise students' awareness of subtle differences between *make* and *do*.

Note that the sample language analysis tasks do not attempt to cover all of the noun collocates observed in the corpus searches. Instead, these activities focus exclusively on collocates that relate to types of mental or academic work. As with the *behind the scenes* approach, it is important for a DDL activity to have a manageable focus. For example, you may decide that your students are already familiar with concrete nouns used with *make*, but are less familiar with idiomatic expressions like *make sense*. Students can always ask follow-up questions about other collocates – what you want to avoid is overwhelming students with too much data. If this happens, it will be difficult for students to identify and describe patterns of use.

Reflection 6.3
- Building on one of your previous investigations (from Reflection 6.1 or 6.2), develop a guided DDL activity that could be used in an L2 classroom.
    - Identify a manageable focus and goal for the in-class investigation.
    - Select, edit, and arrange concordance lines to highlight important patterns of use.
    - Develop a corresponding activity (or set of activities) that engages students in the analysis of the corpus data.

In addition to presenting students with pre-arranged corpus data, teachers also have the option of engaging students directly in their own corpus explorations. One type of student-led DDL activity that can be particularly motivating is an activity which asks students to compare textbook information against actual corpus data. Students can investigate, for example, whether the phrasal verbs, idioms, or useful expressions provided in a textbook chapter are indeed frequently used in spoken or written communication. This type of task also serves as a useful first step in developing corpus analysis skills – students can learn the basics of a particular online corpus interface (e.g., where to type in the keyword, how to generate a frequency list) without the added pressure of analyzing phraseological patterns.

Instructions: Read through the following concordance lines with a partner. You can read each sentence from left to right, but you can also read from top to bottom, focusing on the words *make* and *do*. What words come after *make* and *do*. Do you notice any differences in the types of words that occur after each verb?

They hurried out of her office. 'I think we must	**make**	a decision,' said Mr Grisman. 'And this is it.
Ted had said that she must	**make**	the decision. She had said that Ted was dangerous.
It was time for Megan to speak to Beth. They had to	**make**	a decision together. Did they want Hugh back in their life?
For the moment, they were unable to	**make**	any decisions about their future.
Why had Ashton run away? It didn't	**make**	sense.
We all stared at him. His words did not	**make**	sense at all.
They sat up most of that night, trying to	**make**	sense of these latest events.
she was our teaching a new student – so I didn't have to	**make**	up any more stories about where I'd been.
In that case he might	**make**	up his mind not to marry her under any circumstances
they talk together... Then they	**make**	some story.
'We will	**do**	a lot of scientific experiments.'
We	**do**	a lot of work abroad, and I often go to the Middle East.
other times he's very shy and we have to	**do**	a lot of work to get him to loosen up and relax.
And we've got to	**do**	all the work! I'm going to get out and have a drink.
'The servants	**do**	all the work, don't they?'
'Hurry and	**do**	your cooking now.'
what's the matter with you? Didn't you	**do**	your homework?' 'She didn't have time,' said a boy behind her.
'You wanted someone to	**do**	your ironing for you.'
'and sleep in peace. I'll	**do**	your job for the day and see the Inspector.'
'You mean you	**do**	Your own typing yourself?'

Figure 6.25 Sample DDL concordance line analysis task

Instructions:
I have given your group a set of cards. Each card has a phrase on it. As a group, decide if the phrase is a *mental* activity (something that takes place in your mind) or both a mental and *physical* activity (something you do with your body). Then, place the card under the correct picture below:

Sample word cards:

_____ *a decision*   _____ *your homework*

_____ *choices*   _____ *research*

_____ *sense*   _____ *your job*

_____ *up your mind*   _____ *your work*

Figure 6.26   Sample DDL application task (images retrieved from morgufile.com)

One corpus that is particularly suitable for word frequency investigations is the Michigan Corpus of Upper-Division Student Papers (MICUSP). This corpus is a collection of A student papers written by university seniors and graduate students. When users type in a keyword, they can immediately see how frequently this word is used in student writing across academic disciplines. Figure 6.27 displays the search MICUSP interface. When users first access the MICUSP website, they will see a summary of the student papers included in the corpus. The bar chart indicates how many papers were collected for each discipline, and the pie chart indicates what types of academic papers (e.g., argumentative papers, lab reports) are included in the corpus. Users can perform searches of the entire corpus or can limit searches to a specific discipline or paper type.

Figure 6.27 The MICUSP search interface

One linguistic feature that lends itself to frequency-based searches is linking adverbials such as *however, therefore*, and *furthermore*. These words, often referred to in textbooks as "transition words," are typically taught to students in the form of a long list, and students often have questions about which transition words are preferred over others and how many transitions words they should use in a given essay. While corpus-based resources do provide some information on frequency of use (see, e.g., Conrad, 1999), this information is based on published writing. Students are likely to also be interested in how skilled student writers use these transitions in their academic assignments.

To explore frequency of use in MICUSP, students can simply type the keyword into the search box at the top of the page. After they click search, students will see the bar chart change to show the number of times this word was used in each academic discipline. By clicking on the "per 10,000 words" option above the bar chart, students can see the normed counts, which allows them to compare frequency of use across the disciplines. (A 10,000 word paper would be about a 35-page paper, so a normed count of 10 would indicate the word was used, on average, about 10 times in a long research paper.) Students can also see the total frequency count for the keyword just below the search box. As can be seen in Figure 6.28, the word *however* occurs 3242 times in 698 papers, which means that in most of the papers using *however*, the word appears multiple times.

The keyword can also be viewed in context below the bar chart. The MICUSP interface does not arrange keywords in concordance lines, but rather displays them within several lines of text. As students scroll down these text excerpts, they can see where the word appears in each paper, and can click on the link to that paper to read

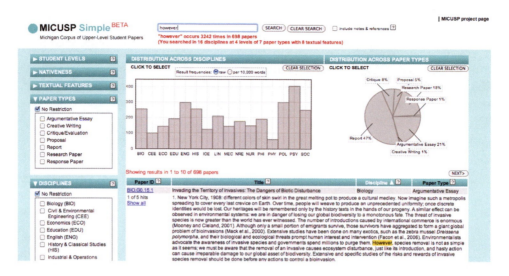

Figure 6.28 MICUSP search results for the keyword *however*

it in its entirety. It is also possible for students to focus on the use of the keyword in a particular academic discipline by clicking on the bar of that discipline, as shown in Figure 6.29. For example, if most of your students plan to take an English course as part of their academic study, you could ask students to look at the use of the word in this discipline specifically. Alternatively, if you have students who represent a variety of majors, you could allow each individual student to choose the discipline that is most relevant to them.

It is also possible to use MICUSP to identify linking adverbials that are used much less frequently. Take, for example, the word *besides*, which is often listed in ESL textbooks as a suitable substitute for *furthermore*. An investigation of this keyword shows that while it does occur in MICUSP, it is much less frequent than *however*, and it is not typically used to link two sentences together. Scanning through the paper samples indicates that most often *besides* is used as a preposition and is followed by either a noun phrase or an *–ing* clause, as in Examples 6.1 through 6.4.

(6.1) <u>Besides</u> neighborhood conditions, which Hector points to as a factor in the choices he has been forced to make, other formative forces include race, ethnicity, socioeconomic status, and instability in the home (Education).

(6.2) <u>Besides</u> trying to influence policy in environmentally beneficial ways, these groups are also interested in maintaining their organizations (Natural Resources & Environment).

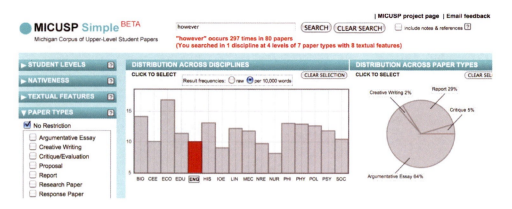

Figure 6.29 Narrowing a search to a specific discipline

(6.3)   There is one major space vehicle producer <u>besides</u> Boeing and Lockheed Martin, and no launch service providers <u>besides</u> Boeing and Lockheed Martin (Economics).

(6.4)   Their ability to connect the personal to the social explains not only why they were so popular, but also offers another forum <u>besides </u>literature and traditional public speaking through which black women expounded on current events and their lives (History).

Although the purpose of student-led DDL is to allow students to take on the role of language researcher, this approach still requires a great deal of planning prior to the in-class exploration. We do not recommend asking students to carry out an investigation before you have had a chance to try it yourself, particularly if students are new to corpus analysis. In the case of linking adverbials, for example, you might carry out your own searches at home, observe important patterns, and then use this information to design an in-class exploration activity.

Reflection 6.4

– Building on a previous investigation (Reflection 6.1, 6.2, or 6.3), design an in-class, student-led DDL activity. Outline steps in the research process that students can complete independently, as a class, or in small groups.

– Now, try out the investigation yourself (before asking your students to do it). What challenges did you encounter? In light of these challenges, how might you modify your original instructions and/or support students as they carry out their own investigations?

Exploring World Englishes and corpora of other languages

The examples provided in this chapter have all been explorations of English language corpora, and most of these corpora represent standard varieties of English spoken in the U.S. and the U.K. However, we also want to highlight the fact that an increasing number of online corpora in other varieties of English and other languages have recently become available to L2 teachers. A corpus that may be of particular interest to teachers who are preparing L2 students for international communication in English is the Vienna-Oxford International Corpus of English (VOICE). This corpus is designed to represent what Seidlhofer (2001) calls *English as a lingua franca*, or English used for the purpose of professional communication in contexts where one's native language is not known by those he is communicating with. As the VOICE website points out:

> The majority of the world's English users are not native speakers of the language, but use it as an additional language, as a convenient means for communicative interactions that cannot be conducted in their mother tongues…. These speakers use English successfully on a daily basis all over the world, in their personal, professional or academic lives.   (VOICE, n.d., p. 1)

On its website, VOICE provides free access to 1 million words of spoken, face-to-face interactions between speakers of English as a Lingual Franca (ELF). Registers represented in the corpus include interviews, press conferences, and professional meetings. Users can download the corpus text files, or they perform keyword searches using the website's interface.

Many corpus linguists are also working to make corpora of other languages available to researchers and teachers. As Lee (2010) notes on his *Bookmarks for Corpus-based Linguists* website, "Monolingual corpora for languages other than English form the fastest-growing group of corpora" (2010, n.p.). Lee (2010) lists well over 100 corpus building projects currently in development, and searchable online corpora are now available for Arabic, German, French, Spanish, Portuguese, and Russian. (See also the resources listed at the end of this chapter.) Complimentary search interfaces and L2 teaching resources in a variety of languages are sure to follow.

Summary

Teachers who are interested in using corpora and corpus-based resources for pedagogical purposes have a number of options available to them:

- A *behind the scenes* approach, where teachers consult corpus-based resources when designing lessons, materials, and tasks.

- A *corpora as a classroom resource* approach, where teachers model the use of corpus-based resources in the classroom and train students in how to use a small set of tools (e.g., corpus-based dictionaries) to investigate their own language questions.
- A *student as researcher* approach, where teachers (1) engage students in guided corpus analysis tasks, using data that has been selected and arranged by the teacher and/or (2) train students to carry out their own investigations of language corpora.

Suggestions for further reading

Bennett, G. (2010). *Using Corpora in the Language Learning Classroom: Corpus Linguistics for Teachers*. Ann Arbor, MI: University of Michigan Press.

Flowerdew, L. (2009). Applying corpus linguistics to pedagogy: A critical evaluation. *International Journal of Corpus Linguistics, 14*, 393–417.

Gavioli, L. (2001). The learner as researcher: Introducing corpus concordancing in the classroom. In G. Aston (Ed.), *Learning with Corpora* (pp. 108–137). Houston, TX: Athelstan.

Reppen, R. (2010). *Using Corpora in the Language Classroom*. Cambridge: Cambridge University Press.

Recommended resources

Corpus-based and corpus-informed English dictionaries
Cambridge Dictionaries Online
<http://dictionary.cambridge.org/us/>

Collins COBUILD English for Learners
<http://www.collinsdictionary.com/dictionary/english-cobuild-learners>

Longman Dictionary of Contemporary English
<http://www.ldoceonline.com/>

Macmillan Dictionary
<http://www.macmillandictionary.com/learn/>

English language corpora (user-friendly and searchable online)
Corpus of Contemporary American English
<http://corpus.byu.edu/coca/>

Corpus of Global Web-Based English
<http://corpus2.byu.edu/glowbe/>

TIME Magazine Corpus
<http://corpus.byu.edu/time/>

MICASE: Michigan Corpus of Academic Spoken English
<http://quod.lib.umich.edu/m/micase/>

MICUSP: Michigan Corpus of Upper-Level Student Papers
<http://micusp.elicorpora.info/>

ELISA (English Language Interview Corpus as a Second Language Application)
<http://www.uni-tuebingen.de/elisa/html/elisa_index.html>

HKCSE: Hong Kong Corpus of Spoken English
<http://rcpce.engl.polyu.edu.hk/HKCSE/>

VOICE: Vienna-Oxford International Corpus of English
<http://www.univie.ac.at/voice/>

Corpora in other languages
Arabicorpus
<http://arabicorpus.byu.edu/>

Corpus del Espanol
<http://www.corpusdelespanol.org/>

Corpus do Portugues
<http://www.corpusdoportugues.org/>

German, French, and Spanish Concordancers (Compleat Lexical Tutor)
<http://www.lextutor.ca/concordancers/>

Russian National Corpus
<http://www.ruscorpora.ru/en/index.html>

Non-English, Parallel, and Multilingual Corpora
<http://www.uow.edu.au/~dlee/corpora2.htm>

WebCorp
<http://www.webcorp.org.uk/live/index.jsp>

Corpuseye
<http://corp.hum.sdu.dk/>

Chapter 7

The dynamic nature of L2 learner language

As we discussed in the Introduction to this book, understanding how to teach the grammar of a language involves more than just an understanding of how grammar is used by speakers and writers in particular contexts. It also requires an understanding of the process of second language acquisition. How do learners integrate new grammatical systems into their existing linguistic repertoires, and in what ways can L2 instruction facilitate this process? In the next two chapters, we turn our attention to these questions. Chapter 7 provides an overview of the study of learner language, which has played a crucial role in our understanding of the L2 acquisition processes. In Chapter 8, we explore the ways in which learner interaction with the linguistic environment (e.g., conversations with native speakers and peers, classroom instruction) can facilitate L2 learning. We begin with a review of some of the earliest attempts to study and characterize learner language and then describe some of the major features of learner language that have been identified in more recent empirical research. Throughout our discussion, we highlight ways in which the study of learner language might help to inform the teaching of grammar in second language classrooms.

Early studies of learner language: L1–L2 comparisons

As we saw in Chapter 2, the field of linguistics in the 1940s and 1950s took a primarily structuralist approach to the study of language. Detailed descriptions of individual languages were provided, and languages were compared against one another to identify key differences. In the world of L2 teaching, the Audiolingual Method made use of these descriptions, through the creation of dialogues which were intended to model how the language was actually spoken. The Audiolingual Method was also influenced by behaviorist theories of language learning, and thus emphasized the importance of repetition and habit formation. L2 learners were charged with the responsibility of unlearning old habits (their L1) so that new habits could be adopted (the L2). This view of L2 learning greatly influenced early approaches to the study of learner language. One of the first theories to be proposed, in the 1950s, was the Contrastive Analysis Hypothesis (CAH), which drew on Lado's (1957) assertion that "those elements that are similar to [a learner's] native language will be simple for him, and those elements that are different will be difficult" (cited in Larsen-Freeman & Long, 1991, p. 53). According to the CAH, differences between the L1 and L2 would result in learner errors, or what is often referred to as *negative transfer*. Learner errors were perceived as unfavorable learning outcomes, and a primary goal of instruction was to eliminate these errors from learner production. Research during this time focused on comparisons of the L1 and L2 grammars and typically did not involve the collection of learner data.

It soon became apparent, however, that differences between the L1 and L2 could not always predict the type of errors that L2 learners would make (Lightbown & Spada, 2013; Mitchell, Myles & Marsdon, 2013; Ortega, 2009). These limitations suggested that if researchers were to achieve a fuller understanding of second language acquisition, they would need to collect and study samples of learner language. A weaker version of the CAH emerged, which posited that L1–L2 comparisons could help to shed light on learner error, but would not always predict the type of errors that learners would make. In a seminal paper, Corder (1967) argued for a more systematic approach to the study of learner errors, one which examined errors in the context of learner production and which attempted to explain why these errors were being made. Errors, Corder argued, were not simply "annoying, distracting… by-products of the process of learning" (p. 162), but rather could serve as an important window into L2 development:

> A learner's errors, then, provide evidence of the System of the language that he is using (i.e. has learned) at a particular point in the course (and it must be repeated that he is using some System, although it is not yet the right System). They are significant in three different ways. First to the teacher, in that they tell him, if he undertakes a systematic analysis, how far towards the goal the learner has progressed and, consequently, what remains for him to learn. Second, they provide to the researcher evidence of how language is learned or acquired, what strategies or procedures the learner is employing in his discovery of the language. Thirdly (and in a sense this is their most important aspect) they are indispensible to the learner himself, because we can regard the making of errors as a device the learner uses in order to learn. It is a way the learner has of testing his hypotheses about the nature of the language he is learning.   (p. 167)

Corder, influenced by the Chomskyan revolution taking place during this time, further argued that L2 learner errors played a role in second language development that was similar to the role that errors played in child language development:

> When a two year old child produces an utterance such as "This mummy chair" we do not normally call this deviant, ill-formed, faulty, incorrect or whatever. We do not regard it as an error in any sense at all, but rather as a normal childlike communication which provides evidence of the state of his linguistic development at that moment.
> (p. 165)

This view of learner errors and learner language development would have a profound effect on the study of learner language in the years to come. First, it would help to establish the collection and analysis of learner production data as a primary research method within the field of second language acquisition. Second, it would help to shift researchers' focus away from predicting and eradicating errors towards a focus on explaining why learner errors occur. Most important, the "why" behind learner errors was now thought to reveal important information about the underlying competence of the L2 learner, or what Corder referred to as "the System." In other words, learner language was not seen as simply a deficient version of the L2, but rather as a variety of language in its own right, with its own grammatical rules and phases of development.

Reflection 7.1

– As an L2 learner, how do you feel about making errors in the target language? Do you view errors as important learning opportunities? What conditions need to be present in order for you to benefit from the errors you make?

– As an L2 teacher, what have you learned from your students' errors? Can you think of times when students' errors were "annoying" or "distracting"? Other times when your students' errors were encouraging or exciting? What contributed to your positive or negative feelings in these situations?

Naming "the System": Selinker's concept of interlanguage

The term most frequently used today to refer to this learner language system is *interlanguage*, which Selinker (1972) describes as derived from both a learners' native language and the target language input she receives from the environment. Interlanguage, according to Selinker, was in constant flux, changing as learners received more input and made more connections and comparisons between the native language and the target. Ideally, interlanguage would gradually evolve into a variety that more closely resembled the target language, and perhaps (though Selinker thought this was rare) could even become indistinguishable from the target.

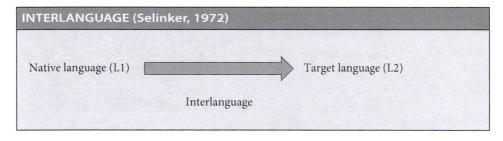

INTERLANGUAGE (Selinker, 1972)

Native language (L1)   →   Target language (L2)

Interlanguage

Selinker argued that the process of second language acquisition could not be understood without consideration of three observable phenomena: the native language system, the target language system, and the interlanguage system. While linguistic research at this time had devoted a considerable amount of attention to the native language (L1) and the target language (L2), little had been done at this point to define or describe a learner's *interlanguage*. And yet, for Selinker, it was the surface structure of interlanguage (the phonology, morphology, and syntax of learner production) that held the key to understanding the underlying psychological processes taking place within the learners' mind.

To support his characterization of interlanguage as a system, Selinker (1972) devotes a great deal of discussion to what he calls *fossilization*:

> Fossilizable linguistic phenomena are linguistic items, rules, and subsytems which speakers of a particular NL [native language] will tend to keep in their IL [interlanguage] relative to a particular TL [target language], no matter what the age of the learner or amount of explanation or instruction he receives.   (p. 215)

According to Selinker, fossilized items (e.g., a students' frequent omission of the third person singular –*s* in spite of a great deal of instruction on third person agreement rules) provide evidence that interlanguage is a system with its own rules, rules that do not always correspond to those of the native or target language. As students learn more about the target language, they may still retain features of their interlanguage, or, after mastering particular target language features, may revert back to interlanguage forms, particularly "when the learner's attention is focused upon new and difficult intellectual subject matter or when he is in a state of anxiety or other excitement" (p. 215). This kind of variability in learner performance suggested that learners were continually working to reorganize the interlanguage system so that it more closely approximated native speaker norms.

Two crucial points that Selinker (1972) makes in this seminal article are: (1) interlanguage is a system which is influenced by, and yet differs from, both the native and target language, and (2) efforts to describe the nature of interlanguage (its phonology, morphology, and syntax) will play a crucial role in our efforts to understand how psychological processes and environmental factors interact with one another as learners move towards a greater understanding of and ability to use the L2. In the decades that followed, a great deal of research would indeed focus on interlanguage development, through the collection and analysis of learner data produced in meaningful contexts. (See Han & Tarone, 2014, for recent reflections on interlanguage and its importance to SLA research over the past 40 years.) These studies would help to provide substantial support for Corder's (1967) and Selinker's (1972) contention that learner language is systematic and rule-governed.

Investigating systematicity in learner language: The morpheme order studies

During this time, three major approaches to the study of learner language began to emerge. The first of these, Error Analysis, addressed Corder's (1967) call for more focused study of learner errors. The goal of many error analysis studies was to identify, classify, and explain particular L2 errors. A second area of research to emerge was what is typically referred to as UG research in SLA, or research which seeks to understand to what extent L2 learners might have access to the innate ability to acquire grammar that they were born with, or what Chomsky refers to as Universal Grammar (see, e.g., Cook, 1993; White, 1989; 2003; Whong, Gil, & Marsden, 2013). This area of research continues today, though makes up only a small proportion of the total body of contemporary SLA research. Much more influential in L2 studies, particularly in the area of L2 pedagogy, is the third strand of research which emerged during this time, one which was concerned with the larger picture of learner language, or the development of the interlanguage system over time. This research answered Selinker's call for the collection and analysis of learner production in meaningful contexts, for the purpose of understanding the complex relationships among the native language, the target language, and the interlanguage system. This area of research also sought to broaden the scope of early Error Analysis studies, to include analysis not just of learner error, but also of learner progress towards target language norms. That is, the central question was no longer "What kind of errors do L2 learners make?" but rather "How and when do learners become capable of producing the correct L2 forms?"

One of the first major foci of this area of research was the order in which particular grammatical forms were acquired by L2 learners. This focus was due, in part, to recent developments in the study of child language acquisition. Studies of children learning English as a native language had found that grammatical morphemes (e.g., the progressive *-ing*, the plural *-s*, the past tense *-ed*) were acquired by children in predictable orders. The first and most famous study of this nature was Brown (1972), a longitudinal study of three children, Adam, Sarah, and Eve. In this study, Brown audiorecorded interactions between the children and their parents over several years. He then analyzed this data to determine at what point particular grammatical morphemes were acquired by each child. Acquisition was defined as the suppliance of a morpheme in an obligatory context (e.g., using plural *-s* when talking about more than one object) more than 90% of the time. Despite differences in the types of conversations each child had with his or her parents, Brown found that all three children mastered the grammatical morphemes in a similar order, with *-ing* being mastered first and the third person irregular form coming last. Table 7.1 displays the order of acquisition observed, using examples provided in Lightbown & Spada (2006, pp. 7–8) and Hudson (2000, p. 127).

Table 7.1 Order of morpheme acquisition observed by Brown (1973)

Age of emergence	Grammatical morpheme	Frequency rank in English (if one of top 10 most frequently used forms)
2 years	Present progressive –*ing* (Mommy runn*ing*)	2
	Prepositions *in* and *on*	
	Plural –*s* (two book*s*)	4
	Irregular past forms (baby *went*)	3
2.5 years	Possessive '*s* (Daddy'*s* hat)	
	Copula in questions (Is Kitty here?)	5
3 years	Articles *the* and *a*	1
3.5 years	Regular past tense –*ed* (she walk*ed*)	6
	Third person singular simple present –*s* (She runs)	7

Brown's findings were replicated in other child language studies, which led second language researchers to wonder whether similar orders of acquisition existed for L2 learners of English. Building on the L1 morpheme order studies, Dulay and Burt (1973) carried out a cross-sectional study with 151 Spanish-speaking children learning English as an L2. To elicit samples of child L2 speech, they used the Bilingual Syntax Measure (BSM), which uses engaging picture and question prompts that young L2 children can understand. In a follow-up study, Dulay and Burt (1974a) found that the vast majority of errors made by the L2 learners were what they considered to be "developmental" in nature, in that they were the same types of errors made by children learning English as an L1 and were not a result of L1 transfer. (Roughly 5% of the errors observed could be traced to L1 influences.) These initial studies suggested that children learning English as an L2 undergo common phases of development which are only minimally influenced by L1 background.

Morpheme order studies were conducted with adult L2 learners as well. The first of these was Bailey, Madden, and Krashen (1974), which found that adult L2 learners experienced an order of morpheme acquisition that was similar to that observed by Dulay and Burt (1973) in their study of child L2 learners. Several studies followed (see Larsen-Freeman & Long, 1991, for a review), and the results suggested that, generally speaking, the order of morpheme acquisition for adult L2 learners was similar across L1 backgrounds. These findings prompted many scholars to explore why some morphemes were typically acquired earlier than others. For example, what makes the –*ing* morpheme easier to master than the –*ed* morpheme? Why might plural –*s* be acquired much earlier than third person singular –*s*?

To address questions like these, Goldschneider and DeKeyser (2001) carried out a research synthesis of 12 morpheme acquisition order studies and investigated the extent to which five "determinants" accounted for the orders of acquisition observed.

These determinants were *perceptual salience* ("how easy it is to perceive or hear a given structure" p. 22), *semantic complexity* ("how many meanings are expressed by a particular form" p. 24), *morphophonological regularity* (whether the form is pronounced differently in different phonological environments; e.g., past tense –*ed* is pronounced as /ɛd/, /d/ or /t/, depending on the sound it follows), *syntactic category* (whether it is a free or bound morpheme, whether lexical or functional), and *frequency* ("the number of times the given structure appears in speech addressed to the learner" p. 30). Goldschneider and DeKeyser found these 5 factors, taken together, explained a large proportion of the variance in the acquisition orders reported in each study. At the same time, Goldscheider and DeKeyser point out that these 5 factors did not account for all of the variation observed, leaving open the possibility that other factors, like L1, play a role in determining the order of L2 morpheme acquisition.

Reflection 7.2

- Keeping Goldschneider and DeKeyser's 5 "determinants" in mind (*perceptual salience, semantic complexity, morphophonological regularity, syntactic category,* and *frequency*) examine the order of morpheme acquisition presented in Figure 7.1. How do these factors help to explain the order of acquisition observed?
- In what ways might an understanding of orders of acquisition help to inform the teaching of grammatical morphemes in L2 classrooms?

Developmental sequences in L2 acquisition

Another outcome of the morpheme order studies was the realization that L2 learners (as well as children learning an L1) did not suddenly acquire a grammatical form, going from 0% accuracy to 100% in a matter of days. Rather, learners experienced what is often referred to as the *U-shaped curve of development* (McLaughlin, 1990). In a U-shaped curve, learners begin using a new grammatical form with relatively high accuracy. Then, for a period of time, accuracy drops, until gradually learners begin using the form with high accuracy again (see Figure 7.1). In the case of the English past tense, for example, learners typically go through a U-shaped curve as they figure out how to use irregular verb forms. Initially, learners use high-frequency irregular past tense forms (e.g., *went, came*) with high accuracy. Eventually, however, learners begin to make errors with past tense forms, using the –*ed* morpheme with irregular verbs (e.g., *goed, camed*). Over time, learners' use of past tense irregular verbs returns to its original rate of accuracy. This process suggests that, as Selinker (1972) had argued, some type of restructuring is taking place within the interlanguage system. Learners' acquisition of grammatical forms does not follow a linear path.

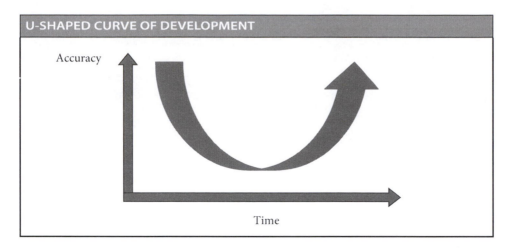

Figure 7.1 U-shaped curve of development

The U-shaped curve helped to focus researchers' attention on not only accuracy of use, but also *emergence* and *attempted use*. That is, studies of learner language began to document when a form was first used by an L2 learner (i.e., emergence), and this use included not only accurate forms but also non-target-like forms (e.g., *He running*). As Bardovi-Harlig (2000) explains, "The chief flaw of morpheme studies.... [is that they] focus on the endpoint of acquisition and not the arguably more interesting process of acquisition.... Focusing on the endpoint of acquisition ignores most of a learner's developmental history" (p. 5).

To better understand the process of L2 acquisition, researchers began to analyze learners' use of particular grammatical forms over time and to investigate the extent to which learners of various L1 backgrounds experienced similar developmental stages. As was found with the morpheme order studies, it is not the case that all learners go through the exact same stages at the exact same time for every grammatical system of a language. However, a number of stages have been identified, stages which are indeed experienced by many L2 learner groups, regardless of L1 and regardless of whether they are learning the L2 in a naturalistic or instructed context. In the following sections we examine why this might be the case, with a focus on three of the most widely-researched grammatical systems: tense and aspect, question formation, and relative clauses.

Tense, aspect, and the lexis-grammar interface

Considering the amount of time L2 teachers devote to teaching verb tenses to L2 learners, it is no surprise that the development of tense and aspect has received considerable attention in the SLA literature. Research on the acquisition of tense and aspect has found that learners pass through predictable phases of development. In English, for example, simple present (*I am a student*) and present progressive (*He is running*) emerge first, followed by simple past (*He left yesterday*). Later in development, learners begin to use present perfect (*I have already eaten*), followed by the tense aspect combinations of present perfect progressive (*He has been running since 5:00*), past perfect (*By the time you got there, he had already left*), and past perfect progressive (*Before moving to the US, I had been studying in Japan*) (Bardovi-Harlig, 2000).

Research on why tense and aspect might emerge in a particular sequence has focused a great deal on both frequency in the input and the inherent semantic properties of particular verbs. That is, many verbs in a language tend to occur with a high frequency in particular tenses and aspects, and this frequency of occurrence is due, in large part, to the meaning the verb typically conveys. This inherent meaning is often referred to as *lexical aspect*. Lexical aspect can be divided into four main categories: *states, activities, accomplishments,* and *achievements* (Vendler, 1967, cited in Bardovi-Harlig & Reynolds, 1995). These lexical categories can be distinguished from one another by considering whether they are *punctual* (occur at a single point in time), *telic* (with a distinct end point), and/or *dynamic* (with action). Andersen (1991) provides a useful visual display of these categories and the relationships among them, as shown in Table 7.2 (adapted from Andersen, 1991; and Bardovi-Harlig & Reynolds, 1995, p. 107).

Table 7.2 Lexical Aspect with examples from English

	States	Activities	Accomplishments	Achievements
Characteristics	−Dynamic −Telic −Punctual	+Dynamic −Telic −Punctual	+Dynamic +Telic −Punctual	+Dynamic +Telic +Punctual
Sample verbs	*know, believe, think*	*rain, write, read, play*	*make a chair, build a house*	*arrive, leave, notice*

As can be seen in Table 7.2, *states* (e.g., *be, have, think, know, want, like*) are verbs which tend to remain constant over time. They express states of being, as well as mental and emotional states. As Yule (2006) explains, no action is being performed by the agent, and these verbs could not be used to answer the question "What do you do?" *Activities* (e.g., *eat, run, swim, walk, work, write*) are dynamic verbs that come with a sense of continual action and no clear end point. *Accomplishments* (e.g., *build a house, write a book, run a mile*) share the same dynamic and durative properties of Activities, but also come with a clear end point that is expressed in the predicate. *Achievements* (e.g., *hit, kick, drop, arrive, leave, notice*) are the only lexical category with all three properties (punctual, telic, dynamic). These verbs express an action that occurs in one instant.

In his Lexical Aspect Hypothesis, Andersen (1991) argues that the lexical aspect of a verb influences the order in which particular tenses and aspects emerge in learner language. Punctual verbs, for example, are likely to be the first verbs to appear in learner language in the past tense, as these actions end immediately after they begin; by the time we are ready to comment on them, they are in the past. For example, we often say things like, "I dropped my pen," but rarely, "I am dropping my pen." The next verb type that would be likely to emerge in past tense would be Accomplishments, as these verb phrases express a clear end point. Verbs which might take much longer to be used in the past tense would be Activities and States. While it is possible to say "I ran" or "I loved it" in particular situations, we much more frequently use these verbs in the present progressive (*I am running*) and the simple present (*I love it*). Thus, it may take learners longer to notice and understand how to use these verbs with past tense meanings.

In response to Andersen's proposal, a number of researchers have investigated L2 learners' acquisition of verbal morphology in English and a number of other languages, including Catalan, Dutch, French, Italian, Japanese, Portuguese, Russian, and Spanish (see Bardovi-Harlig, 2000, pp. 206–211 for a comprehensive list). These studies suggest that there is a general order of L2 acquisition of tense and grammatical aspect and that this order is indeed influenced by lexical aspect. Figure 7.2 summarizes some of Kathleen Bardovi-Harlig's findings regarding English.

As shown in Figure 7.2, much of the research on the Lexical Aspect Hypothesis has focused on simple present, present progressive, simple past, and past progressive. In the earliest stage of acquisition, learners use the base form of the verb to express all tense and aspect meanings. The first morpheme to appear in L2 English is the *-ing* progressive marker. This morpheme is strongly associated with Activity verbs because it expresses a meaning of duration over time. Thus, the first verbs to be inflected with *-ing* in learner language are Activity verbs. The second verb morpheme to appear in learner language is the *-ed* ending (irregular past tense verbs are also used during this time). Learners first use *-ed* with Achievements, then Accomplishments, both of which have distinct end points. In contexts that require the use of an Activity verb in the past tense, learners may still use simple present or present progressive. Activity verbs have no clear end point and thus have a much stronger association with progressive aspect than they do with past tense. States, which most frequently are used to express states of being and emotion that are true at the present time, are not inflected by learners with the past tense until later in the acquisition process.

In English, perfect aspect does not begin to emerge until after learners have been using simple present, progressive aspect, and past tense for some time. Perfect aspect is late-acquired for many of the reasons we reviewed in our discussion of the morpheme order studies. Perfect aspect is not as frequent in the input as the simple tenses, and it has a great deal of semantic complexity. When learners first begin using the present

Simple present

First used with states
(Base form is also used
for all verb types in the
earliest stage of
acquisition)

↑

Present progressive

First used with
Activities, then
Accomplishments, then
Achievements and States

Simple past

First used with
Achievements and
Accomplishments, then
Activities and States

↑

Past progressive

First used with
Activities, then
Accomplishments, then
Achievements and States

Present perfect

↑

Present perfect progressive

↑

Past perfect

Past perfect progressive

Figure 7.2 Observed orders of acquisition for tense and aspect in English (Bardovi-Harlig, 2000)

perfect, they tend to associate it with one meaning only, typically, an action completed in the past (Bardovi-Harlig, 1997). At this stage, learners may use present perfect in contexts where simple past is more appropriate (e.g., In response to the question "What did you do last night?" a learner might respond, "I *have stayed* home.") Though it may appear on the surface that the learner is backsliding or forgetting what has been learned, she is really in the process of restructuring her tense-aspect system. "In spite of the fact that the tense/aspect system as a whole is developing, the rate of appropriate use of individual tense/aspect forms may appear to decline" (Bardovi-Harlig, 1997, p. 415). It is important to keep in mind that the stages of acquisition displayed in Figure 7.2 are not a linear, lockstep progression from one stage to the next. Rather, learners may move forward, revisit earlier stages, and then move forward again, as they sort out the many new meanings and uses associated with each grammatical form.

Reflection 7.3
- As an L2 teacher, how much attention have you paid to lexical aspect? In what ways might teachers integrate lexical aspect into their teaching of verb tense and aspect?
- How might Bardovi-Harlig's (and others') research on tense and aspect help to inform teaching of tense and aspect in L2 classrooms?

Question formation and the Teachability Hypothesis

Research on developmental sequences has important implications for how we approach the teaching of grammar in L2 classrooms. In his Teachability Hypothesis, Pienemann (1984; 1998) posits that learners pass through a set sequence of stages when acquiring grammatical structures and that each stage, starting with stage 1, is a prerequisite for the following stage. He argues further that it is not possible for learners to skip stages, even when they are given instruction which aims to help them do just that. As Pienemann (2013) writes in a recent summary of his Teachability Hypothesis:

> In a number of experiments Pienemann (1984, 1989) tested if the natural order of acquisition "can be beaten" by formal instruction. This test was operationalized by selecting L2 learners on the basis of their current level of L2 acquisition. Two groups were formed (a) with learners at level x and (b) with learners at level x + 1. Both groups were exposed to the same classroom input which focused on level x + 2. It was found that learners at level x + 1 progressed to level x + 2 and that learners at level x did not progress at all.
>
> (p. 5)

Pienemann (1998; 2005) argues that learners' processing abilities constrain their movement from one stage to the next. Early stages involve processing at the individual word level (e.g., asking one-word questions with rising intonation), and later stages involve processing at the phrase and then clause level (e.g., inverting an auxiliary verb and a subject). This progression can be seen in the developmental sequences for question formation in English, as shown in Table 7.3. Stage 1 involves individual words and short phrases, marked with rising intonation. In Stage 2, learners use complete sentences, but have not yet begun to change the word order of the sentence. Later stages involve more complex syntax, with Do- and Wh- fronting, auxiliary verbs, and tags.

Table 7.3 Question formation stages (Kim, 2012)

Developmental stage		Examples
Stage 1:	Single words, formulae, or sentence fragments with rising intonation	Your major?
Stage 2:	Declarative word order, no inversion, no fronting	You have blue jeans? Your cell phone what color?
Stage 3:	Fronting (do-fronting, wh-fronting, no inversion)	Do you have other experience? How much you watch tv show?
Stage 4:	wh+copular, yes/no questions with other auxiliaries, yes/no copula	What's your favorite movie star? Can you give a hint? Have you ever been to the concert? What's the boy doing?
Stage 5:	Inversion in wh-questions with both an auxiliary and a main verb	What degree do you have? How long did you go here?
Stage 6:	Complex questions: tag questions, negative questions, embedded questions	It's better, isn't it? Don't you have pet? Can you tell me where she stays?

To date, a large body of research has demonstrated that learners follow a series of stages that are in line with Pienemann's predictions (Adams, 2007; Loewen & Nabei, 2007; Mackey, 1999, 2006; Mackey & Philp, 1998; McDonough, 2005; McDonough, & Mackey, 2006; Philp, 2003). And many of these studies (e.g., Mackey, 1999; McDonough & Mackey, 2008; Kim, 2012) have found that when learners participate in tasks which target questions that are one stage higher than the learners' current level, learners are able to produce questions at the next developmental stage in subsequent tasks. Just as Pienemann predicted, however, it has not been observed that instruction can result in learners skipping stages and moving to a stage that is two or more levels above their own. A noteworthy implication of this research is the concept of developmental readiness (Han, 2002; Iwashita, 2003; Lightbown, 2013; Mackey & Philp, 1998). In other words, when L2 instruction targets a particular question stage, those learners who are developmentally ready for that stage are the most likely to move to the next level.

Reflection 7.4

– What implications does Teachability Hypothesis have for your own L2 grammar teaching? To what extent do you attempt to evaluate the developmental readiness of your own students?

– How might the concept of Teachability also be applied to the teaching of tense and aspect in L2 classrooms?

Can learners ever skip stages? The case of relative clause acquisition

Though studies of question formation have focused primarily on English, Pienemann (2013) argues that the processing constraints placed on learners are universal, shared by learners of any L2, as well as by children learning their native language. The idea that human language and processing mechanisms share universal properties has also influenced research on relative clauses, as acquisition of this grammatical system appears to involve *typological universals*, or linguistic phenomena that are common across many languages. Many languages have multiple relative clause types and some relative clause types are more structurally complex than others. The Noun Phrase Accessiblity Hierarchy, or NPAH (Keenan & Comrie, 1977) posits that there is a hierarchy of relative clause types, starting from the least complex (and most frequently observed across languages) to the most complex (and least frequently observed across languages). If a language has the most complex type of relative clause, it can be assumed that it also has all other relative clause types. If a language has the second structure on the hierarchy, it can be assumed that it also has the first relative clause type, but not relative clause types three, four, and five. The hierarchy of relative clause types is based upon the grammatical function fulfilled by the relative pronoun in the relative clause. For example, in the sentence *That's the man who ran away*, the relative pronoun is *who* and it is the subject of the relative clause. This is the simplest type of relative clause and is posited to be present in all languages. Relative clause types further down the hierarchy may or may not be present in a given language. Figure 7.3 displays the Noun Phrase Accessibility Hierarchy, moving from least complex and most common across languages (SU) to most complex and less common across languages (OCOMP). (See also Table 7.4.)

SU >	DO >	IO >	OBL/OPREP >	GEN >	OCOMP
subject	direct object	indirect object	oblique	genitive	comparative

Figure 7.3 Noun Phrase Accessibility Hierarchy (adapted from Gass, 2013, p. 230)

From an interlanguage development perspective, although this hierarchy was not meant to predict acquisition order, it was hypothesized (Eckman, 1977) that unmarked items (more frequent, less complex) are acquired earlier than marked items (less frequent, more complex). Moreover, the difficulty of acquiring relative clauses is expected to follow the NPAH. That is, subject relative clauses should be easier to acquire than any other relative clause type, and they can be expected to emerge earliest in learner language. Early support for the NPAH was found by Gass (1979), who examined production data from L2 learners of various L1s. The results showed that with the exception of genitive relative clauses, the frequency and accuracy with which learners produced each relative clause type was as predicted by the hierarchy.

Several studies followed (Doughty, 1988; 1991; Eckman, Bell, & Nelson, 1988; Gass, 1982; Pavesi, 1986; Zobl, 1983), all finding at least partial support for the NPAH. This partial, rather than full, support has generated some debate over whether the NPAH does indeed predict the order of L2 acquisition of relative clauses. Izumi (2003) suggests that the NPAH and one other theory of relative clause acquisition, the Perceptual Difficulty Hypothesis (PDH), may together help to explain L2 relative clause acquisition. The PDH posits that relative clauses which come at the end of a sentence (and which modify a sentence object) are easier to process than relative clauses which are embedded in the middle of a sentence (and which modify a sentence subject). Four main relative clause types receive focus in the PDH: OS (the relative clause modifies the Object of the sentence and contains a Subject relative pronoun), OO (the relative clause modifies the Object of the sentence and contains an Object relative pronoun), SS (the relative clause modifies the Subject of the sentence and contains a Subject relative pronoun), and SO (the relative clause modifies the Subject of the sentence and contains an Object relative pronoun). The PDH predicts the order of acquisition in the following manner: OS > OO > SS > SO. Table 7.4 displays example sentences for both the NPAH and the PDH, in order from easiest (less marked) to most difficult (more marked).

Other scholars have argued that while the NPAH is supported by many studies of the acquisition of English and other European languages, there is less support for the NPAH in studies of East Asian language acquisition. Ozeki and Shirai (2007), for example, analyzed an oral interview corpus from 90 Japanese language learners and found that object relative clause types (direct object, indirect object, object of the preposition) were used more frequently than subject relative clause types, which would seem to go against NPAH predictions. However, as Izumi (2007) points out, several studies of East Asian languages have provided at least partial support for the NPAH.

> It seems to me, therefore, that the issue here is not all or nothing or simply European languages supporting the NPAH versus East Asian languages not supporting the NPAH, but, rather, it is in identifying what factors in addition to the NPAH are involved in creating ease or difficulty in the acquisition of different types of RCs in world languages.
> (p. 352)

One important factor to examine in L2 relative clause acquisition is classroom instruction. If the NPAH serves as a kind of order of acquisition for relative clauses, then Pienemann's Teachability Hypothesis would predict that learners must first master SU relative clauses before they can move on to DO relative clauses, that they must master DO relative clauses before they can move on to IO relative clauses, and so on. However, because the NPAH also suggests that if a language has IO relative clauses it also has DO and SU relative clauses, then it may follow that teaching learners a more

Table 7.4 Relative clause order of difficulty

	4 general types identified for order of difficulty	Corresponding types in NP Accessibility Hierarchy
Least difficult / acquired sooner	OS (noun phrase=object; relative pronoun=subject)	
	The teacher liked <u>the girl</u> [who passed the exam.] O S	**Subject NP** (relative pronoun = subject)
	OO (noun phrase=object; relative pronoun=object)	
	I like <u>the coat</u> [that Mary is wearing.] O O	**Direct Object NP** (relative pronoun = DO)
	Mary likes <u>the man</u> [that I gave the book to.] O O	**Indirect Object NP** (relative pronoun = IO)
	She is the <u>woman</u> [that Tom wants to live with.] O O	**Prepositional Object NP** (relative pronoun = object of prep)
	SS (noun phrase=subject; relative pronoun=subject)	
	<u>The woman</u> [who speaks Russian] is my aunt. S S	**Subject NP** (relative pronoun = subject)
Most difficult / acquired later	SO (noun phrase=subject; relative pronoun=object)	
	<u>The car</u> [that the man drove] was very fast. S O	**Direct Object NP** (relative pronoun = DO)
	<u>The man</u> [that I gave the book to] is my colleague. S O	**Indirect Object NP** (relative pronoun = IO)
	<u>The woman</u> [that Bill is looking for] is beautiful. S O	**Prepositional Object NP** (relative pronoun = object of prep)

Adapted from Izumi (2003, pp. 285–323). Note: Izumi does not include COMP relative clauses in her hierarchy because they are used in some English dialects but not others.

complex relative clause could allow them to, at the same time, acquire the less complex relative clauses on the hierarchy. Research in the 1980s and early 90s (Doughty, 1988; 1991; Eckman, Bell, & Nelson, 1988; Gass, 1982; Pavesi, 1986; Zobl, 1983) did find that when learners mastered a more complex relative clause structure, they could generalize what they had learned to less complex structures that had not been explicitly taught. Doughty (1991) and Izumi (2007) suggest that perhaps, because relative clauses all follow the same general structure (where a relative pronoun fills a gap and is moved to the front of the clause) there is a first stage in which learners figure out how to do this. After this point, a second (and perhaps final) stage involves applying this operation to all of the various relative clause types in the language. If learners first learn the most complex structure as part of their stage one, then it may be fairly easy for them to comprehend and produce all of the other less complex variations.

Reflection 7.5

- As an L2 teacher, how do you typically approach the teaching of relative clauses? What clause types do you highlight when teaching beginner or intermediate learners? What clause types do you typically teach to more advanced students? What clause types seem to be more difficult for your students to master?
- Does research on the Noun Phrase Accessibility Hierarchy give you any new insights into the teaching of relative clauses in L2 classrooms?

Explaining systematicity and variability in learner language

As we have seen in the research reviewed here, learner language has been found to be both systematic and dynamic. Though general orders of acquisition have been observed, so too have many exceptions. Even within one individual learner, we can see signs of a system and deviations from that system. How then might we explain the co-existence of these two phenomena in L2 interlanguage?

One source of variability within the interlanguage system is the process of reorganization or restructuring. In Bardovi-Harlig's (1997; 2000) description of the process of tense/aspect acquisition, for example, learners go through a process of restructuring as they encounter new tense/aspect forms and uses. Linguistic choices that once seemed easy (e.g., use past tense to describe past events) become more complicated as learners realize there is not always a simple one-to-one relationship between form and meaning. These types of realizations help to explain the non-linear, U-shaped curve of development (see Figure 7.1). As learners work to reorganize their interlanguage system, accuracy suffers. As learners begin to sort out the new forms and meanings they have encountered, accuracy improves. Thus, when it comes to L2 grammar pedagogy, it is very important for teachers to understand that variability is a natural part of the acquisition process and that errors do not always mean a failure to learn. In fact, these errors may suggest that a learner is undergoing an important restructuring phase, one which will help them move to a new, more advanced developmental level.

In addition to restructuring, another major explanation for variability in learner language is register, or the situation of use. Just as the grammatical choices of native speakers vary across communicative contexts, so too does the performance of L2 learners. One of the first scholars to focus attention on situational variability was Tarone (1979; 1985; Tarone & Parrish, 1988). Tarone found that some learners were more accurate in their English article use (*a, an, the*) than they were in detecting article errors on a grammaticality judgment task. This finding ran counter to Tarone's (1985) original prediction that the grammaticality judgment task would elicit more accurate forms because this type of task includes a more explicit focus on accuracy than does an oral interview or narrative. Tarone & Parrish (1988) concluded that leaners' greater accuracy in the story-telling tasks could be explained by the characteristics of narrative register.

> Effective story-telling requires that the narrator keep track over time of persons and objects important to the story-line; frequent subsequent mention of such persons and objects must demand the use of [second mention noun phrases], and the marking of such [noun phrases] as referring to "previous" rather than "new" mentions is crucial to the listener's understanding of the story.   (Tarone & Parrish, 1988, p. 34)

In other words, learners may focus more attention on grammatical accuracy if they feel that accurate use is necessary to convey meaning effectively. Accurate use is not only about getting 100% on a grammar test, but also about constructing coherent discourse and achieving communicative goals.

It soon became clear, however, that task demands were just one of many variables which could impact learner performance. In a seminal article which proposes a new framework for the study of learner language, Larsen-Freeman (1997) writes:

> There are many interacting factors at play which determine the trajectory of the developing IL [interlanguage]: the source language, the target language, the markedness of the LI, the markedness of the L2, the amount and type of input, the amount and type of interaction, the amount and type of feedback received, whether it is acquired in untutored or tutored contexts, etc. Then, too, there is a multitude of interacting factors that have been proposed to determine the degree to which the SLA process will be successful: age, aptitude, sociopsychological factors such as motivation and attitude, personality factors, cognitive style… Perhaps no one of these by itself is a determining factor; the interaction of them, however, has a very profound effect.   (p. 151)

Because so many factors are involved in the acquisition and use of language, Larsen-Freeman (1997) proposed that SLA scholars move away from studying variables in isolation and instead move towards viewing both language (in general) and interlanguage (in particular) as a *dynamic, complex system*. A dynamic system is one that changes over time; a complex system is one in which components continuously interact with one another. The behavior of the system is a result of these interactions, and yet, when studied in isolation, the behavior of each individual component cannot predict the behavior of the whole. To illustrate this, Larsen-Freeman (1997) uses the example of a single pebble causing an avalanche, the "camel's back" phenomenon (p. 143). Typically, the movement of a single pebble will not cause an avalanche, but sometimes, it does. Exactly when an avalanche will occur cannot be predicted though an analysis of each individual pebble in the pile. Rather, the cause of the avalanche can only be understood if the numerous interactions between pebbles over a period of time are taken into account. In complex systems (think of the weather as another example), it is possible for unpredictable, seemingly chaotic events to occur.

LANGUAGE AS A DYNAMIC, COMPLEX SYSTEM

- *Language changes over time.*

  "It is common knowledge that the language and grammar of today are not the same as the language and grammar of several centuries ago."   (Larsen-Freeman, 2003, p. 25)
- *Language changes in real-time.*

  "Language users must constantly scan the environment… consider their interlocutors/ readers, and interpret what they are hearing/seeing in order to make decisions about how to respond in accurate, meaningful, and appropriate ways and then carry out their decisions in real time."   (p. 26)
- *Language change is organic.*

  "Language does not change of its own accord. On the other hand, changes in a language are not usually the product of willful attempts on the part of users to alter the code…. Individuals may not intentionally seek to change language, but they do so by their day-to-day interactions in using it…. The behavior of the system as a whole is the result of the aggregate of local interactions."   (p. 30)

When it comes to interlanguage development and the acquisition of second language grammar, a dynamic systems view of language suggests that learner language, like all of language, is in a constant state of change. Learner language changes over time, of course, but also in real-time, through use. It is the day-by-day, minute-by-minute interaction of variables (the L1, the type of input received, the student's motivation, the classroom environment, and so on) which gives rise to the system. Though we cannot predict how the interlanguage system will behave based on the analysis of a single variable (e.g., the learner's L1), we may be able to make more accurate predictions if we take into account the system as a whole.

It is also important to recognize that at times, learner language development may appear chaotic and unpredictable. Though many studies aim to identify clear patterns in development that emerge through the aggregation of learner data (e.g., mean scores on a language assessment), when data is disaggregated, the patterns are often less clear. In an exploratory study which aimed to provide a "dynamical description" of learner performance over time, Larsen-Freeman (2006) collected samples of spoken and written language from five learners studying English in China. In addition to recording group means for accuracy (error rates), fluency (number of words per independent clause), and complexity (number of clauses embedded within an independent clause), Larsen-Freeman also created individual profiles for each learner, to investigate the extent to which each individual learner exhibited patterns that were similar to the patterns of the group. Not surprisingly, Larsen-Freeman found that, although clear patterns could often be identified when group means were calculated, these patterns were not always present in individual learner performance. For example, although the group as a whole improved in their grammatical accuracy over time, some learners actually showed a decrease in accuracy.

Does this mean that the patterns identified in previous research (including studies reviewed earlier in this chapter) no longer mean anything? We would say it is not necessary to disregard previous interlanguage research and start anew. When sample sizes are large enough, mean scores do tell us something about general trends in behavior. However, as qualitative researchers have long pointed out, general trends can never account for the behavior of every individual in the group. There are always exceptions and outliers. Larsen-Freeman's (2006) point is that these exceptions should not be ignored because they muddy the waters a bit. Rather, they should be studied as interesting in their own right. If interlanguage is truly dynamic and complex, then it would follow that for each individual learner, there is a unique set of variables which interact to give rise to his or her interlanguage system. In our own L2 classrooms, we can see that this is clearly the case. Each student brings with them their own set of experiences and attributes (motivations, learning strategies, opportunities to use the L2, feelings about the L2); no set of interacting variables is the same. How then, can we expect each learner's process and outcome to also be the same, even considering our best efforts to teach the language?

More important, perhaps, is for L2 teachers to be aware that several variables are at play, and no single variable (e.g., how well the teacher explained a particular concept, how many hours the student studied that week) is likely to explain a student's performance at any given time. But if we make more efforts to understand how numerous variables interact with one another in the lives of our students and within the confines of our classroom, we may also move one step closer to understanding the nature of L2 grammar development and the role that instruction might play in facilitating this process.

Reflection 7.6
- In what ways does Larsen-Freeman's description of language as a dynamic, complex system relate to the teaching of L2 grammar?
- How might this perspective inform how you approach the design of grammar lessons and the assessment of learner progress?

Revisiting the "target language" and the goal of near-nativeness

The view of interlanguage as a dynamic, complex system also challenges the notion of a "target language" and the assumption that interlanguage development moves in a linear fashion from zero knowledge of the L2 towards "complete" or "native-like" knowledge of the L2. "It has been assumed that successful SLA is accomplished through the acquisition of the rules that bring the learner's performance into greater conformity with the target language" (Larsen-Freeman, 2003, p. 32). This view, according to Larsen-Freeman, represents an "acquisition metaphor" of L2 learning, one that assumes that learning is essentially a process of acquiring some*thing* (e.g., grammar rules) so that it can be applied to a given task (e.g., taking a test, writing an essay, translating a document). A "participation metaphor," on the other hand, emphasizes language acquisition as an act of "doing," rather than a state of "having," a "process of becoming a member of a certain community" (Larsen-Freeman, p. 33).

> While the acquisition metaphor stresses the individual mind and what goes "into it"
> the participation metaphor shifts the focus to the evolving bond between the individual
> and others.   (Sfard, 1998, cited in Larsen-Freeman, 2003, p. 33)

This metaphor of participation has particular relevance to L2 grammar pedagogy, especially when one considers the acquisition-oriented approach taken in many grammar textbooks for L2 learners. The design of many of these textbooks seems to suggest to learners and teachers that language learning is primarily a process of acquiring rules and applying these rules to grammar exercises. What is more, these textbooks assume that there is one grammar to be learned, the "target language," an idealized, somewhat generic, native speaker norm. As we have seen in previous chapters, however, there is no "monolithic" grammar of a language (Conrad, 2000). Different situations of use call for different linguistic choices, and an important goal of L2 grammar instruction is to help learners understand how and why these choices are made.

Thus, if we look at language as a dynamic complex system, then real-time, meaningful, goal-oriented interaction becomes much more important – not only because the ability to communicate meaningfully in particular contexts is a learning goal, but also because learning itself takes place through the act of using language. In Chapters 8 and 9, we look more closely at the role of interaction and collaboration in the L2 grammar acquisition process and examine how carefully designed communication tasks might promote the type of learning-in-action that is so central to a dynamic view of language learning.

If it is not possible to identify one, stable, idealized "target" – or, as Larsen-Freeman puts it, "The target is always moving" (1997, p. 151) – then it is also important to think critically about the concepts of *near-nativeness* or *native-like* competence. These terms are often used to refer to the end-point of acquisition, with the assumption that the interlanguage system will never completely mirror the target language system. But if the goal of L2 acquisition is to participate in a variety of L2 communities and contexts (having dinner with friends who speak the L2, pursuing a graduate degree in the L2, using the L2 when traveling), then mirroring a somewhat vague native speaker target may not be desirable. And, considering the diversity of styles, dialects, and registers used by native speakers of a language, this may not even be possible.

Though numerous scholars have called the idealized native speaker target into question (e.g., Canagarajah, 2004; Cook, 1999; Firth & Wagner, 1997; Jenkins, 2006; Seidlhofer, 2001; Shuck, 2006), Ortega (2010, 2013) argues that the field of second language acquisition still suffers from what she calls a *monolingual bias*, where native speakership *is* defined by birth and monolingualism *is* assumed to be the norm. This is evidenced in the standard research practices of the field, where study participants are given the default label of "non-native speaker" and are described only in terms of their L2 performance on particular tasks, not what they can do as multilinguals functioning in the real world. At the same time, the native speakers of the target language are viewed as superior to those learning the language, even in cases where the native speakers are monolingual (as is often the case with English) and thus have a smaller linguistic repertoire than bi- and multilingual users.

> Language exposure from birth and primary language socialization is seen to confer the linguistic right of legitimate ownership of a language and the advantage of possessing the "purest" form of (monolingual) linguistic competence, one that cannot be altered by later experiences in life. Conversely, the ideology of linguistic birthrights also makes any form of language ownership and linguistic competence that may be developed later in life into less legitimate and less pure. (Ortega, 2013, p. 36)

In a recent corpus-based, critical discourse analysis of the applied linguistics literature, Keck and Ortega (2013) provide empirical evidence for the monolingual bias in L2 research, through the identification of three deficit metaphors which occurred with high frequency across a corpus of over 900 published journal articles: (1) the characterization of learners as generally deficient in some way, through the use of negative statements with primary verbs (*are not, do not*), the modal *cannot*, or an affirmative statement with negative prosody (*have difficulty, need*); (2) the characterization of learner success as partial or possible only under certain conditions, through the use of conditional and concessive clauses (*if, when, although*); and (3) the characterization of learners as passive beneficiaries of particular external forces (e.g., teaching techniques, task conditions) which can bring about learning gains. Examples 7.1 through 7.3, taken from the corpus of applied linguistics literature compiled by Keck and Ortega, illustrate each of these deficit metaphors.

(7.1) *Learners **do not develop** the full spectrum of sociolinguistic registers or the level of cognitive and academic literacy commanded by monolingual native speakers.*

(7.2) ***Even though** learners **can successfully interpret a sentence**, the representations that are created **lack** complex hierarchical structure.*

(7.3) *The teacher **either** provides a recasts or **forces learners to** establish the correct form through elicitation techniques.*

What is particularly troubling about these findings is that these pervasive deficit metaphors *within* the applied linguistics community could serve to reinforce deficit views of language learners that exist *outside* of the research community. For example, when teachers-in-training read the applied linguistics literature, they seek out answers to their questions about how students learn and how second languages should be taught. Discourse that ignores the rich linguistic resources that many language learners bring to the classroom paints an incomplete picture of language acquisition, one which can (unintentionally) result in language teaching practices that make students feel ashamed, rather than proud, of their bilingualism.

Put this way, the consequences of the monolingual bias became painfully clear. All too often, L2 users are made to feel that they are "less rather than more" (Ortega, 2010), that their L2 grammar errors are signs of some inherent deficiency, a deficiency they will always have simply because of where they were born and what language(s) they happened to learn first.

Within our own classrooms, we can also work to move beyond a monolingual bias, towards an emphasis on multilingualism and multicompetence (Cook, 1999). There is no reason why our students, many of whom already speak multiple languages, should feel inferior to those who speak only one. When we encounter learner language, either as L2 researchers or L2 grammar teachers, it is important to keep this bias in mind and to avoid the tendency to focus on what learners cannot do, rather than what they can do. Seeing errors as important signs of progress, as evidence of restructuring and development, is one way we can work against our deficit-oriented tendencies. Recognizing the rich linguistic repertoires our students bring to our classrooms is another. And investigating the ways in which our students use multiple languages to navigate their complex lives is yet another way we can work to recognize and value the unique, talented individuals who come through our classrooms (Canagarajah, 2011; Creese & Blackledge, 2010; Taylor, Bernhard, Garg, & Cummins, 2008). Although much of the L2 literature still uses adjectives like "ungrammatical," "ill-formed," "non-target-like," and "deviant" when describing learner language, we encourage you to consider some more positive alternatives – *creative, amazing, resourceful* (to borrow from the child language acquisition literature) – and, in keeping with the current theme of this chapter: *dynamic* and *complex*.

Reflection 7.7

- As an L2 learner, have you ever felt inferior to native speakers of the language? To what extent do you compare your own abilities against theirs? In what ways have these comparisons been useful? In what ways have they been potentially detrimental to the learning process?
- As an L2 teacher, have you encountered deficit views of L2 learners, either in your school or in your community? How do you respond to this? To what extent do you focus on what your students cannot do, in comparison to what they can do?
- How might L2 teachers and L2 learners work together to combat deficit views of multilingual students?

Summary

-   First coined by Selinker, the term interlanguage refers to the learner's developing language system, one which is influenced by both the native language(s) and the target language.
-   Studies of interlanguage have identified orders of acquisition for grammatical morphemes, as well as developmental sequences for the acquisition of particular grammatical systems. These phases of development are largely influenced features of the input, such as frequency of use, salience, and semantic complexity. Similar orders of acquisition and developmental sequences have been observed in both children learning their native language and adults learning a second language; in both naturalistic and instructed L2 learning contexts; and across a wide range of L1 backgrounds.
-   Learner language can be described as a dynamic, complex system which changes not only over time, but in real time, as learners adjust to the demands of a particular communicative situation.
-   Approaches to the study of learner language which compare learners against an idealized, monolingual norm run the risk of perpetuating deficit views of L2 learners. A more appropriate comparison may be groups of highly successful, multicompetent, multilingual users.

Suggestions for further reading

Bardovi-Harlig, K. (2000). Tense and aspect in second language acquisition: Form, meaning, and use. A Supplement to *Language Learning*, *50*, 1–491.

Han, Z. & Tarone, E. (Eds.). (2014). *Interlanguage: Forty Years Later*. Amsterdam: John Benjamins.

Larsen-Freeman, D., & Cameron, L. (2008). *Complex Systems and Applied Linguistics*. Oxford: Oxford University Press.

May, S. (Ed.) (2013). *The Multilingual Turn: Implications for SLA, TESOL, and Bilingual Education*. New York, NY: Routledge.

Tarone, E., & Swierzbin, B. (2009). *Exploring Learner Language*. Oxford: Oxford University Press.

Chapter 8

Instructed L2 grammar acquisition

Six key theory-practice links

In addition to describing the nature of learner language and the phases that L2 learners pass through as they acquire particular grammatical features, SLA research has also focused extensively on L2 instruction and the ways in which features of the L2 classroom interact with the L2 learning process. A central focus of early research in this area (often referred to as *instructed SLA*) was the language teacher and the important role that he or she played in providing necessary input to L2 learners. As we saw in Chapter 2, many early theories of second language acquisition described the type of teacher input that would be most facilitative to L2 development: proponents of the Audiolingual Method stressed the importance of authentic input, with opportunities for repetition and practice; Krashen's Monitor Model stressed the importance of meaningful, comprehensible input in the L2 classroom; and Long (1980) highlighted the importance of interactionally modified input, or input that is carefully tailored to the needs of the L2 learner through native speaker (or teacher) feedback (e.g., confirmation checks, requests for clarification, and repetitions or paraphrases of learner utterances).

Over the past few decades, however, instructed SLA research has broadened considerably in scope and has achieved what Ortega (2012) refers to as "epistemological diversity" (p. 206). In other words, while instructed SLA research in the 1980s was primarily dominated by a focus on input, interaction, and output, several additional orientations have emerged, all of which offer their own (sometimes competing) theories about how L2 learning works and how L2 instruction can facilitate the learning process. Though published overviews of SLA research differ in their estimates of the precise number of orientations that currently exist, many (e.g., Ellis, 2008; Lightbown & Spada, 2013; Mitchell & Myles, 2013; Ortega, 2009; Skehan, 2003) commonly highlight three major perspectives that have made substantial contributions to our understanding of instructed SLA: interactionist, sociocultural, and cognitive.

The interactionist orientation to SLA examines how the linguistic environment (the input the learner receives) interacts with learners' internal cognitive processes (e.g., noticing, hypothesis testing). This research domain emerged in direct response to Long's Interaction Hypothesis. Key questions explored in this domain which relate directly to L2 grammar pedagogy include: How can teachers promote meaningful interaction in the target language in their own classrooms? To what extent does this interaction promote the acquisition of particular grammatical forms?

The sociocultural orientation to SLA examines L2 learning as it takes place through participation in social interaction (with family members, friends, co-workers, classmates) in particular contexts (local, regional, national, global, historical). Key questions explored in this research domain include: How can teachers encourage learner-learner and learner-teacher collaboration in the classroom? In what ways does students' participation in social interaction contribute to their development of grammatical competence?

The cognitive orientation to SLA examines the role of cognition in second language acquisition. This is not to say that interactionist and sociocultural domains do not account for cognition; both do. However, while interactionist research looks at the interaction between cognition and the environment (e.g., how negative feedback from the environment might prompt noticing) and sociocultural research examines how cognition is developed through social interaction (e.g., how language is first learned through interaction and is then used to mediate thought), cognitive orientations focus primarily on the inner workings of cognition: attention, awareness, information processing, memory storage and retrieval. Key questions explored in this domain include: What role might instruction and practice play in the development of automatic processing and retrieval skills? In what ways do the cognitive demands of a task impact the accuracy, fluency, and complexity of learner language?

Drawing on all three of these research domains, in this chapter, we highlight six key findings which we feel are particularly relevant to the teaching of L2 grammar.

Explicit versus implicit instruction does not have to be an either-or proposition

Over the years, the pendulum has swung away from a structural syllabus, towards entirely meaning-focused Communicative Language Teaching, and back again to at least some focus on grammatical form. While there has been much debate over whether implicit or explicit instruction is superior, the research to date suggests that both approaches have the potential to promote L2 grammar acquisition (Nassaji & Fotos, 2011; Norris & Ortega, 2000). Thus, we feel it is most useful to view explicit and implicit instruction as a continuum, rather than as a dichotomy. On one end of this continuum, we have a *focus on meaning*, or versions of Communicative Language Teaching which involve entirely meaning-focused interaction and no effort on the part of the teacher to shift students' attention to form. On the opposite end, we have what Long (Long, 1996; Long & Robinson, 1998) calls *focus on formS* – a structural syllabus, explicit grammar lessons, rote practice, and no opportunities to interact meaningfully. While

Form-focused instruction

Focus on formS ←——————————————————————→ Focus on meaning

Focus on formS			Focus on meaning
Structural syllabus organized around discreet grammatical items	Explicit instruction + communication about grammar in collaborative tasks (e.g., Ellis & Fotos, 1994)	Communicative task + explicit instruction before or after the task (e.g., Fotos, 1993, 2002; Muranoi, 2000)	Implicit Focus on Form through planned feedback in oral communication tasks (e.g., Doughty & Varela, 1998; Mackey & Philp, 1998; Mackey, 1999)	Implicit Focus on Form through unplanned, reactive feedback in the midst of meaningful communication (e.g., Long & Robinson, 1998)	"Pure" or "strong" versions of Communicative Language Teaching
Decontextualized, rote practice					No explicit grammar instruction or corrective feedback

Figure 8.1 Form-Focused Instruction continuum

few scholars would advocate for either of these extremes, there are many promising approaches in between. These pedagogical options fall under the umbrella term of *form-focused instruction* (Ellis, 2001; Fotos & Nassaji, 2007; Spada, 1997; Spada & Lightbown, 2008), or instruction which aims to draw learners' attention to linguistic form in meaningful contexts.

Just one step to the left of a Focus on Meaning approach, we have Long's *focus on form* (without the –S), where teachers make efforts to draw students' attention to linguistic form in the midst of meaningful communication. Teachers do not plan which forms will be focused on in advance, but rather they observe students in the act of communication and intervene when communication breakdowns occur. This allows for classroom interaction to be primarily meaning-focused, with occasional shifts in attention to vocabulary or grammar forms. Long's focus on form approach is intended for a task-based syllabus, one which is not organized around pre-selected grammatical structures, but rather around "the hundred and one things people do in everyday life, at work, at play, and in between" (Long, 1985, p. 89). In other words, each instructional unit focuses on a particular situation of use and the real-world tasks associated with this context.

For teachers who would like to have some control over what grammatical forms are focused on when, but who also prefer communication tasks over teacher-fronted grammar lessons, planned implicit focus on form is a viable option. In this approach, teachers decide in advance what grammatical forms to target and then design communication tasks that will encourage (or require) the use of those forms. To increase the likelihood that students will attend to the target grammatical forms (without explicitly telling them to do so), teachers can incorporate corrective feedback into the task. For example, Doughty and Varela (1998) designed an instructional intervention in which ESL students in a middle school science class worked collaboratively in groups to carry out and report on science experiments. In their focus on form intervention, Doughty and Varela decided in advance to focus their corrective feedback on students' use of the past tense, a grammatical form that is very important to science reporting. As students discussed the results of the experiments with one another, the teacher (Varela) gave feedback not only on the content of their discussion, but also their use of verb tenses. No explicit explanations of past tense use were provided; rather, Varela used implicit recasts to respond to students' verb tense use. For example, if a student described a past tense event using simple present, the teacher would first repeat the utterance with rising intonation (to get the students' attention) and then would go on to recast the utterance (using the correct past tense form).

Closer to the Focus on FormS end of the continuum would be approaches which attempt to use both meaning-focused communicative tasks and explicit techniques. Sandra Fotos' approach to teaching grammar in English as a Foreign Language (EFL) settings is one example of this. Arguing that Long's focus on form approach is not feasible in many EFL contexts, Fotos (2002) has proposed a three-part grammar lesson in which the teacher introduces the target form to students, engages students in communicative practice, and then reviews the feature with students, responding to any challenges they faced while doing the task. This approach integrates some *focus on formS* (pre-selected grammar features and explicit lessons) with some elements of *focus on form* (meaning-focused communicative tasks that involve some shift in attention to grammar forms).

A Form-Focused continuum allows teachers a good deal of flexibility when it comes to addressing grammar in the L2 classroom. Teachers under pressure to prepare students for grammar-focused exams may find Fotos' approach a practical way to develop both students' declarative knowledge of grammar rules and their communicative competence. Teachers working to help students carry out daily tasks in the L2 with confidence and fluency may favor approaches that shift attention to form through feedback in the midst of communicative activities. And many teachers may find that their approach varies over the course of a semester – that different grammatical features and communication needs call for differing types and amounts of attention to form.

Reflection 8.1

- As an L2 learner, how would you characterize the approaches you have experienced in your second or foreign language classes? Did some classes take a Focus on FormS approach? Did others focus primarily on meaning? Have you experienced classes that fell somewhere in the middle of these two extremes?
- As an L2 teacher, where would you plot your own approach to teaching grammar on the Form-Focused Instruction continuum? What factors (e.g., student needs, instructional context, curricular requirements) influence the choices you make regarding focus on form in the L2 classroom?

Meaning-focused communication tasks can promote the acquisition of L2 grammar

Although the term "Form-Focused Instruction" puts the word "Form" at the fore, the approaches that fall within this middle area of the implicit-explicit continuum typically do not emphasize form over meaning. Rather, these approaches make use of carefully designed communication tasks which place a primary focus on meaning and a secondary focus on grammatical form. As learners work together to understand one another and accomplish a goal, they can, at the same time, be encouraged to use particular grammatical forms or to attend to their own grammatical errors, in ways that do not impede the flow of communication.

This approach to promoting grammar acquisition through communication tasks is often called *task-based interaction*. Since Long's Interaction Hypothesis (1980, 1996), numerous studies have examined the benefits of task-based interaction. Two meta-analyses (Keck, Iberri-Shea, Tracy-Ventura, & Wa-Mbaleka, 2006; Macky & Goo, 2007) have synthesized, quantitatively, the findings of this research, concluding that task-based interaction does indeed promote the acquisition of particular grammatical features which were elicited during task performance. Learners who participate in task-based interaction demonstrate larger gains in L2 grammar acquisition than control groups (learners who received no instruction at all) and comparison groups (learners who received an alternative form of instruction).

Through all of this research, three task features have emerged as particularly important to promoting the acquisition of L2 grammar. First, successful communication tasks often strive to create what Pica, Kanagy, and Falodun (1993) call an *information gap*. That is, each participant in the task has a real need to exchange information with other task participants – if participants do not share this information, they cannot complete the task successfully. Although many alternative task designs exist, Pica et al. argue that an information gap is needed to maximize interaction, as students must ask each other questions and negotiate meaning in order to obtain the information they need. An ideal information gap design is a two-way information gap, or jigsaw task. In this design, all task participants have information they must share with the other members of their group. This encourages the participation of all group members and requires group members to work together towards a shared goal.

TASK-BASED INTERACTION & L2 GRAMMAR ACQUISITION

Communication tasks are more likely to promote grammar acquisition if they:

– *Create an information gap*, or a situation in which each student in a group holds a piece of information that other group members need to know
– *Strive for task-essentialness* by creating obligatory contexts for the target grammatical form(s)
– *Provide opportunities for corrective feedback* in response to student errors

---

Many successful communication tasks also aim for what Loschky and Bley-Vroman (1993) call *task-essentialness*. That is, the task is designed to create obligatory contexts for particular grammatical (or lexical) forms and requires participants to use these forms in order to complete the task successfully. Mackey (1999), for example, used a *spot-the-difference* task to create a need to use targeted question forms. A participant could not identify the differences between her own picture and her partner's picture (hidden from view) without attempting to use and comprehend questions. Loschky and Bley-Vroman place *task-essential* forms (forms needed to carry out a task) on a continuum with *task-useful* forms (learners can more easily complete the task by using the target forms, but are not required to do so) and *task-natural* forms (learners may use the target forms, but it is also possible for them to easily complete the task without these forms). As R. Ellis (2003) points out, task-essentialness is not always possible to achieve (we can't *force* our students to use the forms we want them to!). We believe, however, that it is a worthy goal. An important finding of the Keck et al. (2006) meta-analysis was that task-essential designs resulted in greater acquisitional gains over time than task-useful or task-natural designs. That is, learners who participated in communication tasks which required the use of the target feature demonstrated greater improvement on delayed post-tests (30–60 days after the treatment) than did learners who did not experience task-essential designs.

A third key feature of successful communication tasks is that they often create opportunities for learners to receive feedback on their use of L2 grammar, including *corrective feedback*, or feedback in response to learners' grammatical errors. As we will see in the next section, there are a variety of feedback strategies available to teachers. Feedback can be explicit in nature (e.g., an overt correction of an error) or implicit (e.g., a recast), and it can be planned (e.g., to target past tense errors only) or incidental (e.g., in response to errors as they arise, regardless of error type). An important function of feedback during communication tasks is to promote awareness of and reflection on L2 grammar. Though communication tasks are primarily meaning-focused, feedback during the course of interaction can be used to temporarily shift learners' attention away from meaning towards form (Long, 1996; Long & Robinson, 1998), thus increasing the likelihood that the communication task will promote L2 grammar acquisition.

> **Reflection 8.2**
> – This section highlights features of communication tasks which have been found to promote L2 grammar acquisition: an information gap, task-essentialness, and corrective feedback. In what ways have you, as a teacher (or researcher) aimed to integrate these features into your own instructional task design? What benefits have you observed? What challenges have you encountered?
> – Considering your own experiences as a teacher and a learner, what other task design features do you feel play an important role in promoting L2 grammar acquisition?

Corrective feedback – in many forms – can make a difference

In addition to deciding whether instruction should be primarily implicit or explicit in nature, teachers are also faced with decisions regarding when and how to correct students' grammatical errors. Should I correct every error a student makes? Should I explain the error to the student or just make the correction? Should I simply restate the students' utterance in the correct form and move on? And does any of this feedback make a difference? Does it help my students to improve their grammatical competence?

The answer to the last two questions in the above paragraph should be encouraging – yes, your feedback does make a difference. Numerous studies of corrective feedback have found that this feedback can lead to subsequent acquisition of target grammatical forms (see Bitchener & Ferris, 2012; Mackey, 2012; Nassaji & Fotos, 2011; Russell & Spada, 2006 for reviews). Though there has been some debate over which feedback strategies are better than others, few scholars would argue that teachers use only one type of corrective feedback. Rather, teachers have available to them a repertoire of feedback strategies, all of which can work together to promote noticing and L2 grammar acquisition. For example, Mackey (1999) examined the impact of what she called *interactional feedback* on L2 question development, finding a combination of requests for clarification and recasts to be effective. Muranoi (2000) used a carefully planned sequence of feedback delivery involving requests for repetition, repetitions of the learners' modified feedback, and recasting; all of which he included under the heading of *interaction enhancement*.

One key finding of the research on oral corrective feedback (whether it be a recast, a request for clarification, or an elicitation) is that communication tasks which incorporate frequent feedback into their design lead to greater learning gains than communication tasks with little or no feedback (Li, 2010; Mackey, 2006; Mackey & Goo, 2007; Russell & Spada, 2006). In other words, when learners are focused primarily on meaning as they work to complete information gap tasks, they may not attend to grammatical form unless they receive some kind of feedback in direct response to grammatical errors.

One implicit method of providing feedback that has received considerable attention in SLA research is the *recast*, a conversational strategy in which a person repeats and slightly modifies an utterance made by the person they are in conversation with, for the purpose of either clarifying what was said or highlighting an error. Numerous studies of child-directed speech have found recasts to be the preferred corrective feedback method used by the parents of young children (Saxton, 2010) and, not surprisingly, this has also been found to be the case in studies of teachers interacting with L2 students (Lyster & Ranta, 1997; Mackey et al., 2000; Panova & Lyster, 2002; Moroishi, 2002; Sheen, 2004; Farrokhi, 2007; Yoshida, 2009).

CORRECTIVE FEEDBACK STRATEGIES	
Clarification request	**Example***
Indicating to a student that you did not understand by asking questions such as "Excuse me?" "What did you say?" and "I'm sorry?"	S: *I want practice today, today.* T: *I'm sorry?*
Repetition	**Example**
Repeating an error back to a student, usually with rising intonation or emphasis	S: *Oh my god, it is too expensive, I pay only 10 dollars* T: *I pay? [Repetition with rising intonation]*
Recast	**Example**
Reformulating what a student has said to model and draw attention to a particular form without interrupting the flow of communication	S: *And they found out the one woman run away.* T: *Ok, the woman was running away.* S: *Running away.*
Elicitation	**Example**
Inviting self-repair by repeating part, but not all of what a student has said, usually with rising intonation	S: *And when the young girl arrive, ah, beside the old woman.* T: *When the young girl...?*
Metalinguistic feedback	**Example**
Explaining an aspect of grammar in response to an error, without explicitly providing the correct answer	S: *I see him in the office yesterday.* T: *You need a past tense.*
Direct correction	**Example**
Providing explicit signals to the student that there is an error in the previous utterance	S: *He has catch a cold.* T: *Not catch, caught.* S: *Oh, ok.*

*Examples taken from Nassji & Fotos (2011, pp. 73–78)

In the following conversational excerpt, taken from Mackey and Philp (1998, p. 344), a native speaker recasts an L2 learner in the midst of a communication task:

NNS:	Oh [pause] she go to the zoo and she is she is she fun?
NS:	is she –
NNS:	fun
NS:	is she having fun?
NNS:	having fun
NS:	yeah yeah

In this exchange, the native speaker and the L2 student (labeled NNS, or non-native speaker) are participating in a spot-the-difference task, in which one person is holding a picture that is slightly different from her partner. Each partner must ask the other partner questions to find out how their pictures differ. The L2 learner asks the question "she is she fun?" The native speaker recasts this question by changing its grammatical structure: "Is she having fun?" The learner then repeats part of this recast: "having fun." This can be seen as a type of *implicit corrective feedback* (also called *implicit negative feedback*) in that the recast responds to a grammatical error without explicitly stating that an error has been made. The recast has the potential to draw the L2 learners' attention to the grammatical form of her question without interrupting the flow of the conversation.

Proponents of recasts (Goo & Mackey, 2013; Long, 1996; 2007; Mackey & Philp, 1998; Mackey, 2006) argue that recasts are beneficial for L2 learning because they are unobtrusive, and they provide learners with not only negative evidence (a cue that a grammatical error has been made) but also positive evidence (through the modeling of the correct grammatical form). A number of studies have investigated the impact that recasts might have on the subsequent learning of L2 grammar (e.g., Ammar & Spada, 2006; Nicholas, Lightbown, & Spada, 2001; Nassaji, 2009; Sheen, 2008) and have found recasts to be an effective means for promoting grammar acquisition through task-based interaction. Nevertheless, recasts have been the focus of some intense debate (Goo & Mackey, 2013; Lyster & Ranta, 2013), as some scholars question whether the findings of controlled laboratory studies have relevance to the classroom. It is unlikely that teachers would be able to (or even want to) provide a recast in response to every error made by every student, as is often done in research studies. Because a classroom setting is quite different from a laboratory setting, it is likely that learners' responses to recasts in these two settings might also be different. This was found to be the case in Lyster and Ranta's (1997) oft-cited study of negative feedback in Canadian French immersion settings. Lyster and Ranta found that while recasts were by far the most preferred form of corrective feedback, when compared to other, more explicit feedback types, recasts were found to be least likely to promote an immediate response from the learner. In many cases, there was no evidence that a teacher's recast was noticed or processed by the learner, as the learner did not repeat or modify his utterance after the recast was given. Evidence that a learner has noticed a recast or another form of implicit feedback is often called *uptake*, defined by Lyster & Ranta as "a student's utterance that immediately follows the teacher's feedback and that constitutes a reaction in some way to the teacher's intention to draw attention to some aspect of the participant's initial utterance" (p. 49). While uptake does not guarantee subsequent L2 acquisition, it is seen as an indication that the feedback provided has been noticed, and this noticing, in turn, may facilitate the acquisition process (Ellis, Basturkmen, & Loewen, 2002; Lightbown, 1998; Loewen, 2005).

It is important to note however, that Lyster and Ranta focused on *incidental feedback*, or feedback that arises spontaneously in the course of classroom interaction. Incidental feedback, unlike *planned feedback*, is not designed to address particular aspects of the L2. Incidental feedback also differs from planned feedback in that incidental feedback may not always address errors in form, but may be used to confirm comprehension or clarify the learner's intended meaning. Lyster (1998) argues that when students receive recasts incidentally, they may not perceive them as a type of corrective feedback. The planned recasts used in controlled studies, on the other hand, are delivered in a systematic way, in direct response to particular kinds of L2 grammatical errors. They are also used within communication tasks that create obligatory contexts for the target feature and engage learners in collaboration towards a shared goal. Thus, it may be that recasts delivered within these particular task conditions are more effective than unplanned recasts delivered in the course of whole class activities.

Ellis et al. (2002) and Loewen (2005) argue, however, that both incidental and planned feedback can facilitate the L2 acquisition process. "Planned focus on form has the advantage of providing intensive coverage of one specific linguistic item, whereas incidental focus on form provides extensive coverage, targeting many different linguistic items" (Loewen, 2005, p. 362). In his investigation of incidental feedback provided by teachers in 12 different ESL classes, Loewen was able to link episodes in which learners had received form-focused feedback in the midst of meaningful communication in the classroom (e.g., a recast in response to a grammatical error) to subsequent correct use of the linguistic form on a language test. Loewen found that students were more likely to successfully answer test items if there was some evidence of uptake after the teacher feedback, particularly if that uptake was successful, in that the learner correctly used the linguistic item immediately after the teacher feedback was given. Thus, it can be said that whether planned or incidental, implicit or explicit, corrective feedback has the potential to facilitate the L2 grammar acquisition process. It is important, then, for teachers to develop a repertoire of feedback strategies and to consider how and when these strategies might be used during classroom activities. In Chapter 9, we highlight ways in which teachers might incorporate corrective feedback into grammar-focused communication tasks.

Reflection 8.3

- As an L2 learner, what types of corrective feedback have you experienced? What types do you feel have been most helpful for learning grammar? Least helpful? Why might this be the case?
- As an L2 teacher, do you have a repertoire of feedback strategies that you use in the classroom? If so, what strategies are included, and how do you make decisions about what types of feedback to give when?

Our pedagogical choices are not always determined in advance, but in the moment and in collaboration with L2 learners

While it is important to develop a repertoire of L2 grammar teaching strategies, whether they be approaches to providing feedback on errors or designing informa-tion gap tasks, many of the decisions we make as teachers are not planned in advance, but rather are made in response to what we see happening in our classrooms. Learning is not simply something that takes place after instruction has been given, but rather is "a dynamic social activity that is situated in physical and social contexts" (Johnson, 2006, p. 237). Teachers participate in the learning process not simply by delivering knowledge to learners, but by collaborating with them to achieve particular learning goals. This realization has prompted what many refer to as a "social turn" in second language research and teaching (Johnson, 2006; Lantolf & Thorne, 2007; Ortega, 2010). Sociocultural approaches to SLA are informed by Vygotskian sociocultural theory, which posits that, aside from the most basic, involuntary processes, human cognition develops through interaction with the social environment. We are not born with the fully-functioning capacity to use language to organize our thoughts and experiences, but rather develop this skill through a process of socialization within a particular com-munity (Lantolf & Thorne, 2007).

Central to Vygotsky's sociocultural theory of mind is the Zone of Proximal Devel-opment (ZPD). The most oft-cited definition of the ZPD comes from Vygotsky (1978):

> The distance between the actual developmental level as determined by independent problem solving and the level of potential development as determined through prob-lem solving under adult guidance or in collaboration with more capable peers.
>
> (cited in Lantolf and Thorne, 2007, p. 206)

In this conception, a learner, when working with teachers or more advanced speakers of the language, is able to accomplish tasks that he or she would otherwise not be able to accomplish individually. This is possible because the more advanced adult or peer offers assistance to the learner when needed. This assistance (often called *scaffolding*) can come in the form of explicit instructions or implicit feedback, including many of the strategies highlighted in task-based interaction research. However, within the sociocultural framework, the emphasis is not so much on whether learners notice a particular grammatical form, but rather on the amount of assistance needed to com-plete the task successfully. If learners are given the opportunity to carry out multiple collaborative tasks over a period of time, they are likely to need less and less assistance from their collaborators. Changes in the amount of assistance needed can be seen as signs of development.

This approach to describing and assessing development is exemplified in Aljaafreh and Lantolf (1994), who investigated the collaborative process that takes place in one-on-one tutoring. Aljaafreh and Lantolf recorded the interactions between adult learners and their ESL writing tutor over the course of eight weeks. The tutoring sessions focused on accurate use of four grammatical structures: articles, tense, prepositions, and modal verbs. Aljaafreh and Lantolf documented the accuracy with which the learners used these forms over the course of the study, and they also documented the amount and types of assistance offered by the tutor over time.

During the tutoring session, the tutor asked the student to read the essay draft one sentence at a time. After each sentence, the student would pause and the tutor would ask a general question related to grammatical accuracy (e.g., Is there anything wrong in this sentence?). If the student identified and corrected an error right away, the tutor and the student would move on to the next sentence. If the student was not able to identify an error that was present, the tutor would ask more questions, gradually becoming more and more explicit in their feedback. To characterize the level of explicitness used at different points in the tutoring sessions, Aljaafreh and Lantolf developed a Regulatory Scale, ranging from implicit to explicit, as shown in Figure 8.1.

Regulatory Scale – Implicit (strategic) to Explicit

0. Tutor asks the learner to read, find the errors, and correct them independently, prior to the tutorial.

1. Construction of a "collaborative frame" prompted by the presence of the tutor as a potential dialogic partner.

2. Prompted or focused reading of the sentence that contains the error by the learner or the tutor.

3. Tutor indicates that something may be wrong in a segment (e.g., sentence, clause, line) – "Is there anything wrong in this sentence?"

4. Tutor rejects unsuccessful attempts at recognizing the error.

5. Tutor narrows down the location of the error (e.g., tutor repeats or points to the specific segment which contains the error).

6. Tutor indicates the nature of the error, but does not identify the error (e.g., "There is something wrong with the tense marking here").

7. Tutor identifies the error ("You can't use an auxiliary here").

8. Tutor rejects learner's unsuccessful attempts at correcting the error.

9. Tutor provides clues to help the learner arrive at the correct form (e.g., "It is not really past but some thing that is still going on").

10. Tutor provides the correct form.

11. Tutor provides some explanation for use of the correct form.

12. Tutor provides examples of the correct pattern when other forms of help fail to produce an appropriate responsive action.

Figure 8.2 Aljaafreh & Lantolf's Regulatory Scale (1994, p. 471)

In the Regulatory Scale, 0 represents a phase of development where no help from the tutor is needed. As we move down the scale, more help is needed, and thus the tutor's feedback becomes more and more explicit. At the end of the scale, the tutor exerts a great deal of control over the situation, providing the correct grammatical form, explaining how this form is used, and providing additional examples. In this approach, the choice of implicit versus explicit strategy is based on the amount of assistance needed. Most sociocultural scholars do not ascribe to either an explicit or implicit approach to grammar instruction, but rather see a role for both approaches. (Yet another reason why implicit versus explicit does not have to be an either-or choice.) As Adair-Hauck and Donato (1994) explain:

> A Vygotskain approach to formal explanation belies the simplistic dichotomy of explicit and implicit teaching. While explicit teaching views the teacher as a *depositor of knowledge* and implicit teaching reduces the teacher's role to *provider of linguistic input*, a Vygotskian approach views the teacher as a reflective problem-solver and mediator. (p. 535)

Aljaafreh and Lantolf's (1994) analysis of the recorded tutor-student interactions indicated that, over time, learners needed less explicit feedback, and the locus of control in the tutoring session moved gradually from the tutor to the student. In other words, students were able to internalize the knowledge of grammar that they had initially co-constructed with the tutor, and they were able to arrive at a point at which they could self-regulate their participation in the essay proofreading task. This gradual movement toward self-regulation also roughly paralleled their improvement in written grammatical accuracy over time.

Studies of grammar development within the ZPD have not been limited to student-tutor interaction. Research on the development that takes place through collaboration has also been carried out in L2 grammar classrooms, through observation of both teacher-student and student-student interaction. Anton (1999), for example, investigated the types of instructional strategies that were most conducive to both the negotiation of meaning and the provision of expert assistance within the ZPD. Anton found that learner-centered activities (in which learners took primary responsibility for explaining grammatical rules and constructing grammatical sentences) were more conducive to interaction and collaboration than were teacher-centered activities. Further, inductive lessons, in which learners were asked to look at example sentences and make hypotheses about grammar rules, promoted more collaboration than did deductive lessons, in which the teacher provided extensive explanations of the grammar structures in focus.

Figure 8.2 displays excerpts from two language classes (a college L2 French class and a college L2 Italian class), recorded as part of Anton's study. The excerpt on the left is an example of a collaborative, inductive grammar lesson, while the example on

1. T: So, alors, qu 'est-ce qui se passe ici ? Quelle est la différence ici? Quelle différence est-ce que vous pouvez remarquer ici dans les trois exemples ? (So, what's happening here? What's the difference? What difference can you see in these three examples?)

2. S1: etre. (to be.)

3. T: etre, oui, on utilise le verbe etre, n'est-ce pas? Pour former le passe composse, n 'est-ce pas? Est-ce qu'il y a d'autres différences que vous pouvez remarquer? (To be, yes, we use the verb to be, right? In order to form the past, right? Any other difference that you can see?)

4. S2: new verbs

5. T: oui, rentrer c'est nouveau, n'est-ce pas? Rentrer for the verb to return, right? Ren-trer D'autres, il y a d'autres différences que vous pouvez remarquer? . . . Si non, c'est pas un problème. On va essayer la reponse d ces questions.... (Yes, rentrer is new, right? Rentrer for the verb to return, right? Any other, is there any other difference that you can see? . . . If not, no problem. We are going to practice the answer to these questions. (Focus on form interrupted by oral practice with some questions that include etre in the past, then focus on form resumes)

6. S3: There is something new in the third form, they add an s.

7. T: That's good, that's good, the third one [reading] Paul et Karine . . .

8. S3: because, because it's plural.

9. T: that's good.

10. S3: that's new.

11. T: good, so, she is seeing here Paul et Karine, right? Good, so sortis notice, there is an s at the end of sortis, so they are showing agreement now. The end of your, right? Your past participle, now they show agreement, there is an s because she knows it's Paul et Karine, so it's plural, so we add an s, that's what's happening.

1. T: In this lesson you are doing two important things primarily. We are learning possessive adjectives and another past tense. The Imperfect tense. You've already had the Passato Prossimo. They are both past tenses but they have different uses in Italian. Intricate for the speaker of English, not so intricate for speakers of other Romance languages. Let's talk about possessives first. What's the word for book?

2. Ss: Libro.

3. T: What's the word for house?

4. Ss: Casa.

5. T: OK. Let's get a masculine and singular. The book?

6. Ss: Il libro.

7. T: The house?

8. Ss: La casa.

9. T: That's correct. Now we have a masculine and a feminine. Masculine article il feminine la. We've also learnt that adjectives agree with the nouns they agree with the noun they modify [louder]. An adjective agrees with the noun it modifies. That was important until now, but it becomes more important now in this lesson, so, the . . . the beautiful book il bel libro, the beautiful house la bella casa. Now we are going to adjectives, possessive adjectives, possessive adjectives. Adjectives are words which describe other words, other nouns, pronouns or other adjectives. The beautiful book, beautiful is an adjective, the red book, red is an adjective modifying book. Possessives in English and Italian are also adjectives, possessive adjectives. My house, my is a possessive in Italian, it's next to the noun, it is also an adjective. Now, what did we just say? Adjectives agree with the thing modified. My book, il mio libro. This book is red, il mio libro e rosso. My house is white, la mia casa, adjectives agree with the noun they modify [louder]. So, when you are saying my book, and my house, adjective agree with nouns they modify .

Figure 8.3 Examples of collaborative and non-collaborative grammar explanations (Anton, 1999, pp. 307–309)

the right is an example of a deductive grammar explanation. Anton notes that in the excerpt on the left, the teacher piques students' interest by using open-ended questions (*So what's happening here? What's the difference?*) Students are invited to give their own explanations. Eventually, a student notices the *–s* at the end of the word and offers a hypothesis: because it's plural. The teacher offers her own confirmation, and in this way, both the students and the teacher co-construct the grammar explanation. In the excerpt on the right, on the other hand, the teacher is primarily in control of the grammar explanation. When the teacher does ask the class a question, only one answer is possible (or in some cases, the question is simply rhetorical). Students are not given the opportunity to offer their own explanations of the grammar they are studying.

Though it is the case that in the early phases of development, explicit explanation of rules may be needed (as indicated on Aljaafreh & Lantolf's Regulatory Scale), sociocultural researchers would argue that these explanations should be given only when it is clear that the students cannot come up with the explanations on their own. As Lantolf and Thorne (2007) explain: "Assistance should be graduated – with no more help provided than is necessary because the assumption is that over-assistance decreases the student's ability to become fully self-regulated" (p. 211). In other words, when teachers insist on always giving explicit grammar explanations up-front, students are not given the chance to regulate their own learning, but rather must rely on other (teacher) regulation. Collaborative grammar lessons, on the other hand, help to create an environment in which students build community and gradually move towards self-regulation, a state in which they are fully capable of explaining and using L2 grammar on their own.

Reflection 8.4

– As an L2 teacher, in what ways do you try to create a zone of proximal development in your classroom? What strategies do you use to give graduated assistance to L2 learners?

– When explaining grammar rules in class, to what extent do you collaborate with your students? Are there times when you feel you need to take a deductive approach, explaining for students how the rules work? Are there other times where you prefer to take an inductive approach, letting students figure out the rules for themselves? How do you make these decisions?

L2 learners play an important role in the L2 grammar acquisition of their peers

While Vygotsky's original conception of the ZPD involved a novice working with an expert, sociocultural theories of second language acquisition have expanded this to include L2 learners working with other L2 learners. As Ohta (2000) notes, "Differential competence among peers allows a ZPD to emerge… when no true 'expert' is present"

(p. 55). In recent years Swain and colleagues (e.g., Swain & Lapkin, 1998; 2001; 2002) have focused a great deal of their research on peer collaboration and the important role this collaboration plays in the L2 acquisition process. As we saw in Chapter 2, Swain's research in French immersion settings suggested that input-oriented, content-based, and communicative approaches may not be enough to promote grammar acquisition if students were not given sufficient opportunity to produce output and receive feedback on their utterances. Swain argued that in addition to comprehensible input, output plays a crucial role in the second language acquisition process. Comprehension, Swain explained, is primarily meaning-focused. Learners do not necessarily have to attend to grammatical form in order to grasp the gist of what is being said. Production, or output, on the other hand:

> pushes learners to process language more deeply – with more mental effort – than does input. With output, the learner is in control. In speaking or writing, learners can 'stretch' their interlanguage to meet communicative goals.   (Swain, 2000, p. 99)

Over time, Swain (2000, 2006) has revised her Output Hypothesis, situating it within a sociocultural framework. Second language acquisition, Swain argues, is not simply a process through which a learner receives input, performs cognitive operations, and then produces output. Though the word "output" itself is a noun, for Swain, it is really a verb, as it represents a process in which "the speaker is cognitively engaged in making meaning" (p. 102). In communication, the speaker is not merely a cognitive machine, but a social being. The input-output dichotomy over-emphasizes internal cognitive functions, thus de-emphasizing the important role that collaboration plays in the meaning-making process. When learners are asked to work together to complete a task, they engage in what Swain (2006) calls *languaging*, a process through which learners use language to solve problems, to reflect on what they know and do not know, and to co-construct knowledge about the target language. In other words, language is not simply what learners produce as an object, but is a tool that learners use to mediate the learning process (Lantolf & Thorne, 2007; Swain, 2000). Learners talk to themselves, ask questions, take written notes, correct their own mistakes and the mistakes of others. Through this verbalization, language becomes an object of study (a symbolic artifact), which allows learners to reflect on and perhaps even plan future language use.

To capture the extent to which learners talk about language during collaborative tasks, Swain and Lapkin (1998) developed an analytical tool called the Language Related Episode (LRE). LREs refer to "any part of a dialogue where the students talk about the language they are producing, question their language use, or correct themselves or others" (Swain & Lapkin, 1998, p. 326). Example 8.1 (taken from Kim, 2012, p. 642) displays a grammar-focused LRE in which two learners try to come up with a correct question form.

(8.1)   1   Learner 1:   Does he read… how long? 얼마나가 (ulmanaga) how long 이야
(yiya)?
when asking for time length, do we use "how long"?
2   Learner 2:   어 (uh)
yes
3   Learner 1:   How long read?
4   Learner 2:   How long does he read?
5   Learner 1:   How long does he read?
6   Learner 2:   read book?
7   Learner 1:   yes. How long does he read book?
8   Learner 2:   He reads books for two hours.

In this example, Learner 1 and 2 are exchanging teacher-provided information regarding a person's life during an information gap task. Learner 1 initiates the LRE by asking in Korean how to form a question using the words "how long." Notice, here, that after the learners figured out meaning of the *wh-* question marker in lines 1 and 2 (i.e., how long), they also negotiated *form*, specifically, the syntax required for a "how long" question.

Many studies (e.g., McDonough & Sunitham, 2009; Kim, 2013; Swain, 1998; Swain & Lapkin, 1998, 2001; Tocalli-Beller & Swain, 2007; Watanabe & Swain, 2007; Williams, 2001) have documented the amount and types of LREs that occur during peer interaction and the extent to which these LREs lead to subsequent L2 grammar acquisition. These studies have found that learners frequently shift their attention to language form when in the midst of meaningful communication, sometimes as many as 23 LREs in a 23-minute task (e.g., Swain & Lapkin, 1998). As learners' proficiency levels advance, the number of LREs that occur during peer interaction also tends to increase (Kim & McDonough, 2008; Leeser, 2004; Watanabe & Swain, 2007). At the same time, both matched proficiency pairs and mixed proficiency pairs have been able to successfully resolve grammar-related questions as they arise during collaborative tasks (Watanabe & Swain, 2007). Through the use of tailor-made language tests, researchers have also been able to link LREs to subsequent grammar acquisition (McDonough & Sunitham, 2009; Payant & Kim, in press; Swain & Lapkin, 1998). In many cases, when students negotiate form in an LRE (as in the *"How long read?"* example), they are able to correctly use this form in a subsequent language test. Thus, although early task-based interaction research and research on collaboration focused on learners interacting with or collaborating with teachers or tutors – thus raising questions as to whether peer group work would be as effective – the past two decades of SLA research have provided considerable support for the contention that L2 learners are able to provide one another with feedback that promotes L2 learning (see Philp, Adamns & Iwashita, 2014 for the synthesis of research on the role of learner-learner interaction in SLA).

Reflection 8.5

- As an L2 learner, you have likely been asked to collaborate with your peers in the language classroom. What types of collaboration did you engage in and what role do you think this played in your acquisition of L2 grammar?

- As an L2 teacher, what strategies have you observed your students using when they collaborate with one another in the classroom? In what ways do their feedback and assistance strategies differ from yours? What advantages might peer collaboration have over student-teacher collaboration? What might be some limitations or challenges of peer collaboration?

Our ability to use and acquire language is constrained by limited attentional resources

Thus far in this chapter, we have addressed a number of pedagogical concerns: How to promote both the negotiation of meaning and the noticing of grammatical form in communication tasks, how to provide learners with feedback on the grammaticality of their utterances, how to provide graduated assistance within a zone of proximal development, and how to create opportunities for peer collaboration. We now turn to pedagogical concerns which relate to the inner-workings of cognition: attention, awareness, information processing, memory storage and retrieval. A key concern in this area of L2 research (often referred to as *cognitive SLA*) is learners' attentional resources. For example, is it possible for learners to attend to grammatical form and meaning at the same time? If the complexity of an instructional task increases, will learners spend too much time thinking about how to complete the task and not enough time on language?

These concerns stem from the fact that, when we are learning a new language, our cognitive resources are often strained, and we must devote a great deal of attention to recalling and retrieving the words and phrases needed to communicate meaning. In our native languages, this does not take a great deal of conscious attention – we can retrieve most of the language we need automatically. In a new language, however, retrieval does not come so quickly. In other words, communicating in a language we are in the process of learning often involves *controlled processing*, while communicating in a language we know well typically involves *automatic processing*.

The contrast between these two processes becomes clear when we compare a set of knowledge and skills at two different points in time: when we are first introduced to them and when we have fully mastered them. When we first begin to learn how to drive a car, for example, we need to pay a great deal of conscious attention to the knowledge and behaviors needed to drive the car successfully. We need to remember where the break and the gas pedal are (and if driving a manual car, where the clutch is and how to work the gears), what the rules of the road are (content we have likely studied in a drivers manual), and what actions are required to stop, go, turn, and so on.

Automatic processing, on the other hand, takes very little mental effort. If you are by now an experienced driver, think about the driving you do each and every day. How much conscious reflection is needed? Not much at all. In fact, there may be days where you arrive at work without actually remembering how you got there. You also likely talked on the phone or to passengers, listened to the radio, ate your breakfast, and planned out what you needed to accomplish that day. Multitasking under automatic processing conditions is quite easy, because the knowledge and skills needed to complete the task have been mastered, and no longer require conscious reflection. In automatic processing, our brain responds to stimuli without the need for conscious reflection. In controlled processing, however, the stimulus alone is not enough to trigger the needed action. We must make a conscious decision to retrieve the necessary information. As new drivers, for example, we think about (and even talk out loud about) what needs to happen before every turn.

The concepts of automatic versus controlled processing have important implications for L2 grammar teaching. First, as the car example demonstrates, a task that once required controlled processing can become, through practice, a task that is completed automatically. It is important to remember, however, that the effects of practice are skill-specific (DeKeyser, 1997, 2007). That is, if learners are given repeated practice filling in the blank with the appropriate verb form, over time, they will likely get very good at completing this type of exercise. This skill, however, may not transfer over to situations where the student needs to use multiple verb tenses in a face-to-face conversation or academic essay. Practice and repetition are critical, but equally important are the decisions a teacher makes regarding which skills and tasks are repeated throughout a course. What is practiced in class should have some connection to the real-world tasks that students hope to carry out in the target language.

A second implication of this research is that when learners have limited cognitive resources to devote to language processing, they are more likely to attend to meaning over form, as understanding others and being understood are the primary goals of communication. To address this challenge, VanPatten (1996; 2004) recommends that L2 teachers provide learners with *input processing instruction*, or instruction which aims to help learners develop new processing strategies *before* they are asked to produce output using target grammatical forms. In input processing instruction, practice and feedback are given during input processing, through comprehension-based activities. An example of this is a comprehension task developed by VanPatten and Cadierno (1993), which asks students to listen to sentences in Spanish (the language they are learning) and to match these sentences to a picture that depicts the meaning. To match the pictures and the sentences correctly, students must attend to grammatical form (e.g., pronouns, grammatical morphemes). The goal of instruction is to change learners' default method of processing input, increasing the likelihood that they will attend to and process form.

Research on automatic and controlled processing also has important implications for how teachers design oral communication tasks (which require both comprehension and production). In many cases, learners will need to carry out these tasks using controlled processing. Attentional resources are limited, and choices must be made about how to allocate these resources. Thus, the features of the task (e.g., whether planning time is given, the number of resources learners are asked to consult, the types of decisions learners are asked to make) are likely to impact the amount of attention learners are able to devote to form and meaning during task performance.

Two competing views of learners' attentional resources are presented in Skehan's LImited Capacity Hypothesis (1998) and Robinson's Cognition Hypothesis (2001a; 2001b; 2003; 2005). In his limited capacity hypothesis, Skehan (1998) and Skehan and Foster (1999, 2001) argue that a trade-off exists between attention to form and attention to meaning. When task procedures are complex, learners will focus more on content and less on language form. Furthermore, in Skehan's (1998) view, due to limitations in attentional resources, learners cannot attend to all aspects of language production at the same time. If attention is focused primarily on complexity of language, accuracy is likely to suffer. If attention is focused on accuracy, complexity is likely to suffer. A focus on accuracy is also said to lead to a decrease in the fluency of language produced, as learners may use more time and mental effort to produce more accurate language.

Robinson's Cognition Hypothesis (2001a, 2001b, 2003, 2005, 2011a), however, does not see cognitive capacity as a single resource, but instead argues that learners are able to access multiple and noncompetitive pools of attention. Fluency, accuracy, and complexity may not always be in competition with one another. Robinson further distinguishes between two cognitive dimensions of *task complexity*, as shown in Table 8.1. First, the complexity of an instructional task can be described in terms of (1) the types of reasoning demands the task places on learners, (2) the number of elements learners must attend to when carrying out the task, and (3) the location of these elements in time and space. Robinson calls this dimension of task complexity the *cognitive-conceptual* dimension, and he argues that these elements of task complexity are *resource-directing*, in that they can be manipulated in such a way as to direct learners' attention on making accurate, complex, and appropriate linguistic choices. For example, if learners are asked to make decisions and give reasons for these decisions (+intentional reasoning), to consider multiple sources of information (−few elements), and to narrate events which are displaced in time and space (−here and now), they may be more likely to produce more complex clauses (e.g., with subordinators like *because* and *since*) and to attend to their choice of verb tense and aspect (leading to more accurate language).

Table 8.1 Robinson's cognitive dimensions of task complexity

Cognitive-conceptual (Resource-directing)	Performative-procedural (Resource-dispersing)
+/−few elements	+/−planning
+/−here-and-now	+/−single task
+/−spatial reasoning	+/−task structure
+/−causal reasoning	+/−few steps
+/−intentional reasoning	+/−independency of steps
+/−perspective-taking	+/−prior knowledge

On the contrary, the *performative-procedural* dimension of task complexity is said to be *resource-dispersing*. These elements of the task make increased demands on participants' attentional and memory resources but do not direct them to any element of the linguistic system (Robinson, 2001b, 2005, 2011a). Making tasks more complex along resource-dispersing dimensions – for instance, by requiring learners to perform more than one task simultaneously [−single task] or by providing no prior knowledge support [−prior knowledge] or planning time [−planning time] – leads learners to disperse attention over many nonlinguistic areas during task performance. Thus, while resource-directing elements of a task (reasoning demands, multiple sources of information, multiple time frames) can promote more accurate and complex language use, resource-dispersing elements may take attentional resources away from language, towards other features of the task. When learners are asked to complete multiple task procedures at once, and/or must work with concepts or themes they are unfamiliar with, and/or must perform the task immediately, without time for planning, their language performance may suffer.

Whereas Skehan's limited capacity hypothesis (1998) predicts that tasks can lead either to increased complexity or accuracy but not to both, Robinson's cognition hypothesis claims that making tasks more complex in the resource-directing dimensions can increase both accuracy and complexity (e.g., Robinson, 2001b, 2005, 2007b). Robinson also predicts that increasing task complexity would encourage learners to look for more assistance in the input and attend to linguistic codes that are required for task completion (Robinson, 2001a; Robinson & Gilabert, 2007). This, in turn, has the potential to direct learners' attentional and memory resources to specific L2 structures, providing learning opportunities and thus ultimately leading to interlanguage development, particularly with more developmentally advanced forms (Robinson, 2007a; Robinson, 2007b; Robinson & N. Ellis, 2008).

Robinson's cognition hypothesis has led to a flurry of research on task complexity (see Jackson and Suethanapornkul, 2013 for a recent meta-analysis; as well as Robinson, 2007b, 2011b). Previous studies (e.g., Baralt, 2013; Kim, 2009, 2012; Révész, 2011; Révész, Sachs, & Mackey, 2011; Robinson, 2007b) have examined the role of task complexity in students' language performance in terms of complexity, accuracy, and fluency, as well as in the amount of learners' attention to linguistic features and the subsequent language development. Additionally, researchers (e.g., Kim, 2009; Michel, Kuiken & Vedder, 2007) have also examined how task complexity features might interact with other variables, such as type of task (e.g., information gap or narrative), task condition (monologic vs. dialogic), the grammatical features in focus, and the proficiency levels of the learners. In her 2012 study, Kim designed 4 instructional tasks which differed only in terms of their level of complexity: (a) finding a part-time job, (b) working as a matchmaker, (c) discussing promotion opportunities, and (d) hiring employees. While all of the tasks created a two-way information gap and asked learners to work toward a single solution, the tasks differed in terms of the amount of reasoning required and the number of elements to be considered when making a decision. Table 8.2 summarizes the features of one of the tasks entitled "Finding a part-time job," which had three different task complexity levels. The target grammatical form chosen for the task was question formation, and Kim investigated whether the more complex tasks would promote a greater use of more advanced question forms.

Table 8.2 Kim's (2012) simple and complex tasks

	Simple [−reasoning]	+Complex [+reasoning]	++Complex [++reasoning]
Task input	Profile cards and students' part-time job descriptions	Profile cards and available part-time job descriptions	Profile cards and available part-time job descriptions
Task outcome	Prepare for a report on university students' part-time job	Decide appropriate part-time jobs for students	Decide appropriate part-time jobs for students
Procedure	1. Both learners had profiles of four different university students including their part-time jobs	1. Both learners had profiles of four different university students including their part-time jobs	1. Both learners had profiles of four different university students including their part-time jobs
	2. Both learners were missing some information about each student's background.	2. Both learners were missing some information about each student's background.	2. Both learners were missing some information about each student's background.
	3. In order to complete a report of university students' part-time jobs, both learners collected information from their partners.	3. Based on each learner's background, learners were asked to suggest appropriate part-time jobs for each student. 　　[+few elements] Two considerations should be met for their decision.	3. Based on each learner's background, learners were asked to suggest appropriate part-time jobs for each student. 　　[−few elements] Four considerations should be met for their decision.

Kim (2012) found that, during the instructional tasks, the ++complex group produced a greater number of developmentally advanced questions (Stages 4 and 5) than did the simple and +complex groups. It was also the case that a larger proportion of the ++complex group (82%) advanced a Stage in their question development after participating in their instructional tasks than did the +complex (72%) and simple (64%) groups. What is more, Kim found that most of the students who were not members of the complex or simple groups, but who were taught the same content without the use of task-based interaction, did not advanced in their question development over the same period of time. These findings suggest that, in addition to considering task design features and techniques like interactional demands, task-essentialness, and corrective feedback, teachers may also want to explore the use of more complex, resource-directing tasks in their own L2 classrooms. The key issue here is to provide necessary assistance when learners engage in more complexity tasks which would push them to process and use more advanced forms (see Chapter 9 for suggestions).

Reflection 8.6

– Based on your experience as both an L2 learner and an L2 teacher, which characterization of attentional resources do you find most persuasive: Skehan's limited capacity hypothesis (i.e., fluency, accuracy, and complexity are in competition with one another) or Robinson's cognition hypothesis (i.e., learners are able to access multiple pools of attention)?

– As an L2 teacher, in what ways have you attempted to increase the cognitive complexity of classroom tasks? In what ways have you attempted to decrease task complexity? What relationships do you see between the complexity of the task and the nature of your students' L2 performance (e.g., its complexity, accuracy and fluency)?

– In what ways might VanPatten's input processing instruction help to inform your own design of comprehension and production tasks? Have you ever asked students to attend to grammatical form while processing input, without requiring them to produce any output? If so, how did you do this? In what ways did your students benefit from this task?

Summary

Drawing on the instructed SLA literature, this chapter has highlighted six important theory-practice links which have particular relevance to L2 grammar pedagogy.

– Both implicit and explicit approaches to grammar teaching have a place in the L2 classroom. Though few scholars would advocate for a total Focus on Meaning or a total Focus on FormS, many options are available to teachers along the Form-Focused Instruction continuum, including:

- Implicit focus on form through either reactive or planned feedback.
- Explicit grammar instruction in combination with communication tasks and/or structure-focused collaborative tasks.
- Research on task-based interaction has found that meaning-focused tasks can promote L2 grammar acquisition, particularly when these tasks aim to create an information gap, a convergent goal orientation, obligatory contexts for the target feature, and opportunities for corrective feedback.
- At the same time, not all features of a task can (or should) be determined in advance – learners also benefit when teachers adjust task demands and feedback strategies in the midst of collaboration with L2 learners. Lessons and tasks which aim to provide learners with graduated assistance – no more or less than is needed – have been found to promote L2 grammar acquisition over time.
- Not only teachers, but also learners, play an important role in the L2 acquisition of their peers. Analysis of learner-learner interaction has found that when learners collaborate with one another to complete a task, they focus not only on meaning but also form, they provide one another with useful feedback, and they accomplish goals in the target language that they otherwise could not accomplish alone.
- Communicating in a language that one is in the process of learning can put a strain on cognitive resources. Task designs which allow for planning time and rehearsal and which use content that students are familiar with can help to ease this cognitive load. Teachers can also direct learners' attention to language by asking them to consult resources and make a decision based on the information they have shared with one another. As learners discuss the reasons for their choices, they may be more likely to focus on accuracy and to use more complex sentence structures.

Suggestions for further reading

Ellis, R. & Shintani, N. (2014). *Exploring Language Pedagogy through Second Language Acquisition Research*. London: Routledge.

Lantolf, J. & Poehner, M. (2014). *Sociocultural Theory and the Pedagogical Imperative in L2 Education*. New York, NY: Routledge.

Loewen, S. (2014). *Introduction to Instructed Second Language Acquisition*. New York, NY: Routledge.

Mackey, A. (2012). *Input, Interaction and Corrective Feedback in L2 Learning*. Oxford: Oxford University Press.

Chapter 9

Designing grammar-focused communication tasks

As we saw in Chapter 8, communication tasks have played a central role in instructed second language research over the past few decades. Researchers have used these tasks to investigate how interaction might make input more comprehensible, how oral feedback in response to learner errors might facilitate the noticing of particular linguistic forms, and how students learn from one another as they talk about language. This research has led many scholars to advocate for task-based approaches to L2 instruction and to explore how researcher-designed tasks might be modified to accommodate the dynamic nature of L2 classrooms.

Over time, these efforts to investigate the use of tasks in L2 classrooms have helped to establish the research domain of Task-Based Language Teaching, or TBLT (Ellis, 2003; 2012; Nunan, 2004; Robinson, 2011; Samuda & Bygate, 2008; Shehadeh & Coombe, 2012; Van den Branden, Bygate, & Norris, 2009). Drawing on both general educational theory and second language acquisition theory in particular, TBLT aims to inform the design and use of tasks in the classroom and emphasizes the importance of "what learners are able to *do* with the language" (Norris, 2009, p. 578).

> At its most basic, task-based instruction rejects the notion that knowledge can be learned independently of its application and embraces instead the value of learning by doing, or "experiential learning" (Dewey, 1933). In Dewey's terms, principal elements around which instruction should be built are "activities worthwhile for their own sake" (p. 87), and it is by engaging learners in doing valued activities that relevant declarative and procedural knowledge is developed, learners are motivated to engage with instructional content, and learners develop deep linkages between what they learn and how that learning can be put to use beyond the classroom. (Norris, pp. 578–579)

Norris goes on to explain that classroom tasks function as important "holistic activity structures" which allow students to make connections among linguistic forms, the meanings they express, and the situations in which they are used. If these linkages can be experienced in the classroom, then students may be more likely to make these linkages outside of the classroom, when confronted with real-world communicative situations. A task, then, is not simply any classroom activity, but rather must be designed in such a way as to create opportunities for students to experience important form-meaning-use connections.

Several definitions for the TBLT concept of *task* have been put forth, and most of these definitions involve a set of criteria for determining whether a classroom activity can be labeled as a task or not. As we saw in Chapter 6, Long's (1985) initial definition of a task ("the hundred and one things people do in everyday life," p. 89) emphasized the importance of making classroom tasks correspond in some way to real-world tasks. Though many researchers would argue that classroom tasks need not exactly mirror real-world tasks, most accept Long's argument that classroom tasks be selected and designed in such a way as to directly address the needs, interests, and goals of the language learners. Thus, in TBLT, needs analysis plays a central role in syllabus design (Long, 2005). Efforts are made on the part of the teacher and the language program to identify the real world tasks that students are likely to complete outside of the classroom.

Building on Long's initial proposals (as well as those of Nunan, 1989; and Fotos & Ellis, 1991), Skehan (1998) describes a task as an activity in which:

1. Meaning is primary.
2. There is a communication problem of some type to solve.
3. The activity has some relationship to real-world activities.
4. Task completion is usually required.
5. Task performance can be assessed in terms of the outcome (p. 95).

Skehan's definition does not require that classroom tasks replicate real-world tasks, but that they at least have "some relationship to" what students might experience outside of the classroom. More important for Skehan is that classroom tasks engage learners in meaningful communication, by encouraging them to work together toward a common goal. When these criteria are met, classroom activities are more likely to foster the type of holistic, experiential learning that Norris (2009) emphasizes.

Research in TBLT has also explored how carefully designed tasks can be used in the classroom to create many of the optimal conditions associated with successful second language acquisition. Early recommendations regarding the use of tasks in L2 instruction emphasized the important role that communication tasks can play in making input more comprehensible to language learners, through the negotiation of meaning. In response to Schmidt's (1990) noticing hypothesis, however, new questions emerged. For example, if communication tasks were primarily meaning-focused, would learners pay attention to the accuracy of their utterances? These concerns prompted many researchers to explore how task characteristics (e.g., the roles of the participants, the amount of time provided for planning and rehearsal, the types of feedback provided) might impact the extent to which students attend to grammatical form.

Skehan (2003), in an effort to help teachers navigate the vast TBLT landscape, divides TBLT research into the three major areas of SLA we highlighted in Chapter 8: *interactionist, sociocultural,* and *cognitivist.* Within the *interactionist* domain, TBLT research aims to explore how classroom tasks might be used to create a real need to communicate, to promote a focus on form, to provide opportunities for learners to receive feedback and modify output, and to prepare learners for participation in real-world tasks outside of the L2 classroom. *Sociocultural* approaches to TBLT, according to Skehan, emphasize slightly different considerations. These researchers emphasize the important role that classroom tasks can play in helping learners to build meaning together, to scaffold one another, and to use language for their own purposes. Tasks also provide teachers with opportunities to learn more about what their students know, the strategies they use to help and learn from one another, and the ways in which learners modify classroom tasks to better meet their needs and goals.

The *cognitivist* orientation to TBLT emphasizes yet another set of important task design considerations. Scholars within this orientation often investigate the extent to which task design features impact learners' task performance, or the complexity, accuracy, and fluency of their language production. Some task design features that have received considerable attention in cognitivist TBLT research are task planning (opportunities for learners to plan out what they want to say or do before carrying out the task), task repetition (opportunities to perform the same task multiple times or repeat some aspects of tasks several times), and task complexity (opportunities for learners to engage in high levels of processing, such as decision-making).

Taken together, these TBLT orientations offer many options for second language teachers. Though these orientations represent somewhat separate research domains within applied linguistics, teachers need not choose one orientation over another. Rather, it is important to examine how research in all of these areas can help to inform the decisions that teachers make regarding the use of tasks in their classroom and the role that these tasks might play in promoting L2 grammar acquisition.

Considerations in L2 grammar task design

When integrating communication tasks into L2 grammar instruction, teachers have a number of decisions to make. One of the first considerations is the purpose of the communication task. In an L2 grammar class where target forms are pre-selected (e.g., determined in advance by the teacher and taught using a grammar textbook), communication tasks may be selected based on the extent to which they promote the use of a particular grammatical feature. Task design in this setting involves a consideration of the target form's primary communicative functions: In what contexts will my students be most likely to encounter and/or use these forms? What types of in-class activities might help to prepare students for out-of-class language use? In classrooms organized according to communicative functions, themes, or content, teachers may approach task design from the other way around, starting first with the communicative situation (e.g., writing a narrative essay, ordering food at a restaurant) and moving next to a consideration of form: What grammatical and lexical forms will my students need in order to carry out this task successfully?

Once teachers decide on the purpose of the task and the grammatical features in focus, there are still many decisions to be made. As we will see in this chapter, the three TBLT perspectives on task design highlighted by Skehan (2003) – interactionist, sociocultural, cognitivist – present teachers with many task design considerations. It is unlikely that, for every task a teacher creates, he or she will take into account all three of these perspectives. We do not expect (or even encourage!) teachers to do this for every instructional lesson. What we do expect, is that, for a given classroom task, a teacher will likely prioritize some concerns over others, just as L2 scholars do in their own research. At times, task essentialness and planned feedback may be a central concern, particularly in cases where teachers want to promote the noticing of target grammatical forms. At other times, when teachers are concerned with promoting fluency, they may focus more on task planning, rehearsal, and repetition. It may also be the case that teachers will develop their own personal orientations towards task design, which in turn inform their practice. For example, some teachers may align themselves with sociocultural perspectives on language learning and thus may choose to prioritize collaboration and assistance within the ZPD over other task design concerns.

In the following sections, we explore these task design issues further, providing examples of classroom tasks that emphasize some considerations over others. We begin with the interactionist perspective and considerations related to learner participation, the negotiation of meaning, task-essentialness, corrective feedback, and degree of explicitness. From here, we move to the sociocultural perspective and look at tasks designed to promote collaboration within the ZPD and knowledge co-construction. Finally, we provide examples of tasks designed to address cognitivist concerns, such as task planning, task repetition, and task complexity.

Reflection 9.1

- As you read through this chapter, we encourage you to think about how you might design your own grammar-focused task for a particular classroom context. You can work with a classroom task you have used in the past, or you can think of a new task you'd like to try with your students. Identify the learning objectives for this task, as well as the target grammatical form (or forms).

Promoting interaction through information gap tasks

Within the interactionist domain of TBLT, one of the most important considerations in task design is, not surprisingly, the interaction of participants. In other words, it is crucial that the task provides opportunities for all students to interact and negotiate meaning with their peers. Most scholars agree that one effective way to promote this participation is, as Pica (Pica et al., 1993; Pica, 2005) long argued, through the creation of a two-way information gap. In a two-way information gap task, also called a jigsaw task, each participant in the task holds a piece of information, and each participant must share this information with the members of his group. Jigsaw tasks are convergent in their goal orientation (everyone in the group is working towards the same goal) and there is only one task outcome option. A classic example of a two-way information gap task is the spot-the-difference task, a task that has been used in many interactionist research studies. In a spot-the-difference task, students work in pairs. Each partner holds a picture of an everyday scene (e.g., a park, a living room). The scenes are almost identical, with a few exceptions. The goal of the task is for the students to identify how many differences exist between their pictures. Figure 9.1 displays a spot-the-difference task used in Mackey's (1999) study of L2 question development.

In a task like this, participation of both partners is required, and both learners must respond to their partners' questions as well as initiate questions. If one partner does not participate, it will be impossible for the students to successfully complete the task. It is also important for students to understand one another. If communication breakdowns occur, students will need to negotiate meaning (through requests for clarification, confirmation checks, modified output, and so on). The need to work together towards a shared goal increases the likelihood that these interactional moves will be made, which in turn leads to greater opportunities for language learning than could be achieved through tasks with no interactional requirements and no shared goals.

Picture-based spot-the-difference tasks can be particularly engaging for younger learners, but some older learners may feel that these tasks have little connection to the tasks they need to complete outside of the classroom. It is possible, however, to design spot-the-difference tasks that involve more mature and cognitively demanding comparisons. Pica (2005), for example, describes a series of jigsaw tasks designed for a high school literature class for multilingual students. The tasks were created in response to students' inaccurate use of determiners (e.g., *this, these, some, a/an, the*) in their speech and writing. In these tasks, each partner was given a copy of a typed excerpt of a movie review, as shown in Figure 9.2. The excerpts were almost exactly the same, except for their choice of determiners. Students were asked to compare their versions of the movie review and to discuss which determiner choices were most appropriate.

Figure 9.1 Spot-the-difference task (Mackey, 1999)
Retrieved from http://www.iris-database.org/iris/app/home/about

Though spot-the-difference tasks are one of the most popular jigsaw tasks used in L2 research, they are certainly not the only way to promote the participation of all learners. It is also possible to design tasks in which students contribute their own information to the task, rather than receive teacher-provided information. For example, Nguyen (2009) designed a jigsaw task that asked students to offer advice to a newly arrived international student. Each student in the class received a student profile of an international student who was soon to begin coursework at their university, as shown in Figure 9.3 (adapted from Nguyen, 2009, p. 8). Students were then asked to compose, individually, 5–6 sentences of advice, using modals like *must*, *should*, and *might*.

Jigsaw Passage Versions for Articles and Determiners

Version to Student C	Version to Student D
Sentence #_1_ Stand and Deliver tells the story of a high school mathematics teacher named Jaime Escalante.	Sentence#_1_ Stand and Deliver tells the study of a high school mathematics teacher named Jaime Escalante.
Sentence #___ Escalate motivates them by getting attention.	Sentence # ___Escalante motivates them by getting their attention.
Sentence # ___Students are undisciplined, unmotivated and rebellious.	Sentence # ___The students are undisciplined, unmotivated and rebellious.
Sentence #___ He is asked to teach a class of losers and potential dropouts.	Sentence #___ He is asked to teach a class of some losers and potential dropouts.
Sentence # ___Escalante faces an enormous challenge on the first day of school.	Sentence #___ Escalante faces his enormous challenge on the first day of school.

Figure 9.2 Spot-the-difference task for an academic setting (Pica, 2005, p. 352)

An international student is coming to study at Kenya University! What does she need to know about living in the dormitory in order to have a successful and fun semester here?

- Name: Laura Hinsley
- School, city, country: Boston University, Boston, United States
- Arrival date: August 15, 2009
- Length of stay: Fall semester 2009
- Level, major: Junior, comparative literature
- Accommodation: Dormitory
- Interests: Socializing, reading, going to rock concerts, swimming, singing

Think of some suggestions and write each suggestion on a strip of paper that will be given to you.

Figure 9.3 Example of student-generated material for a jigsaw task

After this individual composing phase, the students formed groups and each student shared the advice they had written. In the final phase of the task, students worked together to compose an email that synthesized the advice of all group members. Thus, through an individual composing phase, Nguyen was able to create a jigsaw task that made use of student-generated material. Each student was required to share their advice, and students worked together to achieve a shared goal. Nguyen's task, like many classroom tasks, also included task design features emphasized in several different TBLT orientations: students had opportunities to compose language collaboratively, and students were given time to plan their language use before producing a final product. Thus, it is often the case that when addressing one particular task design concern (e.g., interaction requirements), teachers are also addressing other, closely related concerns (e.g., opportunities for collaboration and language rehearsal).

TASK DESIGN CONSIDERATIONS: INPUT & INTERACTION

Interaction of participants
-   To what extent will you ensure that all group members participate in the task?
-   Will you assign particular roles to particular students? In what ways will students need to work together to achieve a shared goal?

Task-essentialness
-   How will you try to promote the noticing and/or use of the target feature in your task design?
-   To what extent do you think the task participants will need to comprehend and/or produce the grammatical feature in order to complete the task successfully?

Corrective feedback
-   To what extent will you try to provide form-focused feedback to students as they work to complete the task?
-   Will you plan a systematic approach to feedback in advance (e.g., respond to every student error in a certain way) or will you take a more reactive approach (e.g., offer feedback only during a communication breakdown)?

Degree of explicitness
-   Will the task make use of explicit or implicit instructional techniques for introducing target structures (or some combination of the two)? For example, will you tell students what grammatical feature you would like them to focus on during the task?
-   Will you provide grammar instruction prior to and/or after the task?
-   When offering feedback, will you use implicit techniques (e.g., recasts) or explicit techniques (e.g., correction plus explanation)?

Focus on form through task-essential design and corrective feedback

In addition to ensuring that all students participate in the classroom task, teachers may also want to increase the chances that, as students interact with one another and negotiate meaning, they also at some point turn their attention to particular grammatical forms. One way to encourage the noticing and use of particular grammar forms is to design the task in such a way as to create obligatory contexts for the target feature. Mackey (1999), for example, chose a spot-the-difference task not only because it created a two-way information gap, but also because it required the use of question forms. In this way, the target forms can be said to be task-essential. Students must at the very least attempt to form a question if they are to find out what is in their partner's picture.

In his study of article use and development among Japanese EFL learners, Muranoi (2000) used a picture-description task to create obligatory contexts for the articles *a/ an* and *the*. As shown in Figure 9.4, the students are prompted by keywords to form sentences that describe what is happening in the pictures.

Figure 9.4 Picture description task (Muranoi, 2000, p. 671)

If native speakers of English were to complete this task, they would likely use articles with many of the nouns in the prompts (e.g., girl, boy, picture, park). In this sense, articles are required for grammatical accuracy, though not necessarily to communicate meaning. Muranoi used this task as a pre-test in his study, to assess learners' use of articles prior to his instructional treatment.

In cases like that of articles, where task-essentialness is harder to achieve, teachers may want to use supplemental strategies to draw learners' attention to form during the course of meaningful interaction. This can be done through explicit instruction (e.g., asking students to focus on their use of articles when they complete a task) and/ or through interactional feedback during the task (e.g., the use of recasts in response to learner errors). Muranoi explored the use of both explicit instruction and implicit feedback in his study of L2 article acquisition. His main treatment task was a decision-making task in which students were asked to discuss how profits earned by a company could be spent. To promote a focus on articles in the midst of meaningful communication, Muranoi incorporated planned feedback into his task design. After rehearsing the decision-making task with a peer (with a primary focus on meaning), students had an opportunity to carry out the task with the teacher. When a student made an article error during this phase of the task, the teacher provided the student with a request for repetition, as in Example 9.1. If the student corrected her error, the teacher would repeat the student's correct response back to them. If the student did not correct her error, the teacher responded with another request for repetition, and if the error still persisted, a recast was used to provide the correct form.

(9.1)   Student: I saw rat.
        Teacher: You saw what?
        Student: A rat.
        Teacher: Uh-huh. You saw a rat in your room. That's terrible. (Muranoi, 2000, p. 634)

Though it may not be feasible for teachers to carry out a communication task with every individual student in the class during one class period, it is possible for teachers to select a handful of students in each class to perform a teacher-student role play in front of the class, so that, by the end of the instructional unit, each student has had a chance to receive planned feedback from the teacher.

Another element of task design that is closely related to task-essentialness and planned feedback is developmental readiness. That is, when selecting target forms, teachers may want to consider the developmental levels of students in the class. In the case of question formation, for example, teachers may want to design tasks that target a specific developmental stage, rather than questions in general. This approach can be seen in several of Alison Mackey's studies (e.g., Mackey & Philp, 1998; Mackey, 1999; Mackey & Sachs, 2012). Before students participate in instructional interventions, their developmental level is assessed through diagnostic communication tasks. If learners produce Stage 3 questions, but no Stage 4 questions, or if learners' Stage 4 questions are non-target-like, then interactional feedback may be focused more intensively on Stage 4 questions. As discussed in Chapter 5 in regards to grammar materials development, it is important to keep in mind that classroom tasks need not cover an entire grammatical system, but rather should have a manageable focus, targeting specific meanings, uses, and areas of development.

Options along the implicit-explicit continuum

Creating obligatory contexts for target forms and providing interactional feedback during the course of interaction represent approaches to task design that fall closer to the implicit end of the form-focused instruction continuum. When the focus is primarily on meaning and fluent communication, teachers may wish to engage learners in communication tasks without explicitly instructing them to focus on particular language forms. They may also prefer implicit feedback types, such as recasts, so that the flow of communication is minimally interrupted. In some cases, however, teachers may worry that an entirely implicit approach is not enough to prompt learners to focus on form, and in many cases the students themselves may prefer more explicit strategies.

One approach to increasing the likelihood that learners will attend to target features is to make interactional feedback more explicit. Options include overt correction (telling a student they made an error and then correcting it) and metalinguistic explanation (explaining the relevant grammatical rule). Another approach is to incorporate explicit instruction into the task design. Muranoi, for example, explored how explicit discussions of the target form following a communication task might enhance L2 article acquisition. After task performance, each student participated in a debriefing session. For some students, this debriefing phase was meaning-focused, for others, it was form-focused. In the form-focused debriefing session, the teacher explained:

> why Japanese learners of English tend to make errors with articles…. the teacher also pointed out the important role that the indefinite article plays in communication…. [as well as] the function of the indefinite article in classifying nouns.
>
> (Muranoi, 2000, p. 638)

In other words, each student received his own personal grammar lesson after their task performance! Muranoi found that the students who participated in the form-focused debriefing session demonstrated a greater mastery of article use both immediately and 5 weeks after the treatment tasks than did the students who participated in the meaning-focused debriefing.

Another approach to explicit grammar task design is Ellis and Fotos' grammar consciousness-raising tasks (Fotos, 1993, 1998, 2002; Fotos & Ellis, 1991; 1994). In this type of task, learners are still required to communicate with one another to achieve a shared goal, but unlike many of the information gap tasks we have discussed so far, the content of the task is the grammar feature itself: Learners must work together to develop grammar rules based on their analysis of sample sentences in the target language. Figure 9.5 displays an example of a grammar consciousness-raising task used by Ellis and Fotos (1994) in a study of the L2 acquisition of ditransitive verbs in English. In this task, students worked in pairs or groups of four, and each student was given a task card that contained four example sentences.

Students in groups of 4 – one different card to each member
Students in pairs – two different cards to each member

1. Correct: I asked my friend a question.
1. Incorrect: She asked a question to her mother.
2. Correct: Kimiko reviewed the lesson for John.
2. Incorrect: Kimiko reviewed John the lesson.
3. Correct: The teacher calculated the answers for the students.
3. Incorrect: The teacher calculated the students the answers.
4. Correct: The secretary reported the problem to her boss.
4. Incorrect: The student reported the teacher thematter.
5. Correct: I offered her a cup of tea.
5. Correct: I offered a cup of tea to the president.
6. Correct: The teacher pronounced the difficult word for the class.
7. Correct: I bought many presents for my family.
8. Correct: She cooked a delicious dinner for us.

Figure 9.5 Consciousness-raising task cards (Ellis & Fotos, 1994, p. 626)

Each student took a turn reading aloud the sentences on her card. After this, students were given a list of ditransitive verbs and were asked to collaboratively write down possible correct word order rules for each verb.

Ellis and Fotos found that this task did help Japanese learners of English (students at a community college) to develop explicit knowledge of how these verbs work in English, and they recommend the use of this task type in intermediate and advanced level classes where students are motivated to talk about grammar, such as in cases where high-stakes grammar tests are a part of the curriculum.

Reflection 9.2
– Which interactionist task design considerations are most important to you as an L2 teacher? Why?
– Are there any interactionist task design issues that you typically do not consider when planning lessons, but would like to attend to more in the future?
– Now, think specifically about the grammar-focused task you are working on (see Reflection 9.1). Which interactionist concerns are more important than others for this particular task? How will you address these concerns in your task design?

Promoting collaboration and the co-construction of language knowledge

The task design features described thus far in this chapter – participation require-ments, information gaps, planned feedback, and explicit instruction – emphasize the important role that the teacher can play in classroom second language acquisition. Through carefully designed communication tasks, teachers can create opportunities for learners to attend to grammatical form during the course of meaningful interaction, thus increasing the likelihood that learners will make important connections among the target grammatical feature, its meaning, and its appropriate use. In this section, we turn our attention to the L2 learner and explore how collaborative tasks might be used to promote the co-construction of linguistic knowledge.

TASK DESIGN CONSIDERATIONS: COLLABORATIVE LEARNING WITHIN THE ZPD
Pushed output/languaging
– To what extent will students need to produce language (in speaking or in writing) to complete the task successfully?
– To what extent does the task encourage students to talk about and reflect on the language they are producing?
Collaboration
– In what ways does the task encourage learners to collaborate with other learners and/or the teacher?
– To what extent does the task provide opportunities for learners to accomplish more together than they could alone?
Assistance in the zone of proximal development
– To what extent does the task provide opportunities for assistance that is carefully tuned to the each learner's developmental needs?
– What feedback strategies will be used to provide this assistance?

Two scholars who have played a prominent role in the design of grammar-focused collaborative classroom tasks are Merrill Swain and Sharon Lapkin. One of the most frequently used tasks in Swain and Lapkin's research (e.g., 1998, 2001, 2002) is the dic-togloss task, in which learners listen to an oral dictation at least two times, take notes, and then work in pairs to reconstruct the text they heard using their notes. The primary purpose of this task is to promote collaborative writing, metalinguistic reflection, and the co-construction of linguistic knowledge. When learners are asked to write a text together, they must discuss and negotiate linguistic choices at several levels: morphol-ogy, lexis, syntax, and discourse. Inevitably, this discussion leads to a focus on form, as students ask one another questions about which word in the L2 is most appropri-ate, what verb tense is needed, and so on. It is also likely that students, when working together, are able to produce a text that is developmentally more advanced than what they would produce if working alone (Swain, 2000).

A dictogloss is certainly not the only way to promote collaborative dialogue, however. For example, Swain and Lapkin (1998, 2001, 2002) have also used a jigsaw task in which learners work together to narrate a story told in pictures (see Figure 9.6). In the jigsaw task, one partner holds pictures 1, 3, 5, and 7, and the other partner holds pictures 2, 4, 6, and 8. Each partner takes turns narrating each picture orally; then, the partners work together to write a complete story. This task design creates an information gap (each partner must share what is in her picture) and also pushes learners to co-construct a text both orally and in writing.

Figure 9.6 Jigsaw task used in Swain & Lapkin (2002, p. 300)

Providing assistance in the zone of proximal development

In addition to promoting metalinguistic reflection through collaborative writing tasks, teachers can sequence tasks in such a way as to create opportunities for developmentally appropriate assistance in the zone of proximal development. Ohta (2005) reviews two classroom lessons (in Samuda, 2001 and Yoshimi, 2001) which she feels successfully create a ZPD, without necessarily intending to do so. One important feature of task design that Ohta observed in both of these studies was an instructional phase in which learners had an opportunity to carry out a collaborative task using their own language resources and strategies, without any explicit instruction in the target forms or assistance from the teacher. During this phase, the teacher was able to observe what students were capable of doing without help. Then, in subsequent phases of the task, the teacher provided explicit instruction and interactional feedback that directly addressed the needs she had observed in students' prior task performance.

We can see how this task sequencing might work by looking more closely at Samuda's (2001) study. The focus of Samuda's instructional intervention was four English modal auxiliaries used to express probability and possibility: *must, might, may,* and *could*. In the first phase of the instructional intervention, students were asked to complete a decision-making task. Students were given a bag of objects and were told that the bag contained items found in an individual's pocket. Students were asked to use the items to make inferences about the person's personal characteristics (name, age, sex, marital status) and to guess their identity. Samuda also provided students with a task sheet which asked them to assess how certain they were about their guesses, as shown in Figure 9.7. Students were not, however, given a list of target forms to use. Rather, Samuda designed the first task "to attract initial attention to probability and possibility areas of meaning." (p. 126). In other words, Samuda created a meaningful context for the use of modal forms, but left the task open enough so that the teacher could observe to what extent students would actually use these forms when carrying out the task.

	How certain are you?		
	Less than 50% certain (it's possible)	90% certain (it's probable)	100% certain (it's certain)
Name			
Sex			
Age			
Marital status			

Figure 9.7 Task sheet used in Samuda (2001, p. 127)

As students worked together during this initial phase of the instructional treatment, the teacher participated in some of the students' collaborative dialogue, providing meaning-focused, rather than form-focused feedback. The teacher did, however,
attempt to set the stage for subsequent modal use, by using what Samuda calls *precasts*,
or proactive (rather than reactive) teacher moves that are designed to begin the process of building form-meaning-use connections. In this case, the precasts used by the
teacher provided a semantic category (probability) and then coupled this category with
a target form (*might*). Samuda (p. 129) offers the following example:

(9.2)   S1:   Habits?
        Y: Well first he smokes
        C: But we think uh 50% we think just 50%
        N: Yes just maybe. We're not sure
        T: Oh Yeah? Only 50% What's that?
        S2:   Yes, give proof (laughter)
        N: Because here (showing matchbox). A matchbox
        T: Hmmm, but you're <u>not certain</u> if he smokes, huh? (Looking at matchbox)
        A: Look (opens matchbox). Many matches so maybe he just keep for friend, not
           for him (laughter)
        T: Mmmm I- I guess <u>it's possible</u> he might smoke. It's hard to tell just from this
        A: Yeah, not sure
        S2:   You have more proof?

In the second phase of Samuda's instructional intervention, the teacher provides explicit instruction on how modals can be used to express the meanings of "it's possible,"
"90% certain," and so on. She does this by first eliciting the students' rating of their own
certainty, as shown in Example 9.3 (Samuda, p. 131).

(9.3)   T: So lots of interesting ideas here. Paula, letters, uh schedule, opera, a busy man
        C: Japanese classes
        T: Yeah right, I forgot he's learning Japanese too (laughter)
        N: And golf
        T: Oh yes very busy (laughter). Hmmm let's – why don't we look at how the
           language works here? Just for a minute uhh (looking at objects). Let's see
           now. Did you have anything here you thought was '<u>probable</u>'? Like <u>90%</u>?
        Y: Businessman
        T: Businessman? <u>90%</u>? Ok. So you're <u>90% certain</u> he's a businessman, right?
           Here's another way to say this. You think it's <u>90% certain</u>, so you think he
           must be a businessman. He must be a businessman (writes it on board). So
           this (point to <u>must be</u> on board) is showing how <u>CERTAIN</u> how SURE you
           are. Not <u>100%</u>, but almost <u>100%</u>. <u>90%</u>
        A: So <u>100%</u> is 'be' or 'must'?

> T: 100? 100%? Then you can say he IS a businessman (writes on board). When you when you're NOT 100% certain, you can use must. OK? Not he is a businessman, but he must be a businessman. So 'be' here (pointing to must be on board) is from this verb (pointing to is). Let's uh what other things do you have for probably?

In this approach to task design, Samuda moved from meaning-focused interaction toward a focus on form. This allowed her to establish a *need* for the target form, without actually pushing learners to use the target form from the start.

In addition to this, Ohta (2005) argues that Samuda's task design created an effective zone of proximal development. That is, the initial task phase, in which learners discussed the identity of the person in question, allowed the teacher to observe to what extent learners were already capable of using modals to express how certain they were about their conclusions. Ohta writes:

> The instructional design presented here allowed the teacher to assess the current level of functioning of students and provide support for students to move to a higher level of functioning. With assistance provided through the teacher's implicit and explicit focus on the target forms, learners began using them in their discussion and writing. The teacher's intervention shows expert use of scaffolding as she built on what learners already knew and did with confidence, interweaving new forms and then providing explicit instruction on appropriate use of those forms. This instructional design also exploits the ZPD in providing assistance to students after their need for such assistance was established in the pre-focus phase. In this phase, the students relied on language "mined" from the task worksheet, using lexical expressions of probability rather than modal auxiliaries. It was clear to the teacher that students were unlikely to use the forms without assistance; this exemplifies the ZPD, what a person can do with assistance that they could not have done unaided. The salience of the new forms was also increased because the teacher provided them at the point where they were needed. Using the modals helped students to communicate more effectively, a factor which may make the instructional experience even more powerful in moving students toward retention of the target forms.   (pp. 510–511)

We should point out that Samuda did indeed observe a marked improvement in students' use of modal auxiliaries after they participated in the instructional intervention. In a follow-up task, students were asked to present their final conclusions to the class using a poster to display their decisions. In the first task (filling out the task sheet in Figure 9.7), students had used a total of 73 expressions of probability and possibility (e.g, *maybe, I'm not sure*); however, none of these forms were modal auxiliaries. In the final task (poster presentation), students used roughly the same number of probability/possibilitiy expressions (76), but the breakdown of forms used was much different: Over 38% of the forms use were the modals *must, may, might, and could.*

Reflection 9.3

- As an L2 teacher, have you ever designed activities that allow you to simply observe what students can do without your assistance? If so, what did this task look like and what linguistic forms were targeted?
- What advantages do you see in providing target forms and explanations *after* students have completed a meaning-focused task? What challenges might come with this approach?
- Now, return to the grammar-focused task you are working on (Reflections 9.1 and 9.2). What opportunities do you see in this task for promoting collaboration and assistance within the zone of proximal development?

Preparing students for the task at hand: Task modeling and task planning options

When implementing instructional tasks in the classroom, teachers are well-aware that clear task instructions play a crucial role in the degree to which students will be able to complete the task successfully. Confusion over task procedures can quickly derail a classroom activity, leaving both teachers and students feeling frustrated over missed learning opportunities. In fact, one reason why teachers might feel reluctant to implement a new type of task is students' lack of familiarity with it and the fear that too much class time will be spent explaining task procedures.

From a cognitive perspective, task instructions play a crucial role in determining the extent to which students will have sufficient cognitive resources during the task to devote to language processing and production. Poor instructions prior to a task can result in students devoting most of their attention to figuring out task procedures, rather than expressing meaning fluently and accurately in the target language. Two lines of task-based SLA research, task modeling and task planning, provide useful insights into addressing this pedagogical concern. The first technique, *task modeling*, involves a demonstration of task procedures prior to student engagement in the task, and this can be provided as a technique during pre-task planning time. Such task modeling can not only help to clarify what students are expected to do during the task, but may also promote a greater focus on language form during the task itself. For example, Kim and McDonough (2011) and Kim (2013) both found that students who watched a pre-task modeling video tended to produce more LREs during task performance, and they paid more attention to linguistic forms while planning their task performance. The pre-task modeling video lasted about 2 minutes and demonstrated to students

---

TASK DESIGN CONSIDERATIONS: ATTENTIONAL RESOURCES

Task modeling
-    Will students have a chance to observe a model of task performance before they have a chance to do it themselves?
-    What will be the primary purpose of this modeling phase?

Task planning
-    Will students have an opportunity to plan and rehearse their language use before carrying out the task?
-    Will you offer guided planning with specific techniques (e.g., providing explicit information about grammar or vocabulary)?
-    How much planning time will you provide?

Task sequencing/ repetition
-    Is this task part of a larger sequence of tasks that are designed to promote a particular area of language use?
-    Will students have an opportunity to repeat the task (or a similar type of task) in future classes?

Task complexity
-    What types of reasoning demands will the task place on students? Will the task be situated in the "here and now," or will students need to consider multiple time frames?
-    How many sources of information will students need to consult to complete the task?

---

how to collaborate with one another and how to pay attention to language forms while carrying out tasks collaboratively. Kim and McDonough (2011) found that watching task modeling video also facilitated collaborative pair dynamics.

It is important to note that the purpose of task modeling is not to show or dictate to students what they need to say during the task, but rather is to model how one might engage in the task – how to interact with a partner, how to use task materials, how to talk through language-related questions and challenges. When learners are not accustomed to participating in learner-centered collaborative tasks, task modeling can be particularly useful and is likely more accessible and engaging than lengthy directions on a task worksheet.

To ensure that students have a clear understanding of task procedures and goals, L2 teachers can also provide students with a guided planning phase prior to task performance. The purpose of task planning is to allow students to reflect on and prepare for task demands: What is my role in the task? What are my communicative goals? What language forms will I need to use to achieve these goals? As with task modeling, task planning not only helps students understand task requirements, but impacts student task performance. Studies of task planning (see Ellis, 2005, for a collection of task planning studies) have found that when students have an opportunity to plan their language use, they are more accurate in their production during the task itself, and yet, at the same time, more able to focus their attention on meaning.

In a study of relative clause use in oral task performance, Mochizuki and Ortega (2008) investigated whether Japanese L2 learners of English would produce a greater number of accurate relative clauses if given time to plan for their performance. Mochizuki and Ortega divided their 56 participants into three groups: a no planning condition, an unguided planning condition, and a guided planning condition. In all three conditions, students first listened to a story as they looked at pictures representing the major story scenes. The story itself contained many examples of the target feature, relative clauses using the relative pronoun *which* (e.g., *I like the dog which has long ears*). After this phase of the task, the no planning group was simply asked to retell the story orally. The unguided planning group was given 5 minutes "to prepare for the retelling carefully during their five minutes so that they could convey as many details of the story as possible to the partner" (p. 19). No supporting instructional materials were provided to the students in the unguided group. The guided planning group, on the other hand, was told that relative clauses "may be helpful for their storytelling" and were given a handout that briefly explained in Japanese how to construct a sentence using a relative clause.

Mochizuki and Ortega found that guided planning with explicit information about the target structure resulted in more frequent and more accurate relative clause use than the no planning time or unguided planning time conditions. These findings suggest that task planning may also be a useful tool in promoting learners focus on form. As Ellis (2003) has argued, it is difficult to ensure that learners will use a target feature in a communication task even if the task creates obligatory contexts for that feature. Mochizuki and Ortega were able to address this challenge through guided task planning materials that encouraged learners to use the target form.

Considering the cognitive dimensions of task complexity

Another important consideration when designing tasks is task complexity or difficulty. The appropriate task complexity level can be determined based on several factors, including learners' familiarity with the task content and procedures, learners' proficiency levels, whether learners must produce language under time pressure, and whether learners are required to agree upon a single task solution (Ellis, 2003; Robinson, 2001b; Skehan, 1996).

Robinson (2001b) also makes a distinction between task complexity and task difficulty. As we saw in Chapter 8, *task complexity* involves cognitive factors, or the attentional resources learners must devote to various features of the task. These include *resource-directing factors* (e.g., +/− new elements, +/− here and now, +/− intentional reasoning) and *resource dispersing factors* (e.g., +/− planning, +/− single task, +/− prior knowledge). *Task difficulty*, on the other hand, involves learner factors, including both *affective variables* (e.g., motivation, anxiety, confidence) and *ability variables* (e.g., aptitude, working memory, intelligence). Though teachers should consider both task complexity and task difficulty when planning lessons, Robinson (2011) argues that teachers should focus on features of task complexity if they wish to mediate the learning process and draw learner's attention to linguistic form. Manipulation of resource-directing variables, in particular, have been found to encourage more frequent use of target grammatical forms during task performance, as well as more syntactically complex sentences.

Kim and Tracy-Ventura's study (2011) helps to illustrate how teachers might use Robinson's framework to inform their own classroom task design. The purpose of the study was to investigate the effects of task complexity on the development of simple past tense morphology. The study was conducted in Korean university English classes which followed task-based syllabi. The instructional unit used in the study focused on past events. Because Robinson (Robinson & N. Ellis, 2008) claimed that carrying out more complex tasks would facilitate the learning of developmentally more advanced forms, Kim and Tracy-Ventura analyzed learners' use of simple past morphology with activity and stative verbs only, as these are typically used in the past tense later in development (see Chapter 7). Three different versions of the instructional tasks were created: Simple, +Complex and ++Complex. Kim and Tracy-Ventura operationalized task complexity based on reasoning demands and the number of elements that students must consider when making a decision. For example, in a task which focused on an upcoming mayoral election, learners in all three groups were provided with the same task input (see Figure 9.8). Each student held information that their partner did not have, thus creating an information gap.

Candidate 1 (Taejin Jang)	Candidate 2 (Youngsook Lee)
1. December 01, 1952	5. March 23, 1958
parents, two older sisters, Seoul, are, have, live, books, pictures, read, tell, story, mother	is, fly, America, middle school, business, English, leave, study, move, family
3. February 1985	7. June 1995
Africa, patient, volunteer, hospital help, feel, go, finish, want, build, enjoy, happy	reporter, work, interview, people, meet, like, stay, start, enjoy, social issues, husband, travel

Figure 9.8 An example of Kim & Tracy-Ventura's task input

Top/Left: http://blog.joins.com/media/folderListSlide.asp?uid=fabiano&folder=6&list_id=10037899

Top/Right: http://www.inews365.com/news/article.html?no=236851

Bottom/Left: http://www.egn.kr/news/articleView.html?idxno=4975

Bottom/Right: http://www.chosun.com/culture/news/200504/200504110351.html

For simple tasks, students were required to generate a timeline of life events for two mayoral candidates while exchanging information about the mayoral candidates' previous experiences. For +complex tasks and ++complex tasks, learners also made timelines, but in addition to this, they were asked to make a decision about whom they would vote for. In +complex tasks, students were asked to consider two key factors when deciding how to vote (i.e., amount of leadership experience, knowledge of economics), and in ++complex tasks, students were asked to consider four (i.e., volunteer experience, educational background, amount of leadership experience, knowledge of economics). Figure 9.9 displays the task prompt given to the ++Complex group. The Simple and +Complex groups received the same prompt with the exception of the following:

1. Simple groups did not vote on a candidate and thus were not asked to do item (4).
2. +Complex groups did vote, but they were asked to only consider two of the criteria listed under item (4).

Scenario: Your city will elect a new mayor soon. You and your partner both have four pictures illustrating the life stories of the two candidates, Taejin Jang and Youngsook Lee. You and your partner are organizing a public presentation for the election and will make a brief presentation about the two candidates' previous experiences. Then, decide who should become the mayor of your city and discuss the reasons for your decision with your partner.

Directions:

(1) Between you and your partner, one person has four odd numbered picture cards, and the other has four even numbered picture cards with some key words related to the pictures. Following the numbers, create an overall timeline of the two candidates' life experiences as shown below.

(2) Based on the timeline, develop a detailed life story about the two candidates.

(3) For each picture, describe specific information. For instance, explain what happened at that time in their lives, and elaborate on the story such as including the candidates' feelings at a given time.

(4) Based on the four qualifications provided below, make a decision about who should become the mayor of your city and discuss the reasons for your decision with your partner.

  – Volunteer experience, educational background, amount of leadership experience, knowledge of economics

Note: These instructions were provided to the students in Korean.

Figure 9.9 Kim & Tracy-Ventura's ++complex task prompt

Learners' gains in simple past morphology were measured using picture description tests one week and two weeks after completing the 4 tasks. The results suggested that more complex tasks facilitate the learning of simple past morphology (i.e., higher scores on posttests), especially involving developmentally advanced forms (i.e., activity and stative verbs), as predicted by the Cognition Hypothesis (Robinson, 2001a, 2001b, 2003, 2005). The two complex groups outperformed the simple group, though no significant differences between the +complex and ++complex conditions were found. During the process of evaluating and comparing information, students were pushed to use more advanced and developmentally challenging forms. It appears that the requirement to make decisions (rather than simply exchange information) based on a set of criteria helps learners to focus their attention on target forms, as they need to use these forms when providing a rationale for their decisions. Because more complex tasks are cognitively more demanding, we encourage teachers to also use some of the supportive techniques discussed in this chapter, such as task modeling and guided task planning, so that students understand how they are expected to carry out the task. Translating task instructions into the students' L1 (when possible) can also facilitate this process. When it comes to task complexity, it is important for teachers to remember that as they increase cognitive complexity along the resource-directing dimension (i.e., number of resources to consult, amount of reasoning involved, number of time frames to consider), they should also consider decreasing other areas of complexity, for example, by using topics that are familiar to students and providing adequate time for students to plan for and carry out the task.

Reflection 9.4

- As an L2 teacher, what types of modeling and/or task planning do you typically provide for students before asking them to perform a task on their own? In what ways do you feel these pre-task activities benefit students? More specifically, what role might they play in students' L2 grammar development?
- Have you repeated particular tasks types over the course of an instructional unit or semester? What differences did you observe in task performance when students had a chance to carry out the same task more than once?
- Now, return to the grammar-focused task you are working on (Reflections 9.1, 9.2, 9.3). Can you think of ways you might increase the cognitive complexity of the task, through a manipulation of *resource-directing factors* (+/– new elements, +/– here and now, +/– reasoning demands)? Are there ways you might make the task less complex, in terms of its *resource dispersing factors* (+/– planning, +/– single task, +/– prior knowledge)?

Summary

In this chapter, we have highlighted several grammar task design considerations, drawing on three major areas of TBLT research:

Interactionist
- Promoting interaction and the negotiation of meaning through information gaps and convergent goal orientations.
- Promoting focus on form through task-essentialness, corrective feedback, and explicit instruction

Sociocultural
- Promoting talk about and reflection on language through teacher-learner and learner-learner collaboration
- Withholding explicit instruction until it is clear that learners are not able to use or explain target grammar forms without assistance

Cognitivist
- Reducing cognitive load through task modeling, planning, and repetition
- Directing learners' cognitive resources towards language use through complex task designs (e.g., decision-making based on multiple criteria, consideration of multiple time frames, evaluation of several pieces of information).

Suggestions for further reading

East, M. (2012). *Task-Based Language Teaching from the Teacher's Perspective*. Amsterdam: John Benjamins.

Ellis, R. (2003). *Task-Based Language Learning and Teaching*. Oxford: Oxford University Press.

Long, M. (2015). *Second Language Acquisition and Task-Based Language Teaching*. Malden, MA: Wiley Blackwell

Nassaji, H. & Fotos, S. (2010). *Teaching Grammar in Second Language Classrooms: Integrating Form-Focused Instruction in Communicative Context*. New York NY: Routledge.

Nunan, D. (2004). *Task-based Language Teaching*. Cambridge: Cambridge University Press.

Willis, D., & Willis, J. (2007). *Doing Task-based Teaching*. Oxford: Oxford University Press.

Recommended resources

Task-Based Language Teaching: A Demonstration Module
<http://scholarspace.manoa.hawaii.edu/handle/10125/10623>

Willis-ELT
<http://www.willis-elt.co.uk/index.html>

Instruments for Research into Second Language Learning and Teaching
<http://www.iris-database.org/iris/app/home/index>

Chapter 10

Assessing grammar within a framework of communicative competence

As we saw in Chapter 3, grammatical competence is viewed as one component of communicative competence; it is a resource that speakers and writers draw upon to express meaning and to achieve communicative goals in a wide range of settings. In materials development and teaching, it is important to describe grammar within this framework, and to consider how one might develop lessons and tasks which help students to make important form-meaning-use connections. In this chapter, we explore how such a view of grammar might inform the assessment of L2 grammatical ability. We begin with a discussion of how grammar has been defined for the purpose of assessment, and we provide a general introduction to important assessment concepts. We then explore how grammar ability can be distinguished from other areas of language ability, and highlight important steps in the assessment development process. Finally, we turn our attention to two alternatives to traditional grammar tests: task-based performance assessment and dynamic assessment. We discuss how these approaches might help to inform our understanding of students' abilities to use grammar accurately and appropriately when performing tasks both independently and in collaboration with others.

Defining grammar for the purpose of assessment

When communicative competence became a primary goal of L2 instruction, this impacted not only materials development and teaching methodology, but also L2 assessment. Language tests which focused solely on grammatical accuracy and which consisted largely of multiple choice and fill-in-the-blank items no longer made sense – how could these assessments help us to understand students' abilities to use language meaningfully in a variety of contexts? It soon became clear that designers of L2 assessments would need to consider how grammar knowledge fits into the larger picture of overall language ability

To address this challenge, Bachman and Palmer (1996) proposed a model of communicative language ability. Within this model, Bachman and Palmer identified several subcomponents of Language Knowledge, beginning with two major categories: Organizational Knowledge and Pragmatic Knowledge (see Figure 10.1). Organizational

Knowledge consists of Grammatical Knowledge (knowledge of how language forms are organized to create grammatically correct utterances at the phrase, clause, and sentence level) and Textual Knowledge (knowledge of how utterances are organized to create discourse). Pragmatic Knowledge consists of Functional Knowledge (knowledge of how utterances are used to express intentions and fulfill communicative functions) and Sociolinguistic Knowledge (knowledge of how context impacts the organization of language forms at both the utterance and discourse level).

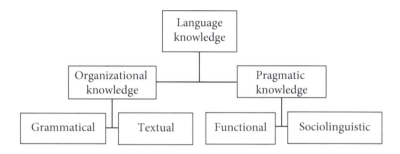

Figure 10.1 Components of language knowledge (Bachman & Palmer, 1996)

In this model, Pragmatic Knowledge is not included as a part of Grammatical Knowledge; rather, Organizational Knowledge (phonemes, morphemes, words, and sentences, texts) is presented as a component that is separate from Pragmatic Knowledge. This conception of grammatical knowledge is different from Larsen-Freeman's (2003) Three Dimensions, where Use (pragmatics) is included as a component of grammar. However, it is important to keep in mind that Larsen-Freeman's model was not developed for the purpose of assessment, but rather is intended to inform L2 teaching. In other words, if the goal of L2 instruction is to foster the development of communicative competence, then grammar instruction should be integrated with pragmatics instruction, so that students understand not only how to form grammatically correct sentences, but how to use them effectively in particular contexts.

Purpura (2004) agrees that test developers should aim to distinguish grammatical ability from other components of communicative competence, as it is possible for students to have greater control over some areas of language and less control over others. For example, some students are able to produce perfectly grammatical sentences but have great difficulty choosing the most appropriate and accepted forms for a given situation. Other students have high levels of sociolinguistic and strategic competence, but have still not acquired some of the most basic grammatical morphemes in the language (as was the case of Wes in Schmidt's 1986 study). These examples suggest that L2 teachers should have some means of assessing the components of communicative competence separately, so that students' strengths and weaknesses can be identified.

In his model of grammatical knowledge, Purpura (2004, 2013) draws on Larsen-Freeman's dimensions of Form, Meaning, and Use. However, rather than representing these components as parts of a whole (i.e., the whole of grammatical knowledge), Purpura treats Form and Meaning as the two main components of grammatical knowledge, and moves Use (Pragmatic Knowledge) to a separate area of language ability (see Figure 10.2). In this model, speakers and writers draw on both grammatical knowledge and pragmatic knowledge to accomplish communicative goals.

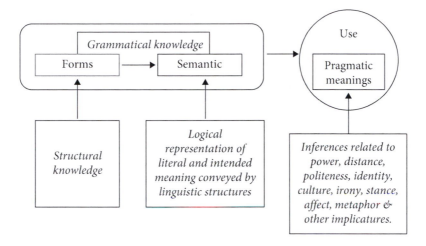

Figure 10.2 Purpura's (2013, p. 5) model of grammatical knowledge

Despite his paring down of what is included within a definition of grammar, Purpura (2004, 2013) still offers a conception of grammatical knowledge that goes far beyond morphology and syntax. Grammatical Form includes graphology and phonology, lexical co-occurrence patterns, and discourse-level forms such as cohesive devices (i.e., forms that hold a text together, showing clear relationships among ideas). Grammatical Meaning consists of both *literal meaning* ("meaning associated with an utterance as the sum of its parts and how these parts are arranged in syntax" p. 62) and *intended meaning* ("meaning associated with the propositional intention that the speaker has in mind while conveying a message" p. 62). Though the inclusion of intended meaning within grammatical meaning suggests some overlap between the grammatical and pragmatic, Purpura suggests that the line between the two be drawn based on the amount of context needed to interpret a speaker's or writer's underlying intention. In other words, within the realm of grammatical meaning, meaning can be inferred based primarily on the inherent semantics of the lexis, morphology, and syntax used. Pragmatic meaning, on the other hand, is inferred primarily based on one's knowledge of context.

Pragmatics refers to…. the relative appropriateness of the utterance within a given context (Why did you say it that way in this context?), to the relative acceptability of the utterance within the general norms of interaction (Is it OK to say that?), or to the naturalness of the utterance in terms of how native speakers might say it (Does this sound like something native speakers would say?)… [and] to the conventionality of the utterance in terms of how speakers from a certain regional or social language variety might express it (Does it sound like something that someone from my social or regional dialect would say?) (Purpura, 2004, pp. 76–77)

Figure 10.3 provides a more detailed account of Purpura's model, with examples of the types of forms that might fall under each category. As can be seen in Figure 10.3, once we get beyond the initial distinction between Grammatical Knowledge and Pragmatic Knowledge, there are many more subcomponents to consider, and for each subcomponent, we could create a taxonomy of all of the forms and meanings an L2 learner would need to know and be able to use to communicate in a variety of contexts. (Purpura, 2013, p. 4, offers an example of what such a taxonomy might look like). How then, are L2 teachers to decide what to focus on in any given grammar assessment? Should we aim to assess form, meaning, and use all at the same time? In some cases might we focus only on grammatical form? In others, only pragmatic knowledge?

The focus and scope of an assessment depends largely on its purpose (see Table 10.1). Assessments used for the purpose of *placement*, for example, are typically broad in scope, and aim to answer questions like: How much grammar does the student know? Would this student be considered to have a beginning level of grammatical knowledge? Intermediate? Advanced? Such questions require test developers to consider what constitutes the whole of grammatical knowledge, as well as various levels of partial knowledge. Classroom-based assessments, on the other hand, are closely linked to course curricula and learning objectives, and thus are much more narrow in scope. A teacher may select areas of grammatical knowledge to be assessed based on state standards, curricular requirements, and topics and tasks covered in a particular instructional unit (Purpura, 2004). Classroom-based assessments can be further divided into *formative, summative,* and *diagnostic* assessments. Formative assessments aim to "evaluate students in the process of forming their competencies and skills with the goal of helping them to continue that growth process" (Brown & Abeywickrama, 2010, p. 7), and thus may cover only a small set of grammatical concepts that were recently addressed in class. Summative assessments measure what students have learned at the conclusion of an instructional unit or at the end of a course (e.g., a final exam), and thus are broader in scope than formative assessments (though still much narrower in scope than placement exams).

Diagnostic assessments can be used at the beginning of a course to identify areas of language knowledge or use that students have already mastered, as well as the areas

Grammatical Knowledge ← ‐‐‐‐‐‐‐‐‐‐‐‐‐‐ → Pragmatic Knowledge

Grammatical Form (accuracy)	Grammatical Meaning (meaningfulness)	Pragmatic Meaning (appropriateness/ conventionality/ naturalness/ acceptability)
SENTENTIAL LEVEL	SENTENTIAL LEVEL	SENTENTIAL OR DISCOURSE LEVEL
Phonological/ graphological forms – Segmental forms – Prosodic forms – Sound-spelling correspondences – Writing systems **Lexical forms** – Orthographic forms – Word formation – Countability and gender restrictions – Co-occurrence restrictions – Formulaic forms **Morphosyntactic forms** – Inflectional affixes – Derivational affixes – Syntactic structures – Simple, compound and complex sentences	**Phonological/ graphological meanings** – Minimal pairs – Interrogatives – Emphasis **Lexical meanings** – Denotation and connotation – Meanings of formulaic expressions – Semantic fields – Collocation **Morphosyntactic meanings** – Time/duration – Passivization – Cause-effect – Factual/counter factual	**Contextual meanings** – Interpersonal **Sociolinguistic meanings** – Social identity markers – Cultural identity markers – Register variation – Social norms, preferences, expectations **Sociocultural meanings** – Cultural meanings – Cultural norms, preferences, expectations **Psychological meanings** – Affective stance (sarcasm, deference, anger, impatience, irony, humor)

Figure 10.3 Purpura's (2004, p. 91) components of grammatical and pragmatic knowledge

in need of development. Diagnostic assessments may also be administered during the course of a student's study in a language program if the student is having persistent learning difficulties (Linn & Gronlund, 2000). In this case, the purpose would be to identify potential causes of these difficulties and to develop a plan for supporting the student during his or her time in the language program.

Table 10.1 Purposes of assessment in instructional contexts

	Placement	Diagnostic	Formative	Summative
Purpose	Place students into levels of a language program	Identify learners' strengths and weakness	Assess and provide feedback on learning progress	Determine to what extent learners have learned what was taught
Example scenario	Prior to each term, the intensive English program administers a placement test to incoming students to identify what level in a program they should enter.	On the first day of the new term, teachers administer a diagnostic test to determine what areas of grammar their students know well and what areas of grammar require more instruction.	Part-way through an instructional unit, teachers administer a quiz to assess how well students understand the concepts covered thus far.	At the end of each textbook chapter, teachers administer a test to assess the extent to which students have learned the concepts covered in the instructional unit.

In the remainder of this chapter, we focus on classroom assessment, as L2 teachers are most likely to design and administer these assessments on a regular basis. For more information on the design of grammar-focused placement tests, we recommend Green and Weir (2004), Purpura (2004), and Chapelle, Chung, Hegelheimer, and Pendar (2010).

Reflection 10.1

– Definitions of grammar for the purpose of assessment (like Purpura's model) typically treat grammatical knowledge as separate from pragmatic knowledge. To what extent do you feel this distinction is useful? How might it impact your approach to assessing your students' L2 grammatical ability?

– Think about the grammar assessments you have used in your own classroom, or grammar assessments you have taken as an L2 student. What aspect of grammatical ability was emphasized most: form or meaning? Why do you think this was the case? To what extent did you or your students need to draw on pragmatic knowledge when carrying out these assessment tasks?

Classroom-based assessment: Important terminology

Before we survey the many assessment options available to L2 teachers, it is first important to define a few key assessment concepts. Thus far in this chapter, we have discussed *grammatical knowledge* as it relates to overall communicative competence, and we have also discussed the importance of helping students develop their *ability to use* grammar in meaningful contexts. In assessment, a distinction is drawn between *knowledge* and *ability*, and both of these concepts relate to *language performance*. Purpura (2004) defines *knowledge* as "a set of informational structures available for use in long-term memory" (p. 86). Language *ability*, then, is the "capacity to utilize mental representations of language knowledge built up through practice or experience in order to convey meaning" (p. 86). Both knowledge and ability are theoretical constructs which cannot be directly measured. Instead, we must observe *language performance* (e.g., student performance on a grammar test, student performance in a communication task) and use this as a basis for making inferences about underlying knowledge and ability. When discussing knowledge and ability in the context of L2 grammar assessment, Purpura (2004) draws a distinction between *grammatical knowledge* and *metalinguistic knowledge*. Grammatical knowledge is a set of language structures (phonemes, graphemes, lexis, morphemes, syntax, discourse organizers) that can be retrieved and used during communication. Metalinguistic knowledge, on the other hand, is a set of "informational structures that relate to linguistic terminology" (p. 88). While grammatical knowledge is a necessary component of grammatical ability (i.e., it is the resource that makes communication possible), metalinguistic knowledge is not. While knowing *about* language is certainly helpful, students must also have a store of grammatical structures in long-term memory to draw upon when communicating. In many cases, language users possess grammatical knowledge and the ability to use it, but not the corresponding metalanguage to describe what they know. Thus, assessments of underlying grammar ability cannot simply focus on metalanguage, but rather must include some kind of meaningful language performance.

GRAMMATICAL KNOWLEDGE, ABILITY, AND PERFORMANCE	
Grammatical knowledge	A set of language forms (phonological, graphological, lexical, morphological, syntactic, discourse) and their associated meanings, stored in long-term memory
Grammatical ability	The capacity to realize grammatical knowledge accurately and meaningfully in testing or other language-use situations
Grammatical performance	The observable manifestation of grammatical ability in language use
Metalinguistic knowledge	A set of informational structures related to linguistic terminology (Purpura, 2004, pp. 85–91)

Two other key concepts that are easily confused are the terms *assessment* and *test*. Thus far in this chapter we have used the word assessment, but for many of us, assessment conjures up images of our own stressful experiences taking high-stakes exams. Brown and Abeywickrama (2010) define assessment as "an ongoing process that encompasses a wide range of methodological techniques," (p. 3) including informal techniques such as classroom observation and practice worksheets, as well as more formal techniques, like grammar tests. A test, then, is a type of assessment with particular characteristics. As Linn and Gronlund (2000) explain, a test "typically consists of a set of questions administered during a fixed period of time under reasonably comparable conditions for all students" (p. 31). Additionally, a test measures a test-taker's performance based on explicit procedures or rules, such as a scoring rubric (Bachman, 1990). Because test design procedures and basic principles of assessment (e.g., reliability, validity, washback) are covered extensively elsewhere (see, e.g., Bachman & Palmer, 1996; 2010; Brown & Abeywickrama, 2010; Purpura, 2004; Linn & Gronlund, 2000), we will not provide those details here. Instead, we aim to provide general guidelines for identifying an assessment's purpose and evaluating the ways in which assessment tasks connect to language use in the real world.

Designing classroom-based assessments of L2 grammar ability

In the L2 classroom, teachers may design assessments for both formative and summative purposes, or to diagnose student strengths and weaknesses at the start of a course or instructional unit. In all of these cases, there are important steps that teachers should follow in order to design an assessment that measures what it intends to measure in a fair, practical, and meaningful way.

STEPS IN CLASROOM-BASED GRAMMAR ASSESSMENT

1. Identify a purpose and focus for the assessment
2. Define the constructs to be assessed (i.e., specific areas of grammatical form and meaning) and the target language use domain (i.e., the real-world context in which students would need to use these forms and meanings)
3. Develop assessment tasks that (a) correspond to tasks within the target language use domain and (b) require the use of target grammatical forms and meanings

(adapted from Purpura, 2004, pp. 102–109)

Identifying a purpose and focus for the assessment. The first step in development is identifying a purpose and focus for the assessment. Is the assessment for diagnostic, formative, or summative purposes? What general areas of grammatical ability will be assessed? In what contexts do you hope students will be able to use the grammar they are learning? Table 10.2 provides an example statement of purpose for a classroom-based diagnostic assessment.

Table 10.2 Defining a purpose and focus for an assessment

Assessment scenario	Example statements of purpose and focus
I would like to administer a diagnostic assessment before I begin an instructional unit on the use of tense and aspect in personal introductions	– To measure students' ability to use tense/ aspect forms and meanings accurately and appropriately when providing a brief personal introduction (e.g., where I am from, where I have lived, where I live now). – To identify tense/aspect forms and meanings that students demonstrate full control over – To identify tense/aspect forms and meanings that students have not yet mastered and/or avoid using

Defining the constructs and the target language use (TLU) domain. The next steps involve providing a more detailed description of the grammatical forms and meanings to be assessed and the context in which students will need to use these forms and meanings. The former is typically referred to as the *constructs* to be assessed, and the latter is what Bachman and Palmer (1996) call the *target language use (TLU) domain*, or the relevant real-world context for language use. In the diagnostic assessment featured in Table 10.2, for example, we identify an area of grammar (tense and aspect) and a situation of use (personal introductions). But within these broad categories, many grammatical forms and meanings are possible, and many TLU domains are relevant (e.g., a language class, a dinner party, a job interview). Thus, it is important for teachers to define the parameters for the assessment. In some cases, teachers may begin with a TLU domain in mind, and from there work to identify important grammatical forms and meanings. Conversely, teachers may begin with a set of target grammatical forms (e.g., those listed in a textbook chapter), and from there identify a relevant TLU domain. Selection of the TLU domain and target forms can be informed by the theme and learning objectives of the instructional unit, curricular requirements, and learners' needs and goals.

Another important step in this process is to identify *target language use (TLU) tasks* (Bachman & Palmer, 1996) that exist within the TLU domain. In Table 10.2, the teacher has already taken a step toward identifying a TLU task by specifying the purpose for which students may shift from one tense or aspect to another in discourse. If we focus on the TLU domain of a language class, then a relevant TLU task within this domain would be introducing oneself to classmates during the first week of the semester. This process of defining the relevant assessment constructs, the TLU domain, and TLU tasks helps teachers to understand what types of information their assessment can provide and what information it cannot. As Purpura (2004) reminds us, "every grammar-test development project begins with a desire to obtain (and often provide) information about how well a student knows grammar in order to convey meaning in some situation where the target language is used" (p. 103). If we clearly define the constructs and the TLU domain, then we can use our assessments to make inferences about the abilities that our students have to use grammar in particular communicative contexts.

Table 10.3 provides example definitions of assessment constructs, a TLU domain, and a TLU task for a diagnostic assessment of students' ability to use tense and aspect in personal introductions.

Table 10.3 Defining constructions, TLU Domain, and TLU tasks

	Example descriptions
Constructs (grammatical forms and meanings to be assessed)	– Past tense (both regular and irregular) to express actions that were completed at a specific point in time in the past (e.g., I graduated from high school in May, 2008)
	– Present perfect to express states which began in the past and are still true now (e.g., I have lived in Boise for 3 years)
	– Simple present to express facts about me (e.g., I speak Arabic, Somali, and English)
Target Language Use Domain	– A language class in an Intensive English Program
Target Language Use Task	– Introducing oneself to classmates at the start of a semester

An essential part of defining the constructs and the TLU domain is what Purpura (2004) calls *needs analysis*, or the collection and analysis of language samples from the target language use domain. For example, if we have decided that our TLU domain is the professional workplace and the TLU task is explaining to others what you did before you decided on your career and what you do now, then it would be helpful to collect sample conversations of the same nature from fluent speakers of the target language. (Fortunately, for this career-oriented TLU task, a collection of interviews already exists, as part of the ELISA corpus: <http://www.uni-tuebingen.de/elisa/html/elisa_index.html>). If easy access to language samples is not available, then it is also helpful for teachers to think through how they would carry out the task themselves. For example, if you want your students to be able to introduce themselves to their classmates both in speaking and in writing, then, as a teacher, you might take the first step of completing these tasks yourself. This not only helps you to create useful models of the language you expect, but also allows you to analyze your own choice of grammatical forms and meanings.

Developing assessment tasks. Once a TLU domain and TLU task(s) have been identified, it is now time to develop an assessment task which corresponds to the TLU task(s) (Bachman & Palmer, 1996; 2010; Purpura, 2004). As we saw in Chapter 9, in the Task-Based Language Teaching literature, *tasks* are typically viewed as activities in which the focus is on meaning (not form) and learners use language to solve problems and/or accomplish goals (Skehan, 1998). Similarly, for the purpose of assessment, Bachman and Palmer (1996) define a *language use task* as "an activity that involves individuals in using language for the purpose of achieving a particular goal or objectives in a particular situation" (p. 44). Two key task design features are emphasized in both the TBLT literature and the L2 grammar assessment literature:

- Tasks should correspond in some way to real-world (or TLU domain) tasks
- Tasks should create obligatory contexts for target grammatical forms and meaning (i.e., should strive for task essentialness).

To help teachers address authenticity in their task design, Bachman and Palmer (1996; 2010) have developed a framework for comparing features of a selected assessment task with features of an existing TLU task. Table 10.4 displays these features, along with question prompts that teachers can use to reflect on their own assessments.

As Bachman and Palmer (1996) and Bachman (2002) point out, an exact match between the TLU task and the assessment task is highly unlikely and may even be undesirable.

> First, not all TLU tasks will engage the areas of ability we want to assess. Second, some TLU tasks may not be practical to administer in an assessment in their entirety. Thirdly, some TLU tasks may not be appropriate or fair for all test-takers if they presuppose prior knowledge or experience that some test-takers may not possess.
>
> (Bachman, 2002, p. 460)

Thus, we encourage teachers to consider what features of the TLU task are feasible to include in the assessment task, and which features are not, and how differences between the TLU task and the assessment task might impact the inferences they make regarding students' L2 ability.

Purpura (2004) further argues that classroom contexts themselves can be considered relevant TLU domains. That is, if students are planning to use the target language in formal instructional contexts, then assessment tasks that correspond to typical instructional tasks (including high-stakes language tests) can be considered to be authentic in much the same way that real-world tasks are. He encourages L2 teachers to consider both *real-life domains* (domains that exist outside the walls of the classroom) and *language-instruction domains* (domains that exist within a classroom or school setting).

In the assessment literature, then, assessment tasks include not only communication tasks that attempt to mirror real-world tasks, but also more traditional test tasks, like fill-in the blank and multiple choice. Though these less interactive methods of

Table 10.4 Comparing the assessment task and the TLU task*

	Characteristics of TLU task	Characteristics of assessment task
Setting:	*In what ways will the setting for the assessment task and the TLU task differ?*	
– Physical characteristics – Participants – Time of task		
Input:	*In what ways will the assessment task and TLU task differ in terms of the linguistic characteristics and content of the input?*	

– Format
– Language characteristics
  – Organizational
  – Pragmatic
– Topical content		

Expected response:	*In what ways will the assessment task and TLU task differ in terms of the linguistic characteristics and content of the student's output?*	

– Format
– Language characteristics
  – Organizational
  – Pragmatic
– Topical content		

Relationship between input and response:	*In what ways will the assessment task differ from the TLU task in terms of (a) the level of interaction involved (One-way communication? Two-way communication?), (b) how much input is provided (Short sentences? Long texts?), and (c) to what extent students need information not included in the input (e.g., knowledge of social norms) to make decisions about the appropriate response?*	
– Interactiveness – Scope – Directness		

* Note: Adapted from Bachman (April, 2010, p. 9).

assessment may feel inauthentic as compared to the communication tasks featured in Chapter 9, it is possible to design these test items in such a way as to establish a correspondence between the assessment and the target language use task. To illustrate how this might work, Purpura (2004) provides example test items developed for an assessment of students' ability to use target grammatical forms and meanings in the context of a university chemistry lab. The target language use domain identified for the test was an English for Engineering course, which included a focus on chemical engineering. Selected target language use tasks included: "Write a lab report based on an experiment" and "Describe lab materials, procedures and cause effect relationships" (p. 106). The grammatical constructs to be measured included passive voice and causative verbs in the past tense. To assess students' abilities to use these grammatical forms both accurately and meaningfully in the TLU domain, the test developers constructed test items that corresponded to sentences that one might find in a written lab report, as shown in Examples 10.1 and 10.2.

(10.1)   Water is then _____ to the solution.
       ___1. add   ___3. added
       ___2. adds   ___4. adding

(10.2)   This ___ the litmus paper blue.
       ___1. turned   ___3. changed
       ___2. makes   ___4. produces

While this type of assessment task differs from the TLU task of writing a lab report in a number of ways (e.g., in the format of the expected response and the time on task), the assessment task and TLU task share organizational features – both require the use of passives and causative verbs to describe what happened in an experiment. Purpura (2004) emphasizes the importance of task-essentialness for grammar test design, arguing that a grammatical test task should be "designed to elicit scoreable grammatical performance within a TLU domain, where without the requisite knowledge or ability the test-taker would not be able to complete the task successfully" (p. 112). One advantage that these items have over more open-ended items (e.g., an assessment that asks students to write a mock lab report) is that they allow teachers to control the areas of grammar they want to assess – with open-ended responses, there is a chance that students will not use all of the target grammatical forms, thus making it more difficult to make inferences about their underlying grammatical knowledge.

Reflection 10.2

- Using Table 10.2 as a guide, identify a focus and purpose for an L2 grammar assessment you would like to develop for your students.
- Next, using Table 10.3 as a guide, define the areas of grammar to be assessed, the target language use domain, and the relevant target language use task(s).
- Finally, sketch out a plan for an assessment that (a) will allow you to observe students' use of target grammatical forms and meanings, and (b) has some connection to the target language use task(s). Using Table 10.4 as a guide, compare your assessment tasks to the TLU tasks. In what ways are they similar? In what ways are they different?

Task-based performance assessment

In addition to assessing grammatical ability as separate from (but related to) other components of communicative competence, teachers may also want to assess students' ability to successfully perform particular language tasks, such as ordering a drink at a coffee shop, making a doctor's appointment, or (continuing with Purpura's example) writing a lab report. In this situation, the ability to use grammar accurately and appropriately plays an important role in task performance, but it is not the whole of task performance. Other areas of language ability, such as pragmatic competence, also play a role, and thus an overall assessment of students' task performance will need to include an assessment of these multiple ability components.

Task-based performance assessment refers to an approach in which the goal of assessment is to make inferences about a student's ability to perform a real-world task. As Long and Norris (2000) explain:

> Task-based language assessment takes the task itself as the fundamental unit of analysis motivating item selection, test instrument construction, and the rating of task performance. Task-based assessment does not simply utilize the real-world task as a means for eliciting particular components of the language system, which are then measured or evaluated; instead, the construct of interest is performance of the task itself.
>
> (cited in Norris, Hudson, and Bonk, 2002, p. 395)

Task-based performance assessments differ from assessments of L2 grammar tests in a number of important ways. First, L2 grammar assessments aim to elicit the production of particular forms and meanings, so that inferences can be made about underlying grammatical ability. L2 grammar assessment tasks should have some correspondence to a TLU task, but they need not replicate a real-world task. Other considerations, such as the need to create obligatory contexts for the grammatical forms to be assessed, may outweigh authenticity concerns. Task-based performance assessments, on the other hand, are designed to maximize authenticity and typically correspond to a task-based syllabus. That is, if teachers have identified a set of tasks that their students need to be able to do in the target language, and they have organized instruction around these tasks, then task-based performance assessments can be used to evaluate to what extent students have learned to perform these target tasks. Figure 10.4 displays sample assessment tasks developed for Korean language courses at the University of Hawaii at Manoa (Brown, Hudson, & Kim, 2001, pp. 103–119).

TASK-BASED PERFORMANCE ASSESSMENT

In task-based performance assessment, Long's (1985) notion of *task* guides assessment development. Assessment tasks are selected and developed based on a needs analysis of what students do (or hope to do) in the target language "in everyday life, at work, at play, and in between" (p. 89). Information gathered during a student's performance on a classroom assessment task is used to make inferences about the student's ability to accomplish similar tasks in the real world.

Area: Transportation
Theme: Getting a driver's license

Task: Gathering information on getting a driver's license

Prompt: You are going to get a driver's license. You find a driver's license test center nearest to where you currently live and its phone number in an information booklet on getting a driver's license. Only a phone number for the automated audio response system (ARS) is available, but you would like to talk to the person at the information desk in person. So when calling this ARS number, you have to first listen to the menu options and then press the number that allows you to talk to the person. While talking to him, you ask questions, e.g., the test due date, test time and cost, and write down the necessary information.

Realia/Materials: Booklet on getting a driver's license, including map with your place and nearest driver's license test center marked; telephone, ARS messages prerecorded on tape and cassette tape player.

Area: Illness, Injury, and Medicine
Theme: At the hospital

Task: Describing your symptoms to a doctor

Prompt: You have become ill and go to a hospital. You go to the reception desk and listen to the receptionist's instructions as to how to fill out a medial treatment application form. After completing this form and waiting for your turn, you finally see a doctor in her office. Describe your symptoms and answer any questions your doctor may have concerning your illness.

Realia/Materials: Medical treatment application form

Area: At school
Theme: Registration

Task: Calling your academic supervisor regarding course selection

Prompt: It is toward the end of the semester. You have to see your academic supervisor regarding course selection for next semester. When you call her at her office to make an appointment, her answering machine is on. While listening to her greeting message, you learn that she asks students who call her for course selection consultation to leave a course selection-related message and she will get back to them with her feedback on students' course selection. You call her and this time write down what she wants you to say in your message. When you call her again, you have to politely leave a message that is loud enough, clear, and to the point.

Realia/Materials: Telephone with answering machine; your academic supervisor's greeting message prerecorded on tape, which asks you to tell her your name, the reason for calling, courses you want to take next semester and your phone number; list of courses you want to take next semester; your phone number.

Figure 10.4 Sample performance tasks (Brown, Hudson, & Kim, 2001, pp. 103–119)

In task-based performance assessment, grammatical constructs to be measured may not be defined in the early stages of assessment development. Rather, teachers begin by conducting a formal needs analysis of what students do or hope to do in the target language. From here, teachers select target real-world tasks and describe their characteristics. This process is similar to Bachman and Palmer's (1996) framework for describing TLU tasks, in that the mode, the interaction between input and response, and the types of organizational and pragmatic knowledge needed to complete the task are considered.

Byrnes, Crane, Maxim, and Sprang (2006) describe how members of a German foreign language program in the U.S. worked to revise their curriculum so that tasks played a central role in both instruction and assessment. Byrnes et al. offer their own conception of task, one that is informed by systemic-functional approaches to the study of language use: "We imagine task not primarily, much less exclusively, as transactional, interactive, oral communicative exchanges of daily life, but as oriented toward textuality and literacy in a range of areas of public language use" (p. 86). As the goal of the German program is to prepare students to use German in professional and academic life – contexts which require high levels of literacy – Byrnes et al. focused on the development of *genre-based tasks*. In genre-based tasks, a *genre* is viewed as a goal-oriented activity which takes the form of a text (either spoken or written). In this text, lexis, grammar, and discourse structures are used in conventionalized ways to express meaning within a particular discourse community. Example genres within the German curriculum include personal narratives, journal entries, short stories, film reviews, service encounters, newspaper articles, and political speeches (p. 94). A *genre-based task*, then, is a task in which students interact with, respond to, and/or create particular genres. "Textual genres used in instructional units serve as models or as topical bases for students' performance" (Byrnes et al., p. 94).

In the German program that Byrnes et al. describe, this notion of genre also informs the design of task-based performance assessment. Figure 10.5 displays a performance assessment used in the program's Level III. As can be seen from the prompt, the expectations for task performance are clearly outlined, and they include information about the task's communicative purpose, its genre conventions, required rhetorical moves, and the grammatical forms and meanings that are essential to composing a successful appeal. In this example, then, we can see that assessment of grammatical ability still plays a role in task-based performance assessment, and it is possible to score lexis, grammar, and discourse (i.e., components Purpura's construct of grammatical ability) as separate from other aspects of task performance.

In sum, task-based performance assessments allow teachers to evaluate the extent to which students are able to perform the types of tasks they are likely to encounter in personal, professional, and academic contexts. As Norris et al. (2002) argue, this addresses an important need within language education:

Level III: German Stories, German Histories
Political Appeal

Task: Public appeal

As an engaged student and citizen, you are well informed about hot topics and problems at Georgetown University as well as around the world. At this point, you are actively involved with a particular topic/problem. To address this problem, you will write a public appeal, or manifesto, which you will want to present publicly and publish. Your appeal should have the following parts:
- An engaging title,
- A description of the problem,
- One or more suggestions for solving the problem, and
- An appeal for concrete action.

The goal of your appeal is to motivate the audience to act. The style of your appeal (formal, informal) depends on the particular audience that you want to read.

Content

The political appeals that we have worked on in class ("For our Country" and the appeal by Stefan Heym) serve as the basis for this assignment. Particulary relevant are organizational structure and rhetorical means employed by the model texts.

The following points need to be present in your appeal:
- You define the topic of the appeal: it can pertain to either (world) politics or life at Georgetown University
- Your audience and your relationship to this group must be clearly identifiable
- Place and date of your public presentation of the appeal
- Description of the problem, including background information regarding and consequences of the problem
- Suggestion(s) for solving the problem, e.g., via presenting alternatives or contrasts
- Appeal for concrete action – What should the readers/listeners do?
- Signature(s): individual or as a fictive group

Language Focus

At the discourse level: Describing, justifying, persuading, calling for action
At the sentence level: Complex syntax (focus on the correct verb position):
- Relative clauses for describing
- Temporal clauses for defining time periods
- Dependent clauses for justifying (e.g., "because")

Use of adjectives to describe (focus on correct adjective endings)

Imperative sentences addressed to the audience to call for action

At the word level: Vocabulary relevant for the chosen topic
Use of rhetorical devices typical of a public appeal

Writing process: Preparation worksheet, essay, and revision; first version due; final version due

Length: 1.5–2 pages; double-spaced, with typed Umlauts

Assessment criteria:
The three categories of task, content, and language focus are weighted equally. The overall grade is an average of the three grades for these categories.

Figure 10.5 Sample genre-based performance assessment task (Byrnes et al., 2006, p. 103)

> Language teachers, subject matter teachers, language learners, potential employers and others frequently want to know whether or not, or the degree to which, a learner can utilize language in order to accomplish specific target communication tasks, ranging from the survival-related to the job-specific or academic. (p. 396)

Focusing on the pedagogic value of performance assessment in L2 classrooms, Shohamy and Inbar (2006) list several additional benefits:

> Performance tasks require learners to engage in problem solving activities that require utilizing high level cognitive strategies such as analyzing, comparing and generalizing. In addition, since tasks do not presume a single correct answer they generate a variety of outcomes. Performance tasks are related to "real world" experiences and therefore necessitate the activation of prior knowledge, and encourage the authentic use of the target language as a means for accessing information in various subject areas. Performance tasks also provide opportunities for peer interaction, such as pair and group work, as well as provide learners with opportunities for reflection, self-evaluation and peer assessment. (Shohamy & Inbar, 2006, p. 2)

In terms of grammar assessment specifically, task-based performance assessments allow teachers to examine how students use grammar as a resource for accomplishing task goals and to what extent students have control over the forms and meanings needed to carry out the task successfully. In this regard, the information gained from task-based performance assessments can provide a useful supplement to the types of information obtained through more traditional and form-focused grammar tests.

Reflection 10.3

- As an L2 teacher, have you used task-based performance assessments in your classroom? If so, in what ways did these assessments help you to learn more about your students' L2 grammar ability?
- As an L2 learner, have you ever experienced task-based performance assessment? If so, what was this experience like? How did it compare to more traditional language tests?
- How might task-based performance assessments be used to assess L2 grammar ability? Should they be used in conjunction with more traditional tests? In place of grammar tests? What are some advantages and disadvantages of traditional and task-based approaches?

Dynamic assessment

Task-based performance assessment has its roots in Task-Based Language Teaching and is informed by interactionst approaches to the study of second language acquisition. Similarly, sociocultural approaches to second language research have also led to new innovations, particularly in the area of L2 *dynamic assessment*. Dynamic assessment (DA) is an approach informed by Vygotsky's concept of the zone of proximal development, or the distance between what a learner can do alone and what she can do with assistance (see Chapter 8). Proponents of dynamic assessment argue that "important information about a person's ability can be learned by offering assistance during the assessment itself" (Lantolf & Poehner, 2004, p. 2). Such assessment has the potential to offer a more nuanced picture of a student's language ability. Whereas an accuracy score on an L2 grammar assessment may suggest that a student has not mastered particular forms and meanings, a dynamic assessment can help teachers to gauge whether students need a great deal of assistance when carrying out a task, or whether students need a minimal amount of prompting, and thus may soon be ready to perform the task without assistance. A key aim of dynamic assessment is to make inferences about the future. As Minick (1987) writes, dynamic assessment can be:

> a means of gaining insight into the kinds of psychological processes that the child might be capable of in the next or proximal phase of development and a means of identifying the kinds of instruction, or assistance that will be required if the child is to realize these potentials.   (cited in Poehner & Lantolf, 2005, p. 240)

DYNAMIC ASSESSMENT
In dynamic assessment, Vygotsky's concept of the *zone of proximal development* guides assessment development. Though assistance from a teacher or test administrator in the assessment process is typically prohibited, as it may give some students an unfair advantage, in dynamic assessment, assistance during the task is used to gather more detailed information about the learner's developmental level, to create learning opportunities, and to identify potential areas of focus for future instruction. (Poehner, 2005)

Two major approaches have gained attention in the L2 literature recently: *interventionist* DA and *interactionist* DA (Poehner & Lantolf, 2005). In an interventionist approach, researchers ask students to carry out a performance assessment task without assistance (as a pre-test), to carry out the same task again (perhaps 3–5 times) with assistance, and to then carry out the task one last time without assistance (as a post-test). Prior to assessment, the researcher develops a standardized approach to providing assistance during the task. Then, during the assistance phase, the researcher uses this instrument to note how often assistance is given (e.g., the number of hints or prompts) and how explicit the assistance is (as done in Aljaafreh & Lantolf's Regulatory Scale), and this information is converted into a numeric score indicating learning potential (Poehner, 2005).

In interactionist DA, qualitative techniques, rather than quantitative ones, are used to assess learning potential. Scales for characterizing assistance are not developed in advance of assessment, but rather during the process of assessment, and rich descriptions of interactions between the student and the task mediator are provided. The aim here is to explore how DA might (a) offer teachers new insights into students' language abilities that could not otherwise be obtained through more traditional assessment techniques, (b) facilitate language development, (c) identify areas of language ability that could benefit from future instructional interventions, and (d) develop learners' abilities to perform similar tasks in other contexts (Poehner, 2005).

DA is often characterized as a form of formative assessment because it is administered multiple times throughout the course of an instructional unit and provides learners with developmentally appropriate feedback on their performance (Poehner & Lantolf, 2005). Anton (2009), however, also found DA to be useful for placement purposes. She argues that both traditional test scores and analyses of dynamic assessment interactions were needed to make decisions about how to place individual students into a Spanish language program. For example, in an oral story-retelling task, Anton noted that some students switched into the simple present tense, even though they were recounting past tense events. When learners had a chance to do the task again with assistance, they differed in the number of prompts and hints needed to notice and correct their tense shifting. One student, for example, needed only brief prompting to remind him that he was recounting past events and he was able to switch back to past tense with ease. Another student needed much more explicit feedback, including prompts that asked her to choose between two verb forms provided by the mediator. Although both of these students would have received similar accuracy scores on the unassisted oral re-telling task, the use of dynamic assessment allowed the researcher to make distinctions between the two students' ability levels that she otherwise would not have made.

Reflection 10.4

- As an L2 teacher, have you used dynamic assessments in your own classroom? If so, in what ways did these assessments help you to learn more about your students' L2 grammar ability?
- As an L2 learner, have you ever experienced dynamic assessment? If so, what was this experience like? How did it compare to more traditional language tests?
- How might dynamic assessment be used to assess L2 grammar ability? Could you envision, for example, having students complete a grammar test individually, and then again with assistance? Or, could you ask students to carry out a task-based performance assessment alone, and then again in collaboration with you? Practically speaking, how might this be done, and what types of information would you want to collect throughout the process?

Evaluating student performance

In addition to making decisions about what types of assessments to use in the L2 classroom, teachers also must develop methods for evaluating student performance on these assessments. Purpura (2004) provides a comprehensive overview of scoring methods that can be used for L2 grammar tests, including right/wrong scoring and partial credit scoring (e.g., assigning some credit for accurate form and some credit for accurate meaning) as well as rating scales for test tasks that require more extended responses. Because our main interest in this chapter is alternatives (or complements) to traditional grammar tests, we will focus our attention on rubrics and scoring schemes that have been developed for both task-based performance and dynamic assessments.

Rubrics for scoring task-based performance assessment. Because task-based performance assessment has become a central component of many L2 language programs, The American Council on Teaching Foreign Languages (ACTFL, 2012) recently developed *Performance Descriptors for Language Learners*, which can be used both to carry out formative and summative assessments of students' abilities to perform tasks that have been practiced in class, as well as to assess overall proficiency or place students in levels of a language program. ACTFL has developed performance descriptors for three major modes of performance:

–   *Interpersonal*: Active negotiation of meaning among individuals (e.g., conversation, reading and writing via text messages or social media)
–   *Interpretive*: Interpretation of what the author, speaker, or producer wants the receiver of the message to understand (e.g., reading websites, stories, articles; listening to speeches, messages, songs; viewing video clips of authentic materials)
–   *Presentational*: Creation of messages (e.g., writing messages, articles, reports; telling a story, giving a speech, describing a poster; visually representing [through] video or PowerPoint) (ACTFL p. 7).

Each performance task used in a classroom can be classified into one of these three categories. Then, within each mode, performance descriptors can be used by teachers to answer two fundamental questions: (1) What are the parameters for the language learner's performance? and (2) How well is the language learner able to be understood and to understand (ACTFL, 2012, pp. 8–9)?. The first question concerns the range of learner performance. In other words, can the student perform at a particular level (novice, intermediate, advanced) within a small range of task types (i.e., a limited number of communicative functions, contexts, and content areas) or a broad range (i.e., a wide variety of communicative functions, contexts, and content areas)? The second question concerns what ACTFL refers to as Language Control, Vocabulary, Communication Strategies, and Cultural Awareness, which can be said to represent components of language ability.

To assist teachers in using the ACTFL performance descriptors in classroom task-based assessment, the Consortium for Assessing Performance Standards (Foreign Language Educators of New Jersey, 2013) has compiled a set of performance assessment tasks and corresponding rubrics (see Thematically Organized Assessment Tasks in the Recommended Resources at the end of this chapter). These tasks are organized by theme (e.g., Art Appreciation, Work and Career) and ACTFL proficiency levels. Figure 10.6 displays a sample task and Figure 10.7 displays a scoring rubric for the task developed by Franco (2013). As can be seen in Figure 10.7, this rubric allows teachers to give specific feedback to students on their L2 grammar use, in the context of their overall task performance.

TOA Title: Stress in der Schule: was kann man tun?

Task Title: Schlafen inder Schule: was hältst du davon?

Theme: Health

Level: Pre-Advanced

Age Group: 15 -18 years

National Standards Goals: Communication Cultures   Comparisons

Communicative Mode: Interpersonal

Time Frame: Depends on class size; per pair of students about 10 minutes, plus self-evaluation and peer evaluation

Description of Task:
After reading the article "Trend-Sport Schlafen" you wonder if the idea of taking a nap to increase performance during the day should be adapted in American schools.To find out more about the possible advantages and disadvantages of sleeping to fight stress at school, you turn to the German exchange student at your school. In your conversation, ask each other questions about different measures to fight stress used in the US and Germany and discuss whether short naps during the school day might be a solution to stress.

Make sure to ask and respond to questions and elaborate as much as you can, based on the reading as well as your previous knowledge. Use different time frames to describe what has been going on in other countries and what could be done in the US.

Materials Needed: Tape recorder or video camera to record student performance

Teacher Notes: Students will work in pairs with one student taking over the role of the German exchange student and the other playing an American student at his or her school. This is an oral assessment, and students should not use notes or read off a prepared text.

Figure 10.6 Sample performance assessment task (Franco, 2013, p. 6)

Pre-Advanced Interpersonal Rubric: **Stress in der Schule: was kann man tun?**

	EXCEEDS EXPECTATIONS	MEETS EXPECATIONS	DOES NOT MEET EXPECTATIONS
Language Function	Describes in past, present and future with detail most of the time. Is very accurate in present, past and future.	Narrates and describes some of the time in past, present and future. Is most accurate in present tense and is less accurate when speaking in past and future.	Is most accurate in the present tense. Accuracy decreases significantly when speaking in past and future.
Communication Strategies	Sustains and/or redirects conversation and is able to clarify in many different ways. Involves partners all the time. Is able to circumlocute and self-correct. Speaks with fluency.	Sustains conversation and sometimes is able to clarify. Involves partner most of the time. Is able to circumlocute and self-correct at times. Unnatural pauses may disrupt the flow.	Shows limited ability to sustain conversation and/or clarify. Is not able to involve partner in conversation. Is not able to circumlocute successfully. Repeated unnatural pauses disrupt the flow.
Comprehensibility	Is easily understood by native speakers, even those unaccustomed to interacting with language learners.	There may be some confusion about the message but generally understood by those unaccustomed to working with language learners.	Generally understood by those used to interacting with language learners.
Vocabulary	Consistently uses an extensive and topic-related vocabulary to complete the task.	Uses an adequate vocabulary to complete the task.	Uses vocabulary insufficient to complete the task, little or no-topic–related vocabulary and/or English.
Cultural Awareness	Compares and contrasts many different cultural practices.	Compares and contrasts some cultural practices.	Compares and contrasts few or no cultural differences.

Figure 10.7 Sample performance assessment rubric (Franco, 2013, p. 7)

Techniques for dynamic assessment. With any task-based performance assessment (or grammar test for that matter), it is also possible to integrate dynamic assessment techniques, so that students have an opportunity to perform the task both individually and with assistance. It is also possible to record information about the amount and type of assistance given along with numeric scores or ratings obtained through grammar tests and performance assessments. This allows teachers to see what levels of performance a student can reach:

– individually, prior to any assistance: this helps teachers to diagnose strengths and areas of difficulty and to plan future instructional interventions;
– with assistance: this helps teachers to assess how much and what types of assistance the student needs and to make inferences about the learner's next phase of development; and
– individually, after assistance has been given: this allows teachers to assess in what ways the process of dynamic assessment may have facilitated language development.

Fahmy (2013) developed a method for assessing the performance of L2 learners of Arabic on the Department of Defense's Oral Proficiency Interview (OPI), using both a standardized rating scale and a coding scheme for graduated assistance within the zone of proximal development. Students completed the Oral Proficiency Interview individually, with trained OPI testers, and then participated in several dynamic assessment sessions in which they carried out the OPI interview with assistance from the researcher (who was also the teacher of the students' Arabic course). Fahmy recorded what grammatical forms students needed assistance with during the task and what level of explicitness was needed to help students self-correct:

1. [Implicit] hint that reflected that the teacher-researcher did not accept the answer
2. Repeating broadly the erroneous utterance
3. Repeat[ing] the specific erroneous utterance
4. Naming the syntactical deficiency
5. Providing the student with the answer along with its explanation.

(Fahmy, 2013, p. 79)

These notes were taken down on a scoring sheet that also included performance indicators for the OPI. Notes about the grammatical forms and meanings that students needed the most assistance with can serve as a useful complement to descriptors of independent task performance, thus providing yet another source of information for making inferences about students' underlying grammatical ability.

Reflection 10.5

– Return to your notes from Reflection 10.2. In this Reflection, you sketched out ideas for an L2 grammar assessment task. Now that you have read more about task-based performance assessment and dynamic assessment, do you have new ideas about how you might design this task?

– What approaches could you use to score students' performance on this assessment task? Will you develop a rubric with several components? Devise a scoring scheme that awards points for both form and meaning? Will your feedback be focused only on grammar, or also on other areas of language ability?

– If using dynamic assessment, how might you describe the amount and types of assistance needed by your students during the assessment task?

Summary

– For the purpose of assessment, *grammatical knowledge* is typically defined as a knowledge of language forms (phonological, graphological, lexical, morphological, syntactical, discourse) and their inherent meanings. *Grammatical ability* is the capacity to retrieve and use these forms in communication. Grammatical knowledge and ability cannot be observed directly; we make inferences about students' knowledge and ability based on their language performance.

– A number of steps are involved in the development of L2 grammar assessments:
    – Defining the purpose and focus for the assessment
    – Identifying the areas of grammatical knowledge and meaning to be assessed
    – Identifying a target language use (TLU) domain
    – Selecting relevant target language use (TLU) tasks within this domain
    – Designing assessment tasks that correspond in some way to TLU tasks

– Task-based performance assessment is an approach to assessment which aims to maximize authenticity – assessment tasks are designed in such a way as to mirror, as much as possible, real-world tasks. This approach allows teachers to examine how students use grammar as a resource for accomplishing task goals and to what extent students have control over the forms and meanings needed to carry out the task successfully.

– Dynamic assessment is an approach to assessment in which teachers provide graduated assistance to students during the assessment task. Dynamic assessment allows teachers to observe how much and what types of grammar-focused assistance students need to accomplish task goals, which in turn can help to inform future instruction.

Suggestions for further reading

Bachman, L. & Palmer, A. (2010). *Language Assessment in Practice: Developing Language Assessments and Justifying their Use in the Real World.* Oxford: Oxford University Press.

Brown, D. & Abeywickrama, P. (2010). *Language Assessment: Principles and Classroom Practices.* White Plains, NY: Pearson Longman.

Poehner, M. (2008). *Dynamic Assessment: A Vygotskian Approach to Understanding and Promoting L2 Development.* New York: Springer.

Purpura, J. (2004). *Assessing Grammar.* Cambridge: Cambridge University Press.

Shohamy, E. & Inbar, O. (2006). Assessment of Advanced Language Proficiency: Why Performance-Based Tasks? (CALPER Professional Development Document 0605). University Park, PA: The Pennsylvania State University, CALPER.

Recommended resources

ACTFL Performance Descriptors
<http://www.actfl.org/publications/guidelines-and-manuals/actfl-performance-descriptors-language-learners>

Equipped for the Future Assessment Resource Collection
<http://eff.cls.utk.edu/assessment/default.htm>

NCSSFL-ACTFL Can-Do Statements
<http://www.actfl.org/publications/guidelines-and-manuals/ncssfl-actfl-can-do-statements>

Thematically Organized Assessment Tasks
<http://flenj.org/CAPS/toas.shtml>

Virtual Assessment Center (Center for Advanced Research on Language Acquisition)
<http://www.carla.umn.edu/assessment/vac/index.html>

Chapter 11

Reflections and suggestions for further study

In the introduction to this book, we proposed a framework for pedagogical grammar which highlights three major areas of research and teaching: Grammar Description, L2 Grammar Acquisition, and L2 Grammar Instruction (see Figures 1.1 and 1.2). We also provided a set of question prompts designed to help teachers reflect on their own pedagogical approaches within these three areas. Now, in our conclusion, we would like to return to these questions.

Table 11.1 displays the three major areas of pedagogical grammar, along with the question prompts provided in Figure 1.2. Before reading further, please take some time to respond to these prompts and to reflect on how your responses have (or have not) changed since beginning this book.

In Chapter 1, we also identified aspects of L2 teaching which can be informed by pedagogical grammar research:

- Development of classroom materials
- Analysis of the language my students produce
- Lesson and task design
- Assessment of student learning

In Chapters 3 through 10, we explored how research in the areas of Grammar Description, L2 Grammar Acquisition, and L2 Grammar Instruction might inform the decisions that teachers make in their own classrooms. We focused, in particular, on evaluating and adapting existing materials, using online corpora, designing grammar-focused tasks, and assessing L2 grammar ability. Though these chapters cover several aspects of instruction and several research domains, we feel that it is possible to identify themes that run across these domains.

1. **The importance of making Form-Meaning-Use connections**. In much of the pedagogical grammar research, grammar is viewed as a resource for expressing meaning and accomplishing communicative goals in particular contexts. L2 grammar instruction should address all three of these dimensions and should aim to help students develop both a *knowledge of* and an *ability to use* grammar.
2. **The importance of authenticity**. Descriptions of grammar should be based on empirical investigations of actual language use, instruction should address the registers and tasks that are most relevant to students' lives, and assessments should have some connection to real-world contexts.

Table 11.1 Reflections on the three major areas of pedagogical grammar

Grammar Description
– What is grammar?
– How does grammar interact with other linguistic systems?
– How can it best be described to L2 students?
L2 Grammar Acquisition
– What does it mean to "acquire" the grammar of a language?
– How and when does this acquisition take place?
– What role does instruction play in this process?
L2 Grammar Instruction
– What relevance does pedagogical grammar research have for my own classroom context?
– In what ways can it inform my grammar teaching?

3. **The importance of addressing not just grammar, but lexicogrammar.** Investigations of language use and language acquisition have shown that grammar and lexis do not operate independently of one another; rather, language users often retrieve and process multiword strings as single units of meaning. Phenomena such as collocation, phraseology, and formulaic sequences deserve attention in L2 grammar instruction.

4. **The importance of developmentally appropriate instruction.** Learner language is not simply a deficient version of the L2, but a variety of language in its own right, with its own grammatical rules and phases of development. Instruction that is tailored to students' developmental levels can facilitate the L2 grammar acquisition process.

5. **The importance of communication tasks in the L2 classroom.** Research on the relative effectiveness of different instructional approaches, whether informed by interactionist, sociocultural, or cognitivist orientations, clearly demonstrates that carefully designed, meaning-focused communication tasks can promote the acquisition of L2 grammar. Interaction and collaboration play a crucial role in development, as they provide learners with opportunities to receive comprehensible input, to test hypotheses about grammar, to receive corrective feedback and graduated assistance, and to notice grammatical forms they have not yet fully acquired. These tasks, whether used as classroom activities or for the purpose of assessment, also provide teachers with important information regarding what their students know and are able to do in the target language.

Table 11.2 provides space for you to identify three pedagogical grammar themes that are most important to you as an L2 teacher. You can choose from themes we have listed here, or identify additional themes that you feel that run across the domains of Grammar Description, L2 Grammar Acquisition, and L2 Grammar Instruction. For each theme, you can list related concepts, research findings, and/or resources (as a way to review the content covered in this book), and you can reflect on how each theme connects to your own teaching practices (e.g., the way you approach materials development, task design, or grammar assessment).

In conclusion, we would like to draw attention to areas of research which do not receive coverage in this book but which nevertheless have relevance to pedagogical grammar. As with any published work, space limitations require authors to make difficult decisions about what can and cannot be included. Thus, we would like to offer several suggestions for further study.

The first major area with particular relevance to L2 grammar teaching is research on the role of corrective feedback in second language writing development. In this book, we focus our discussion of corrective feedback and its use in oral communication tasks, primarily because this research has sought to investigate empirical links between such feedback and subsequent grammar acquisition. However, we also recognize the important role that grammar-focused feedback on written compositions can play in grammar development. For study in this area, we recommend Dana Ferris'

Table 11.2

Theme #1:

Relevant concepts/research findings/resources:

Connections to my own teaching practices:

Theme #2:

Relevant concepts/research findings/resources:

Connections to my own teaching practices:

Theme #3:

Relevant concepts/research findings/resources:

Connections to my own teaching practices:

work (e.g., Bitchener & Ferris, 2012; Ferris, 2011), as well as the plethora of articles published in the *Journal of Second Language Writing* on this topic.

Another area we regret not covering more fully is the use of learner corpora for L2 research and teaching. Sylviane Granger (e.g., Granger, 2014; Granger, Hung, & Petch-Tyson, 2002) has done a substantial amount of work in this area. Learner corpora has been used to investigate patterns in learner error, to inform materials development, and to develop engaging data-driven learning activities for the classroom. We would also be remiss if we did not mention the increasingly important role that technology plays in the teaching and learning process. Several researchers (e.g., Blake, 2000; Darhower, 2002; Salaberry, 2000; Sauro, 2009) have explored how computer-mediated communication (CMC) tasks might help to facilitate L2 development, including the acquisition of grammar. These studies help to expand our understanding of interaction and collaboration in L2 learning, as some (e.g., Baralt, 2013) have found that the role of task design and the provision of corrective feedback differ significantly in face-to-face interaction and CMC environments. Gonzalez-Lloret and Ortega (2014) offer a comprehensive review of research in this area.

Another area to consider is Aptitude-Treatment Interaction (ATI) research, which aims to explore the interactions among individual differences (e.g., age, motivation, language aptitude), instructional approaches, and the acquisition of particular grammatical structures. Research on language aptitude has found, for example, that a higher language aptitude is beneficial when students are asked to discover grammar rules for themselves, but may not provide an advantage when the rules are presented explicitly; and that higher language aptitude may also explain why some adults who begin learning a language late in life reach high levels of success, while many others do not (DeKeyser, 2012). For a recent review of research in this area, we recommend Vatz, Tare, Jackson, and Doughty (2013).

Finally, we feel it is important to highlight that much of the research on second language teaching and learning to date has focused on literate language users with a substantial amount of educational experience, particularly at the university level. Recently, however, some researchers have worked to expand the domain of inquiry, by examining non-traditional L2 students, such as recently relocated refugees and pre- and emerging-literate learners (Tarone & Bigelow, 2005; 2007; Tarone, Bigelow, & Hansen, 2009). Continued investigation of these learner populations will no doubt play a crucial role in informing L2 grammar pedagogy in the years to come.

Reflection 11.1

– Compare your reflections in this chapter with those of your classmates or colleagues. What themes received the most attention in your reflections? Why do you think this was the case?
– What do you feel are the most important things you have learned from this book? What areas of pedagogical grammar do you hope to pursue further in the future?

References

Adair-Hauck, B., & Donato, R. (1994). Foreign language explanations within the zone of proximal development. *The Canadian Modern Language Review, 50*, 532–557.

ACTFL. (2012). *Performance Descriptors for Language Learners*. Alexandria, VA: American Council on the Teaching of Foreign Languages.

Adams, R. (2007). Do second language learners benefit from interacting with each other? In A. Mackey (Ed.), *Conversational Interaction in Second Language Acquisition* (pp. 29–51). Oxford: Oxford University Press.

Aljaafreh, A., & Lantolf, J. P. (1994). Negative feedback as regulation and second language learning in the zone of Proximal development. *Modern Language Journal, 78*, 465–483. DOI: 10.1111/j.1540-4781.1994.tb02064.x

Ammar, A., & Spada, N. (2006). One size fits all? Recasts, prompts and L2 learning. *Studies in Second Language Acquisition, 28*, 543–574. DOI: 10.1017/S0272263106060268

Andersen, R. W. (1991). Developmental sequences: The emergence of aspect marking in second language acquisition. In T. Huebner & C. A. Ferguson (Eds.), *Crosscurrents in Second Language Acquisition Theories*. Amsterdam: John Benjamins.

Antón, M. (1999). The discourse of a learner-centered classroom: Sociocultural perspectives on teacher-learner interaction in the second language classroom. *The Modern Language Journal, 83*, 303–318. DOI: 10.1111/0026-7902.00024

Antón, M. (2009). Dynamic assessment of advanced second language learners. *Foreign Language Annals, 42*, 576–598. DOI: 10.1111/j.1944-9720.2009.01030.x

Aston, G. (Ed.). (2001). *Learning with Corpora*. Houston, TX: Athelstan.

Bachman, L. (April, 2010). Developing Language Assessments and Justifying their Use. Workshop presented at *The 5th UC Language Consortium Conference on Theoretical & Pedagogical Perspectives*. San Diego, CA. Retrieved from <http://uccllt.ucdavis.edu/events/fifth_conf/pres_files/lbachman/workshop_handout.pdf>

Bachman, L. & Palmer, A. (1996). *Language Testing in Practice: Designing and Developing Useful Language Tests*. Oxford: Oxford University Press. DOI: 10.1177/026553229601300201

Bachman, L. & Palmer, A. (2010). *Language Assessment in Practice: Developing Language Assessments and Justifying their Use in the Real World*. Oxford: Oxford University Press.

Bailey, N., Madden, C., & Krashen, S. D. (1974). Is there a "natural sequence" in adult second language learning? *Language Learning, 24*, 235–243. DOI: 10.1111/j.1467-1770.1974.tb00505.x

Baralt, M. (2013). The impact of cognitive complexity on feedback efficacy during online versus face-to-face interactive tasks. *Studies in Second Language Acquisition, 35*, 689–725. DOI: 10.1017/S0272263113000429

Bardovi-Harlig, K. (1997). Another piece of the puzzle: The emergence of the present perfect. *Language Learning, 47*, 375–422. DOI: 10.1111/0023-8333.00015

Bardovi-Harlig, K. (2000). *Tense and Aspect in Second Language Acquisition: Form, Meaning, and Use*. Oxford: Blackwell.

Bardovi-Harlig, K., & Reynolds, D. W. (1995). The role of lexical aspect in the acquisition of tense and aspect. *TESOL Quarterly*, 29, 107–131. DOI: 10.2307/3587807

Bennett, G. R. (2010). *Using Corpora in the Language Learning Classroom: Corpus Linguistics for Teachers*. Ann Arbor MI: University of Michigan Press.

Biber, D., Johansson, S., Leech, G., Conrad, S., Finegan, E. (1999). *Longman Grammar of Spoken and Written English*. London: Longman.

Biber, D., & Conrad, S. (2001). Quantitative corpus-based research: Much more than bean counting. *TESOL Quarterly*, 35, 331–336. DOI: 10.2307/3587653

Biber, D., Conrad, S., & Cortes, V. (2004). "If you look at…": Lexical bundles in university teaching and textbooks. *Applied Linguistics* 25, 371–405. DOI: 10.1093/applin/25.3.371

Biber, D., Conrad, S., & Reppen, R. (1998). *Corpus Linguistics: Investigating Language Structure and Use*. Cambridge: Cambridge University Press. DOI: 10.1017/CBO9780511804489

Biber, D., Johansson, S., Leech, G., Conrad, S., & Finegan, E. (1999). *The Longman Grammar of Spoken and Written English*. London: Longman.

Biber, D., & Reppen, R. (2002). What does frequency have to do with grammar teaching? *Studies in Second Language Acquisition*, 24, 199–208. DOI: 10.1017/S0272263102002048

Bitchener, J., & Ferris, D. R. (2012). *Written Corrective Feedback in Second Language Acquisition and Writing*. New York, NY: Routledge.

Blake, R. (2000). Computer mediated communication: A window on L2 Spanish interlanguage. *Language Learning & Technology*, 4, 120–136.

Brown (1973). *A First Language: The Early Stages*. Cambridge, MA: Harvard University Press.

Brown, D. (2007). *Teaching by Principles: An Interactive Approach to Language Pedagogy*. (3rd ed.). White Plains, NY: Pearson Longman.

Brown, D., & Abeywickrama, P. (2010). *Language Assessment: Principles and Classroom Practices*. White Plains, NY: Pearson Longman.

Brown, J. D., Hudson, T., & Kim, Y. (2001). *Developing Korean Language Performance Assessments* (Research Note #27). Honolulu HI: University of Hawai'i, Second Language Teaching & Curriculum Center.

Bybee, J. (2008). Usage-based grammar and second language acquisition. In Robinson, P., & Ellis, N. (Eds.), *Handbook of Cognitive Linguistics and Second Language Acquisition* (pp. 216–236). New York, NY: Routledge.

Byrnes, H., Crane, C., Maxim, H. H., & Sprang, K. (2006). Taking text to task: Issues and choices in curriculum construction. Special issue on task-based learning in the *ITL International Journal of Applied Linguistics*, 152, 85–110.

Canagarajah, S. (2004). Subversive identities, pedagogical safe houses, and critical learning. In B. Norton & K. Toohey (Eds.), *Critical Pedagogies and Language Learning* (pp. 116–137). Cambridge: Cambridge University Press. DOI: 10.1017/CBO9781139524834.007

Canagarajah, S. (2011). Codemeshing in academic writing: Identifying teachable strategies of translanguaging. *The Modern Language Journal*, 95, 401–417. DOI: 10.1111/j.1540-4781.2011.01207.x

Canale, M., & Swain, M. (1980). Theoretical bases of communicative approaches to second language teaching and testing. *Applied Linguistics*, 1, 1–47. DOI: 10.1093/applin/1.1.1

Celce-Murcia, M. (1975). English Structure in Context: An Area of Research for ESL Specialists. *Workpapers in Teaching English as a Second Language*, Vol. 9. University of California, Los Angeles. ERIC document 121100: http://files.eric.ed.gov/fulltext/ED121100.pdf

Celce-Murcia, M. (1990). Discourse analysis and grammar instruction. *Annual Review of Applied Linguistics*, 11, 135–151. DOI: 10.1017/S0267190500002002

Celce-Murcia, M. (1991). Grammar pedagogy in second and foreign language teaching. *TESOL Quarterly*, 25(3), 459–480. DOI: 10.2307/3586980

Celce-Murcia, M. (2002). Why it makes sense to teach grammar in context and through discourse. In E. Hinkel & S. Fotos (Eds.), *New Perspectives on Grammar Teaching in Second Language Classrooms* (pp. 119–133). Mahwah, NJ: Lawrence Erlbaum Associates.

Celce-Murcia, M., & Larsen-Freeman, D. (1999). *The Grammar Book: An ESL/EFL Teacher's Course.* (2nd ed.). Boston, MA: Heinle & Heinle.

Chapelle, C. A., Chung, Y. R., Hegelheimer, V., Pendar, N., & Xu, J. (2010). Towards a computer-delivered test of productive grammatical ability. *Language Testing*, 27, 443–469. DOI: 10.1177/0265532210367633

Chomsky, N. (1959). Review of *Verbal Behavior* by B. F. Skinner. *Language*, 35, 26–58. DOI: 10.2307/411334

Chomsky, N. (1975). *Reflections on Language*. London: Temple Smith.

Conrad, S. (1999). The importance of corpus-based research for language teachers. *System*, 27, 1–18. DOI: 10.1016/S0346-251X(98)00046-3

Conrad, S. (2000). Will corpus linguistics revolutionize grammar teaching in the 21st century? *TESOL Quarterly*, 34, 548–60. DOI: 10.2307/3587743

Conrad, S. (2001). Variation among disciplinary texts: A comparison of textbooks and journal articles in biology and history. In S. Conrad & D. Biber (Eds.) *Multi-dimensional Studies of Register Variation in English* (pp. 94–107). Harlow, UK: Pearson Education.

Conrad, S., & Biber, D. (2002). *Real Grammar: A Corpus-Based Approach to English*. White Plains, NY: Pearson Longman.

Conrad, S. (2004). Corpus linguistics, language variation, and language teaching. In J. Sinclair (Ed.), *How to Use Corpora in Language Teaching* (pp. 67–85). Amsterdam: John Benjamins. DOI: 10.1075/scl.12.08con

Cook, V. J. (1993). *Linguistics and Second Language Acquisition*. London: Macmillan.

Cook, V. (1999). Going beyond the native speaker in language teaching. *TESOL Quarterly*, 33, 185–209. DOI: 10.2307/3587717

Corder, S. P. (1967). The significance of learner's errors. *International Review of Applied Linguistics in Language Teaching*, 4, 161–170. Retrieved from <http://files.eric.ed.gov/fulltext/ED019903.pdf>

Cortes, V. (2004). Lexical bundles in published and student disciplinary writing: Examples from history and biology. *English for Specific Purposes*, 23, 397–423. DOI: 10.1016/j.esp.2003.12.001

Cortes, V. (January, 2013). Waiting for the revolution. Plenary talk presented at the *American Association for Corpus Linguistics*. San Diego, CA.

Coxhead, A. (2000). A new academic word list. *TESOL Quarterly*, 34, 213–238. DOI: 10.2307/3587951

Crease, A., & Blackledge, A. (2010). Translanguaging in the bilingual classroom: A pedagogy for learning and teaching? *The Modern Language Journal*, 94, 103–115. DOI: 10.1111/j.1540-4781.2009.00986.x

Csomay, E. (2004). Linguistic variation within university classroom talk: A corpus-based perspective. *Linguistics and Education*, 15, 243–274. DOI: 10.1016/j.linged.2005.03.001

Csomay, E., & Cortes, V. (2009). Lexical bundle distribution in university classroom talk. *Language and Computers*, 71(1), 153–168.

Cummins, J. (2008). Teaching for transfer: Challenging the two solitudes assumption in bilingual education. In N. Hornberger (Ed.), *Encyclopedia of Language and Education* (pp. 1528–1538). Dordrecht: Springer. DOI: 10.1007/978-0-387-30424-3_116

Curzan, A., & Adams, M. (2012). *How English Works: A Linguistic Introduction.* (3rd ed.). Boston, MA: Longman.

Darhower, M. (2002). Interactional features of synchronous computer-mediated communication in the intermediate L2 class: A sociocultural case study. *CALICO Journal*, 19, 249–277.

DeKeyser, R. (1997). Beyond explicit rule learning: Automatizing second language morphosyntax. *Studies in Second Language Acquisition*, 19, 195–221. DOI: 10.1017/S0272263197002040

DeKeyser, R. (2007). Situating the concept of practice. In R. DeKeyser (Ed.), *Practicing in a Second Language: Perspectives from Applied Linguistics and Cognitive Psychology* (pp. 1–18). Cambridge: Cambridge University Press.

DeKeyser, R. (2012). Interactions between individual differences, treatments, and structures in SLA. *Language Learning*, 62, 189–200. DOI: 10.1111/j.1467-9922.2012.00712.x

Doughty, C. (1991). Second language instruction does make a difference. *Studies in Second Language Acquisition*, 13, 431–469. DOI: 10.1017/S0272263100010287

Doughty, C. *The Effect of Instruction on the Acquisition of Relativization in English as a Second Language.* (January 1, 1988). Dissertations available from ProQuest. Paper AAI8816121. Retrieved from <http://repository.upenn.edu/dissertations/AAI8816121>

Doughty, C., & Varela, E. (1998). Communicative focus on form. In C. Doughty & J. Williams (Eds.), *Focus on Form in Classroom Second Language Acquisition* (pp. 114–138). Cambridge: Cambridge University Press.

Dulay, H. C., & Burt, M. K. (1973). Should we teach children syntax? *Language Learning*, 23, 245–258. DOI: 10.1111/j.1467-1770.1973.tb00659.x

Dulay, H. C., & Burt, M. K. (1974a). Errors and strategies in child second language acquisition. *TESOL Quarterly*, 8, 129–136. DOI: 10.2307/3585536

Dulay, H. C., & Burt, M. K. (1974b). Natural sequences in child second language acquisition. *Language Learning*, 24, 37–53. DOI: 10.1111/j.1467-1770.1974.tb00234.x

Eckman, F. R. (1977). Markedness and the contrastive analysis hypothesis. *Language learning*, 27, 315–330. DOI: 10.1111/j.1467-1770.1977.tb00124.x

Eckman, F., Bell, L., & Nelson, D. (1988). On the generalization of relative clause instruction in the acquisition of English as a second language. *Applied Linguistics*, 9, 1–20. DOI: 10.1093/applin/9.1.1

Ellis, N. C. (2002). Frequency effects in language processing. *Studies in Second Language Acquisition*, 24, 143–188.

Ellis, N. C. (2008). The dynamics of second language emergence: Cycles of language use, language change, and language acquisition. *The Modern Language Journal*, 92, 232–249. DOI: 10.1111/j.1540-4781.2008.00716.x

Ellis, N. C., Simpson-Vlach, R., & Maynard, C. (2008). Formulaic language in native and second language speakers: Psycholinguistics, corpus linguistics, and TESOL. *Tesol Quarterly*, 42, 375–396.

Ellis, R. (1993). The structural syllabus and second language acquisition. *Tesol Quarterly*, 27, 91–113. DOI: 10.2307/3586953

Ellis, R. (1998). Teaching and research: Options in grammar teaching. *TESOL Quarterly*, 32, 39–60. DOI: 10.2307/3587901

Ellis, R. (2001). Introduction: Investigating form focused instruction. *Language Learning*, 51(s1), 1–46. DOI: 10.1111/j.1467-1770.2001.tb00013.x

Ellis, R. (2003). *Task-based Language Learning and Teaching.* Oxford: Oxford University Press

Ellis, R. (Ed.). (2005). *Planning and Task Performance in a Second Language.* Amsterdam: John Benjamins. DOI: 10.1075/lllt.11

Ellis, R. (2006). Current issues in the teaching of grammar: An SLA perspective. *TESOL Quarterly*, 40, 83–107. DOI: 10.2307/40264512

Ellis, R. (2008). Explicit form-focused instruction and second language acquisition. In B. Spolsky & F. M. Hult, *The Handbook of Educational Linguistics*. Malden MA: Blackwell.

Ellis, R., Basturkmen, H., & Loewen, S. (2002). Doing focus-on-form. *System*, 30, 419–432. DOI: 10.1016/S0346-251X(02)00047-7

Eskildsen, S. W. (2009). Constructing another language – Usage-based linguistics in second language acquisition. *Applied Linguistics*, 30(3), 335–357. DOI: 10.1093/applin/amn037

Fahmy, M. M. (2013). *The Effect of Dynamic Assessment on Adult Learners of Arabic: A Mixed-Method Study at the Defense Language Institute Foreign Language Center*. Unpublished Doctoral Dissertation, University of San Francisco.

Farrokhi, F. (2007). Teachers' stated beliefs about corrective feedback in relation to their practices in EFL classes. *Research on Foreign Languages journal of Faculty of Letters and Humanities*, 49, 91–131.

Ferris, D. (2011). *Treatment of Error in Second Language Student Writing*. Ann Arbor, MI: University of Michigan Press.

Fillmore, C. J. (1992). Corpus linguistics or computer-aided armchair linguistics. In J. Svartvik (Ed.), *Directions in Corpus Linguistics. Proceedings of Nobel Symposium* (Vol. 82, pp. 35–60). Berlin: De Gruyter.

Firth, A., & Wagner, J. (1997). On discourse, communication, and (some) fundamental concepts in SLA research. *The Modern Language Journal*, 81, 285–300. DOI: 10.1111/j.1540-4781.1997.tb05480.x

Flowerdew, L. (2012). *Corpora in Language Education*. New York, NY: Palgrave Macmillan.

Foreign Language Educators of New Jersey. (2013). *Thematically Organized Assessment Tasks*. Retrieved from <http://flenj.org/CAPS/toas.shtml>

Fotos, S. (1993). Consciousness raising and noticing through focus on form: Grammar task performance versus formal instruction. *Applied Linguistics*, 14, 385–407. DOI: 10.1093/applin/14.4.385

Fotos, S. (1994). Integrating grammar instruction and communicative language use through grammar consciousness-raising tasks. *TESOL Quarterly*, 28(2), 323–351. DOI: 10.2307/3587436

Fotos, S. (2002). Structure-based interactive tasks for the EFL grammar learner. In E. Hinkel & S. Fotos (Eds.), *New Perspectives on Grammar Teaching in Second Language Classrooms* (pp.135–154). Mahwah, NJ: Lawrence Erlbaum Associates.

Fotos, S., & Ellis, R. (1991). Communicating about grammar: A task-based approach. *TESOL Quarterly*, 25(4), 605–628. DOI: 10.2307/3587079

Fotos, S. & Nassaji, H. (Eds.) (2007). *Form-Focused Instruction and Teacher Education: Studies in Honour of Rod Ellis*. Oxford: Oxford University Press.

Francis, G. (1993). A corpus-driven approach to grammar: Principles, methods and examples. In M. Baker, G. Francis, & E. Tognini-Bonelli (Eds.), *Text and Technology: In Honour of John Sinclair* (pp. 137–156). Amsterdam: John Benjamins.

Francis, G., & Sinclair, J. (1994). 'I bet he drinks Carling Black Label': A riposte to Owen on corpus grammar. *Applied Linguistics*, 15(2), 190–202. DOI: 10.1093/applin/15.2.190

Franco, S. (2013). Thematically Organized Assessment: German. In Foreign Language Educators of New Jersey, *Thematically Organized Assessment Tasks*. Retrieved from <http://flenj.org/CAPS/toas.shtml>

Fries, C. (1940a). *American English Grammar*. New York, NY: Appleton Century Crofts.

Fries, C. (1940b). *English Word Lists: A Study of Their Adaptability for Instruction*. Washington, DC: American Council on Education.

Fries, C. (1955). American linguistics and the teaching of English. *Language Learning*, 6, 1–22. DOI: 10.1111/j.1467-1770.1955.tb00828.x

Fries, P. (2010). Charles C. Fries, linguistics and corpus linguistics. *ICAME Journal*, 34, 89–119.

Gardner, D., & Davies, M. (2007). Pointing out frequent phrasal verbs: A corpus-based analysis. *TESOL Quarterly*, 41, 339–359.

Gas, S. (1979). Language transfer and universal grammatical relations. *Language Learning*, 29, 327–344. DOI: 10.1111/j.1467-1770.1979.tb01073.x

Gass, S. (1982). From theory to practice. In M. Hines & W. Rutherford (Eds.), *On TESOL '81: Selected Papers of the Fifteenth Annual Conference of Teachers of English to Speakers of Other Languages* (pp. 129–139). Washington, DC: TESOL.

Goldschneider, J. M., & DeKeyser, R. M. (2001). Explaining the "natural order of L2 morpheme acquisition" in English: A meta-analysis of multiple determinants. *Language Learning*, 51, 1–50. DOI: 10.1111/1467-9922.00147

Goo, J., & Mackey, A. (2013). The case against the case against recasts. *Studies in Second Language Acquisition*. 35, 127–165. DOI: 10.1017/S0272263112000708

Granger, S. (2012). How to use foreign and second language learner corpora. In A. Mackey & S. Gass (Eds.), *Research Methods in Second Language Acquisition: A Practical Guide*. Oxford: Wiley-Blackwell.

Granger, S. (Ed.). (2014). *Learner English on Computer*. New York, NY: Routledge.

Granger, S., Hung, J., & Petch-Tyson, S. (Eds.). (2002). *Computer Learner Corpora, Second Language Acquisition and Foreign Language Teaching*. Amsterdam: John Benjamins. DOI: 10.1075/lllt.6

Grant, L., & Bauer, L. (2004). Criteria for re-defining idioms: Are we barking up the wrong tree? *Applied Linguistics*, 25, 38–61. DOI: 10.1093/applin/25.1.38

Green, A. B., & Weir, C. J. (2004). Can placement tests inform instructional decisions? *Language Testing*, 21, 467–494. DOI: 10.1191/0265532204lt293oa

Halliday, M. A. K. (1977). *Language as Social Semiotic: The Social Interpretation of Language and Meaning*. Baltimore, MD: University Park Press.

Han, Z. (2002). A study of the impact of recasts on tense consistency in L2 output. *TESOL Quarterly*, 36(4), 543–72. DOI: 10.2307/3588240

Han, Z. & Tarone, E. (Eds.). (2014). *Interlanguage: Forty Years Later*. Amsterdam: John Benjamins.

Harris, T. (2001). Linguistics in applied linguistics: A historical overview. *Journal of English Studies*, 3(2), 99–114.

Hudson, G. (2000). *Essential Introductory Linguistics*. Malden, MA: Blackwell.

Hulstijn, J., & Schmidt, R. (Organizers) (March, 2013). *Cognitive and Social Approaches in Applied Linguistics*. Colloquium presented at the *American Association of Applied Linguistics*, Dallas, TX.

Hunston, S. (2002). *Corpora in Applied Linguistics*. Cambridge: Cambridge University Press. DOI: 10.1017/CBO9781139524773

Hunston, S., & Francis, G. (1998). Verbs observed: A corpus-driven pedagogic grammar. *Applied Linguistics*, 19(1), 45–72. DOI: 10.1093/applin/19.1.45

Hymes, D. H. (1972). On communicative competence. In J. B. Pride & J. Holmes (Eds.), *Sociolinguistics* (pp. 269–293). New York, NY: Penguin Books.

Iwashita, N. (2003). Negative feedback and positive evidence in task-based interaction. *Studies in Second Language Acquisition*, 25, 1–36. DOI: 10.1017/S0272263103000019

Izumi, S. (2003). Comprehension and production processes in second language learning: In search of the psycholinguistic rationale of the output hypothesis. *Applied Linguistics*, 24, 168–96. DOI: 10.1093/applin/24.2.168

Izumi, S. (2007). Universals, methodology, and instructional intervention on relative clauses. *Studies in Second Language Acquisition*, 29, 351–359. DOI: 10.1017/S0272263107070210

Jenkins, J. (2006). Points of view and blind spots: ELF and SLA. *International Journal of Applied Linguistics*, 16, 137–162. DOI: 10.1111/j.1473-4192.2006.00111.x

Johnson, K. E. (2006). The sociocultural turn and its challenges for second language teacher education. *TESOL Quarterly*, 40, 235–257. DOI: 10.2307/40264518

Johnson, J. S., & Newport, E. L. (1989). Critical period effects in second Language: The influence of
maturational state on the acquisition of English as a second language, *Cognitive Psychology*, 21,
60–99. DOI: 10.1016/0010-0285(89)90003-0

Keck, C. (2013). Corpus Linguistics in Language Teaching. In Chapelle (Ed.), *The Encyclopedia of
Applied Linguistics*. Blackwell Publishing. DOI: 10.1002/9781405198431.wbeal0256

Keck, C., & Ortega, L. (October, 2013). Deficit views of language learners in applied linguistics
discourse: A corpus-based critical discourse analysis. Paper presented at the *Second Language
Research Forum*, Provo, UT.

Keck, C., Iberri-Shea, G., Tracy-Ventura, N., & Wa-Mbaleka, S. (2006). Investigating the empirical
link between task-based interaction and acquisition: A quantitative meta-analysis. In J. M. Norris
& L. Ortega (Eds.), *Synthesizing Research on Language Learning and Teaching* (pp. 91–131).
Amsterdam: John Benjamins. DOI: 10.1075/lllt.13.08kec

Keenan, E. L., & Comrie, B. (1977). Noun phrase accessibility and universal grammar. *Linguistic
inquiry*, 8(1), 63–99.

Kennedy, G. (1998). *An Introduction to Corpus Linguistics*. New York, NY: Longman.

Kim, Y. (2012). Task complexity, learning opportunities and Korean EFL learners' question development. *Studies in Second Language Acquisition*, 34, 627–658. DOI: 10.1017/S0272263112000368

Kim, Y. (2013). Effects of pretask modelling on attention to form and question development. *TESOL
Quarterly*, 47, 8–35. DOI: 10.1002/tesq.52

Kim, Y., & McDonough, K. (2011). Using pretask modeling to encourage collaborative learning opportunities, *Language Teaching Research*,15(2), 1–17. DOI: 10.1177/1362168810388711

Kim, Y., & Tracy-Ventura, N. (2011). Task complexity, language anxiety and the development of past
tense. In P. Robinson (Ed.), *Task Complexity: Researching the Cognition Hypothesis of Language
Learning and Performance* (pp. 287–306). Amsterdam: John Benjamins.
DOI: 10.1075/tblt.2.18ch11

Kramsch, C. (2000). Second language acquisition, applied linguistics and the teaching of foreign
languages. *The Modern Language Journal*, 84(3), 311–326.

Krashen, S. (1982). *Principles and Practice in Second language Acquisition*. Oxford: Pergamon. Retrieved from <http://www.sdkrashen.com/>

Lantolf, J., & Poehner, M. (2004). *Dynamic Assessment in the Language Classroom*. (CALPER Professional Development Document CPDD-0411). University Park, PA: The Pennsylvania State
University, Center for Advanced Language Proficiency Education and Research.

Lantolf, J., & Thorne, S. (2007). Sociocultural theory and second language learning. In B. VanPatten
& J. Williams (Eds.), *Theories in Second Language Acquisition: An Introduction* (pp. 197–220).
New York, NY: Routledge.

Larsen-Freeman, D. (1997). Chaos/complexity science and second language acquisition. *Applied
Linguistics*, 18, 141–165. DOI: 10.1093/applin/18.2.141

Larsen-Freeman, D. (2003). *Teaching Language: From Grammar to Grammaring*. Boston, MA: Heinle.

Larsen-Freeman, D. (2006). The emergence of complexity, fluency, and accuracy in the oral and written production of five Chinese learners of English. *Applied Linguistics*, 27, 590–619.
DOI: 10.1093/applin/aml029

Larsen-Freeman, D., & Long, M. (1991). *An Introduction to Second Language Acquisition Research*.
London: Longman.

Lewis, M. (1993). *The Lexical Approach*. Hove, UK: Language Teaching Publications.

Li, S. (2010). The effectiveness of corrective feedback in SLA: A meta-analysis. *Language Learning*, 60, 309–365. DOI: 10.1111/j.1467-9922.2010.00561.x

Lightbown, P. M. (2013). Learner readiness. In C. Chapelle (Ed.), *The Encyclopedia of Applied Linguistics*. Hoboken, NJ: Wiley-Blackwell.

Lightbown, P. M., & Spada, N. (2013). *How Languages are Learned* (4th ed.). Oxford: Oxford University Press.

Linn, R. & Gronlund, N. (2000). *Measurement and Assessment in Teaching*. (8th ed.). London: Prentice Hall.

Liu, D. (2011). The most frequently used English phrasal verbs in American and British English: A multicorpus examination. *TESOL Quarterly*, 45, 661–688. DOI: 10.5054/tq.2011.247707

Loewen, S. (2005). Incidental focus on form and second language learning. *Studies in Second Language Acquisition*, 27, 361–386. DOI: 10.1017/S0272263105050163

Loewen, S., & Nabei, T. (2007). Measuring the effects of oral corrective feedback on L2 knowledge. In A. Mackey (Ed.), *Conversational Interaction in Second Language Acquisition: A Collection of Empirical Studies* (pp. 361–377). Oxford: Oxford University Press.

Long, M. H. (1980). *Input, interaction, and second language acquisition*. Unpublished doctoral dissertation. University of California, Los Angeles.

Long, M. H. (1985). Input and second language acquisition theory. In S. M. Gass & C. G. Madden (Eds.), *Input in Second Language Acquisition* (pp. 377–393). Rowley, MA: Newbury House.

Long, M. H. (1991). Focus on form: A design feature in language teaching methodology. *Foreign Language Research in Cross-cultural Perspective*, 2, 39–52. DOI: 10.1075/sibil.2.07lon

Long, M. H. (1996). The role of the linguistic environment in second language acquisition. In W. C. Ritchie & T. K. Bhatia (Eds.), *Handbook of Second Language Acquisition* (pp. 413–468). New York, NY: Academic Press.

Long, M. H. (Ed.) (2005). *Second Language Needs Analysis*. Cambridge: Cambridge University Press.

Long, M. H. (2007). *Problems in SLA*. Mahwah, NJ: Lawrence Erlbaum Associates.

Long, M. (2015). *Second language acquisition and task-based language teaching*. Malden, MA: Wiley Blackwell.

Long, M. & Robinson, P. (1998). Focus on form: Theory, research, and practice. In C. Doughty & J. Williams (Eds.), *Focus on Form in Classroom Second Language Acquisition* (pp. 15–41). Cambridge: Cambridge University Press.

Loschky, L. & Bley-Vroman, R. (1993). Grammar and task-based methodology. In G. Crookes & S. Gass (Eds.), *Tasks and Language Learning* (pp. 123–167). Clevedon, UK: Multilingual Matters.

Lyster, R. (1998a). Recasts, repetition, and ambiguity in L2 classroom discourse. *Studies in Second Language Discourse*, 20, 51–81. DOI: 10.1017/S027226319800103X

Lyster, R. (1998b). Negotiation of form, recasts, and explicit correction in relation to error types and learner repair in immersion classrooms. *Language Learning*, 48, 183–218. DOI: 10.1111/1467-9922.00039

Lyster, R., & Ranta, L. (1997). Corrective feedback and learner uptake: Negotiation of form in communicative classrooms. *Studies in Second Language Acquisition*, 20, 37–66.

Lyster, R., & Ranta, L. (2013). Counterpoint piece: The case for variety in corrective feedback research. *Studies in Second Language Acquisition*, 35, 167–184. DOI: 10.1017/S027226311200071X

Mackey, A. (1999). Input, interaction, and second language development: An empirical study of question formation in ESL. *Studies in Second Language Acquisition*, 21, 557–587. DOI: 10.1017/S0272263199004027

Mackey, A. (2006). Feedback, noticing and second language development: An empirical study of L2 classroom interaction. *Applied Linguistics*, 27, 405–430. DOI: 10.1093/applin/ami051

Mackey, A. (2012). *Input, interaction and corrective feedback in L2 classrooms*. Oxford: Oxford University Press.

Mackey, A., Gass, S., & McDonough, K. (2000). How do learners perceive interactional feedback? *Studies in Second Language Acquisition*, 22, 471–497. DOI: 10.1017/S0272263100004022

Mackey, A., & Goo, J. (2007). Interaction research in SLA: A meta-analysis and research synthesis. In A. Mackey (Ed.), *Conversational Interaction in Second Language Acquisition: A Series of Empirical Studies* (pp. 407–453). Oxford: Oxford University Press.

Mackey, A., & Philp, J. (1998). Conversational interaction and second language development: Recasts, responses, and red herrings? *The Modern Language Journal*, 82, 338–356. DOI: 10.1111/j.1540-4781.1998.tb01211.x

Martinez, R., & Schmitt, N. (2012). A phrasal expressions list. *Applied Linguistics*, 33, 299–320. DOI: 10.1093/applin/ams010

Matthiessen, Christian M. I. M., & Halliday, M. A. K. (1997). *Systemic Functional Grammar: A first Step into the Theory*. Macquarie University. Retrieved from <http://web.uam.es/departamentos/filoyletras/filoinglesa/Courses/LFC-SFL/FirstStep.html>

McCarthy, M. (2008). Accessing and interpreting corpus information in the teacher education context. *Language Teaching*, 41, 563–574. DOI: 10.1017/S0261444808005247

McDonough, K. (2005). Identifying the impact of negative feedback and learners' responses on ESL question development. *Studies in Second Language Acquisition*, 27, 79–103. DOI: 10.1017/S0272263105050047

McDonough, K., & Mackey, A. (2006). Responses to recasts: Repetitions, primed production, and linguistic development. *Language Learning*, 56, 693–720. DOI: 10.1111/j.1467-9922.2006.00393.x

McDonough, K., & Mackey, A. (2008). Syntactic priming and ESL question development. *Studies in Second Language Acquisition*, 30, 31–47 DOI: 10.1017/S0272263108080029

Meunier, F., & Gouverneur, C. (2009). New types of corpora for new educational challenges. In K. Aijmer (Ed.), *Corpora and Language Teaching* (pp. 179–201). Amsterdam: John Benjamins. DOI: 10.1075/scl.33.16meu

McLaughlin, B. (1990). Restructuring. *Applied linguistics*, 11(2), 113–128.

Mindt, D. (1997). Complementary distribution, gradience and overlap in corpora and in ELT: Analysing and teaching the progressive. *Language and Computers*, 19, 227–238.

Mitchell, R., Myles, F., & Marsden, E. (2013). *Second Language Learning Theories*. (3rd ed.). New York, NY: Routledge.

Mochizuki, N., & Ortega, L. (2008). Balancing communication and grammar in beginning-level foreign language classrooms: A study of guided planning and relativization. *Language Teaching Research*, 12, 11–37. DOI: 10.1177/1362168807084492

Muranoi, H. (2000). Focus on form through interaction enhancement: Integrating formal instruction into a communicative task in EFL classrooms. *Language Learning*, 50, 617–673. DOI: 10.1111/0023-8333.00142

Nassaji, H. (2009). The effects of recasts and elicitations in dyadic interaction and the role of feedback explicitness. *Language Learning*, 59, 411–452. DOI: 10.1111/j.1467-9922.2009.00511.x

Nassaji, H., & Fotos, S. (2004). Current developments in research on the teaching of grammar. *Annual Review of Applied Linguistics*, 24, 126–145. DOI: 10.1017/S0267190504000066

Nassaji, H., & Fotos, S. (2011). *Teaching Grammar in Second Language Classrooms: Integrating Form-Focused Instruction in Communicative Context*. London: Routledge.

Nattinger, J. R., & DeCarrico, J. S. (1992). *Lexical Phrases and Language Teaching*. Oxford: Oxford University Press.

Nguyen, X. (2009). *Form-Focused Task*. Unpublished manuscript submitted for ENG 653, San Francisco State University.

Nicholas, H., Lightbown, P. M., & Spada, N. (2001). Recasts as feedback to language learners. *Language Learning*, 51, 719–758. DOI: 10.1111/0023-8333.00172

Norris, J. M. (2009). Task-based teaching and testing. In M. Long & C. Doughty (Eds.), *Handbook of Language Teaching* (pp. 578–594). Malden, MA: Blackwell. DOI: 10.1002/9781444315783.ch30

Norris, J. M., Brown, J. D., Hudson, T. D., & Bonk, W. (2002). Examinee abilities and task difficulty in task-based second language performance assessment. *Language Testing*, 19, 395–418. DOI: 10.1191/0265532202lt237oa

Norris, J. M., & Ortega, L. (2000). Effectiveness of L2 instruction: A research synthesis and quantitative meta-analysis. *Language Learning*, 50, 417–528. DOI: 10.1111/0023-8333.00136

Odlin, T. (Ed.). (1994). *Perspectives on Pedagogical Grammar*. Cambridge: Cambridge University Press. DOI: 10.1017/CBO9781139524605

O'Keeffe, A., & Farr, F. (2003). Using language corpora in initial teacher education: Pedagogic issues and practical applications. *TESOL Quarterly*, 37, 389–418. DOI: 10.2307/3588397

O'Keeffe, A., McCarthy, M., & Carter, R. (2007). *From Corpus to Classroom: Language Use and Language Teaching*. Cambridge: Cambridge University Press. DOI: 10.1017/CBO9780511497650

Ohta, A. S. (2000). Rethinking interaction in SLA: Developmentally appropriate assistance in the zone of proximal development and the acquisition of L2 grammar. In J. P. Lantolf (Ed.), *Sociocultural Theory and Second Language Learning* (pp. 51–78). Oxford: Oxford University Press.

Ohta, A. S. (2005). Interlanguage pragmatics in the zone of proximal development. *System*, 33(3), 503–517. DOI: 10.1016/j.system.2005.06.001

Ortega, L. (2003). Doctoral Seminar in SLA: Innovative Research On Pedagogical Grammar. Course syllabus. Course syllabus for ENG 703, English Department, Northern Arizona University.

Ortega, L. (2009). *Understanding Second Language Acquisition*. London: Hodder Education.

Ortega, L. (March, 2010). The bilingual turn in SLA. Plenary talk presented at the *American Association of Applied Linguistics*, Atlanta, GA.

Ortega, L. (2013). Ways forward for a bi/multilingual turn for SLA. In S. May (Ed.), *The Multilingual Turn: Implications for SLA, TESOL, and Bilingual Education* (pp. 32–52). London: Routledge.

Ozeki, H., & Shirai, Y. (2007). Does the noun phrase accessibility hierarchy predict the difficulty order in the acquisition of Japanese relative clauses? *Studies in Second Language Acquisition*, 29, 169–196. DOI: 10.1017/S0272263107070106

Panova, I., & Lyster, R. (2002). Patterns of corrective feedback and uptake in an adult ESL classroom. *TESOL Quarterly*, 36, 573–595. DOI: 10.2307/3588241

Pavesi, M. (1986). Markedness, discoursal modes, and relative clause formation in a formal and an informal context. *Studies in Second Language Acquisition*, 8, 38–55. DOI: 10.1017/S0272263100005829

Philp, J. (2003). Constraints on "noticing the gap": Nonnative speakers' noticing of recasts in NS-NNS interaction. *Studies in Second Language Acquisition*, 25, 99–126. DOI: 10.1017/S0272263103000044

Pica, T. (2005). Classroom learning, teaching, and research: A task-based perspective. *Modern Language Journal*, 89, 339–352. DOI: 10.1111/j.1540-4781.2005.00309.x

Pica, T., Kanagy, R., & Falodun, J. (1993). Choosing and using communication tasks for second language instruction and research. In G. Crookes & S. Gass (Eds.), *Tasks and Language Learning: Integrating Theory and Practice* (pp. 9–34). Clevedon, UK: Multilingual Matters.

Pienemann, M. (1984). Psychological constraints on the teachability of languages. *Studies in Second Language Acquisition*, 6, 186–214. DOI: 10.1017/S0272263100005015

Pienemann, M. (1998). *Language Processing and Second Language Development: Processability Theory*. Amsterdam: John Benjamins. DOI: 10.1075/sibil.15

Pienemann, M. (Ed.). (2005). *Cross-linguistic Aspects of Processability Theory*. Amsterdam: John Benjamins. DOI: 10.1075/sibil.30

Pienemann, M. (2013). Processability theory and teachability. In C. Chapelle (Ed.), *Encyclopedia of Applied Linguistics*. Hoboken, NJ: Wiley-Blackwell.

Poehner, M. E. (2005). *Dynamic Assessment of Oral Proficiency among Advanced L2 Learners of French*. Unpublished Doctoral dissertation, The Pennsylvania State University.

Poehner, M. E., & Lantolf, J. P. (2005). Dynamic assessment in the language classroom. *Language Teaching Research*, 9, 233–265. DOI: 10.1191/1362168805lr166oa

Purpura, J. (2004). *Assessing Grammar*. Cambridge: Cambridge University Press. DOI: 10.1017/CBO9780511733086

Reppen, R. (2010). *Using Corpora in the Language Classroom*. Cambridge: Cambridge University Press.

Rivers, W. M. (1981). *Teaching Foreign-language Skills*. Chicago IL: University of Chicago Press.

Robinson, P. (2001a). Task complexity, cognitive resources, and syllabus design: A triadic framework for examining task influences on SLA. In P. Robinson (Ed.), *Cognition and Second Language Instruction* (pp. 287–318). Cambridge: Cambridge University Press. DOI: 10.1017/CBO9781139524780.012

Robinson, P. (2001b). Task complexity, task difficulty, and task production: Exploring interactions in a componential framework. *Applied Linguistics*, 22(1), 27–57. DOI: 10.1093/applin/22.1.27

Robinson, P. (2003). The cognition hypothesis, task design, and adult task-based language learning. *Second Language Studies*, 21(2), 45–105.

Robinson, P. (2005). Cognitive complexity and task sequencing: Studies in a componential framework for second language task design. *International Review of Applied Linguistics in Language Teaching*, 43, 1–32. DOI: 10.1515/iral.2005.43.1.1

Robinson, P. (2007a). Criteria for classifying and sequencing pedagogic tasks. In M. Del Pilar García Mayo (Ed.), *Investigating Tasks in Formal Language Learning* (pp. 7–26). Clevedon, UK: Multilingual Matters.

Robinson, P. (2007b). Task complexity, theory of mind, and intentional reasoning: Effects on L2 speech production, interaction, uptake and perceptions of task difficulty. *International Review of Applied Linguistics in Language Teaching*, 45, 193–213.

Robinson, P. (2011a). Task-based language learning: A review of issues. *Language Learning*, 61, 1–36. DOI: 10.1111/j.1467-9922.2011.00641.x

Robinson, P. (2011b). Second language task complexity, the cognition hypothesis, language learning, and performance. In P. Robinson (Ed.), *Second Language Task Complexity: Researching the Cognition Hypothesis of Language Learning and Performance* (pp. 3–38). Amsterdam: John Benjamins. DOI: 10.1075/tblt.2.05ch1

Robinson, P., & Ellis, N. C. (2008). An introduction to cognitive linguistics, second language acquisition, and language instruction. In P. Robinson & N. C. Ellis (Eds.), *Handbook of Cognitive Linguistics and Second Language Acquisition* (pp. 2–24). New York, NY: Routledge.

Robinson, P., & Gilabert, R. (2007). Task complexity, the cognition hypothesis and second language learning and performance. *International Review of Applied Linguistics*, 45, 161–176.

Römer, U. (2005). *Progressives, Patterns, Pedagogy: A Corpus-driven Approach to English Progressive Forms, Functions, Contexts and Didactics*. Amsterdam: John Benjamins. DOI: 10.1075/scl.18

Römer, U. (2011). Corpus research applications in second language teaching. *Annual Review of Applied Linguistics*, 31, 205–225. DOI: 10.1017/S0267190511000055

Russell, J., & Spada, N. (2006). The effectiveness of corrective feedback for the acquisition of L2 grammar: A meta-analysis of the research. In J. Norris, & L. Ortega (Eds.), *Synthesizing Research on Language Learning and Teaching* (pp. 133–164). Amsterdam: John Benjamins.

Salaberry, M. R. (2000). Pedagogical design of computer mediated communication tasks: Learning objectives and technological capabilities. *The Modern Language Journal*, 84, 28–37. DOI: 10.1111/0026-7902.00050

Samuda, V. (2001). Guiding relationships between form and meaning during task performance. In M. Bygate, P. Skehan, & M. Swain (Eds.), *Researching Pedagogic Tasks: Second Language Learning, Teaching, and Testing*. New York, NY: Pearson Longman.

Savignon, S. J. (1972). *Communicative Competence: An Experiment in Foreign-language Teaching*. Philadelphia, PA: Center for Curriculum Development.

Sauro, S. (2009). Computer-mediated corrective feedback and the development of L2 grammar. *Language Learning & Technology*, 13, 96–120.

Saxton, M. (2010). *Child Language: Acquisition and Development*. Thousand Oaks, CA: Sage.

Schmidt, R. (1983). Interaction, acculturation and the acquisition of communicative competence. In N. Wolfson & E. Judd (Eds.), *Sociolinguistics and Language Acquisition* (pp. 137–174). Rowley, MA: Newbury House.

Schmidt, R. (1995). Consciousness and foreign language learning: A tutorial on attention and awareness in learning. In R. Schmidt (Ed.), *Attention and Awareness in Foreign Language Learning* (pp. 1–63). Honolulu, HI: University of Hawai`i, National Foreign Language Resource Center.

Schmidt, R. W. (1990). The role of consciousness in second language learning. *Applied linguistics*, 11, 129–158. DOI: 10.1093/applin/11.2.129

Schmidt, R., & Frota, S. (1986). Developing basic conversational ability in a second language: A case study of an adult learner of Portuguese. In R. R. Day (Ed.), *Talking to Learn: Conversation in Second Language Acquisition* (pp. 237–326). Rowley, MA: Newbury House.

Searle, J. (June, 29, 1972). Chomsky's revolution in linguistics. *The New York Times*. Retrieved from: <http://www.nybooks.com/articles/archives/1972/jun/29/a-special-supplement-chomskys-revolution-in-lingui/>

Seidlhofer, B. (2001). Closing a conceptual gap: The case for a description of English as a lingua franca. *International Journal of Applied Linguistics*, 1, 133–158. DOI: 10.1111/1473-4192.00011

Selinker, L. (1972). Interlanguage. *International Review of Applied Linguistics in Language Teaching*, 10, 209–231. DOI: 10.1515/iral.1972.10.1-4.209

Sheen, Y. (2004). Corrective feedback and learner uptake in communicative classrooms across instructional settings. *Language Teaching Research*, 8, 263–300. DOI: 10.1191/1362168804lr146oa

Sheen, Y. (2008). Recasts, language anxiety, modified output and L2 learning. *Language Learning*, 58, 835–874.

Shohamy, E., & Inbar, O. (2006). Assessment of Advanced Language Proficiency: Why Performance-Based Tasks? (CALPER Professional Development Document 0605). University Park, PA: The Pennsylvania State University, CALPER.

Shuck, G. (2006). Racializing the nonnative English speaker. *Journal of Language, Identity, & Education*, 5, 259–276. DOI: 10.1207/s15327701jlie0504_1

Simpson, R., & Mendis, D. (2003). A corpus-based study of idioms in academic speech. *TESOL Quarterly*, 37, 419–441. DOI: 10.2307/3588398

Sinclair, J. M. (Ed.). (1987). *Looking Up: An Account of the COBUILD Project in Lexical Computing.* London: Collins.

Sinclair, J. M. (1991). *Corpus, Concordance, Collocation.* Oxford: Oxford University Press.

Sinclair, J. M. (Ed.). (2004). *How to Use Corpora in Language Teaching.* Amsterdam: John Benjamins. DOI: 10.1075/scl.12

Skehan, P. (1998). *A Cognitive Approach to Language Learning.* Oxford: Oxford University Press.

Skehan, P., & Foster, P. (2001). Cognition and tasks. In P. Robinson (Ed.), *Cognition and Second Language Instruction* (pp. 183–205). Cambridge, UK: Cambridge University Press. DOI: 10.1017/CBO9781139524780.009

Skehan, P. (2003). Task-based instruction. *Language Teaching*, 36, 1–14. DOI: 10.1017/S026144480200188X

Skehan, P., & Foster, P. (1999). The influence of task structure and processing conditions on narrative retellings. *Language Learning*, 49, 93–120. DOI: 10.1111/1467-9922.00071

Spada, N. (1997). Second language classroom research: Some answers…. more questions. *TESL Ontario Newsletter*, Fall, 1997.

Spada, N., & Lightbown, P. M. (2008). Form focused instruction: Isolated or integrated? *TESOL Quarterly*, 42, 181–207.

Swain, M. (1985). Communicative competence: Some roles of comprehensible input and comprehensible output in its development. *Input in Second Language Acquisition*, 15, 165–179.

Swain, M. (2000). The output hypothesis and beyond: Mediating acquisition through collaborative dialogue. In J. P. Lantolf (Ed.), *Sociocultural Theory and Second Language Learning* (pp. 97–114). Oxford: Oxford University Press.

Swain, M., & Lapkin, S. (1989). Canadian immersion and adult second language teaching: What's the connection? *The Modern Language Journal*, 73, 150–159. DOI: 10.1111/j.1540-4781.1989.tb02537.x

Swain, M., & Lapkin, S. (1998). Interaction and second language learning: Two adolescent French immersion students working together. *The Modern Language Journal*, 82, 320–337. DOI: 10.1111/j.1540-4781.1998.tb01209.x

Swain, M., & Lapkin, S. (2001). Focus on form through collaborative dialogue: Exploring task effects. In M. Bygate, P. Skehan & M. Swain (Eds.), *Researching Pedagogic Tasks: Second Language Learning, Teaching and Testing.* Harlow, UK: Longman.

Tarone, E. (1979). Interlanguage as chameleon, *Language Learning*, 29, 181–191. DOI: 10.1111/j.1467-1770.1979.tb01058.x

Tarone, E. (1985). Variability in interlanguage use: A study of style-shifting in morphology and syntax. *Language Learning*, 35, 373–403. DOI: 10.1111/j.1467-1770.1985.tb01083.x

Tarone, E., & Bigelow, M. (2005). Impact of literacy on oral language processing: Implications for second language acquisition research. *Annual Review of Applied Linguistics*, 25, 77–97. DOI: 10.1017/S0267190505000048

Tarone, E., & Bigelow, M. (2007). Alphabetic print literacy and processing of oral corrective feedback in L2 interaction. In A. Mackey (Ed.), *Conversational Interaction in Second Language Acquisition: A Series of Empirical Studies* (pp. 101–121). Oxford: Oxford University Press.

Tarone, E., Bigelow, M. & Hansen, K. (2009). *Literacy and Second Language Oracy.* Oxford: Oxford University Press.

Tarone, E., & Parrish, B. (1988). Task-related variation in interlanguage: The case of articles. *Language Learning*, 35, 373–403. DOI: 10.1111/j.1467-1770.1985.tb01083.x

Taylor, L. K., Bernhard, J. K., Garg, S., & Cummins, J. (2008). Affirming plural belonging: Building on students' family-based cultural and linguistic capital through multiliteracies pedagogy. *Journal of Early Childhood Literacy*, 8, 269–294. DOI: 10.1177/1468798408096481

Tomasello, M., (2009). *Constructing a Language: A Usage-based Theory of Language Acquisition*. Cambridge, MA: Harvard University Press.

Tyler, A. (2010). Usage-based approaches to language and their applications to second language learning. *Annual Review of Applied Linguistics*, 30, 270–291. DOI: 10.1017/S0267190510000140

Van Ek, J. A. (1976). Significance of the threshold level in the early teaching of modern languages. *Bulletin of the Council of Europe*. <http://www.eric.ed.gov/contentdelivery/servlet/ERICServlet?accno=ED131700>

Vatz, K., Tare, M., Jackson, S. R., & Doughty, C. I. (2013). Aptitude-treatment interaction studies in second language acquisition. In G. Granena, & M. Long (Eds.), *Sensitive Periods, Language Aptitude, and Ultimate L2 Attainment* (pp. 273–291). Amsterdam: John Benjamins. DOI: 10.1075/lllt.35.11vat

Vygotsky, L. S. (1978). *Mind in Society: The Development of Higher Psychological Processes*. Cambridge, MA: Harvard University Press.

Wang, W. (2003). How is pedagogical grammar defined in current TESOL training practice? *TESL Canada Journal*, 21, 64–78.

West, M., & West, M. P. (Eds.). (1953). *A General Service List of English Words: With Semantic Frequencies and a Supplementary Word-list for the Writing of Popular Science and Technology*. London: Addison-Wesley Longman.

White, L. (1989). *Universal Grammar and Second Language Acquisition*. Amsterdam: John Benjamins. DOI: 10.1075/lald.1

White, L. (2003). *Second Language Acquisition and Universal Grammar*. Cambridge: Cambridge University Press. DOI: 10.1017/CBO9780511815065

Whong, M., Gil, K. H., & Marsden, H. (Eds.). (2013). *Universal Grammar and the Second Language Classroom*. Dordrecht: Springer. DOI: 10.1007/978-94-007-6362-3

Wilkins, D. A. (1976). *Notional Syllabuses*. Oxford: Oxford University Press.

Wray, A. (1998). Protolanguage as a holistic system for social interaction. *Language & Communication* 18, 47–67. DOI: 10.1016/S0271-5309(97)00033-5

Wray, A., & Perkins, M. R. (2000). The functions of formulaic language: An integrated model. *Language & Communication*, 20, 1–28. DOI: 10.1016/S0271-5309(99)00015-4

Wulff, S., Ellis, N. C., Römer, U., Bardovi-Harlig, K., & Leblanc, C. J. (2009). The acquisition of tense–aspect: Converging evidence from corpora and telicity ratings. *The Modern Language Journal*, 93, 354–369. DOI: 10.1111/j.1540-4781.2009.00895.x

Yoshimi, D. R. (2001). Explicit instruction and JFL learners' use of interactional discourse markers. In K. R. Rose & G. Kasper (Eds.), *Pragmatics in Language Teaching* (pp. 223–244). Cambridge: Cambridge University Press. DOI: 10.1017/CBO9781139524797.016

Yule, G. (2006). *Explaining English Grammar*. Oxford: Oxford University Press.

Zobl, H. (1983). Markedness and the projection problem. *Language Learning*, 33, 293–313. DOI: 10.1111/j.1467-1770.1983.tb00543.x

Index